Coyote has many magical powers, but they do not always work in his favor. His own trickery fools him. He is the master trickster who tricks himself. No one is more astonished than Coyote at the outcome of his own tricks. He falls into his own trap. And yet he somehow manages to survive. He may be banged and bruised by the experience, but he soon goes on his way to even *greater error*, forgetting to learn from his mistakes. He may have lost the battle, but he is never beaten.

Source: Jamie Sams & David Carson, *Medicine Cards.* New York: St. Martin's Press, 1999.

Thanks for your help,
Alan.
Coyote Jack

COYOTE JACK

DRAWING MEANING
FROM LIFE AND VIETNAM:

A Memoir

BY JACK LYNDON THOMAS

lyndonjacks publications
Houston, Texas
2006

Copyright © 2006 by Jack Lyndon Thomas

Hardcover: 0-9659843-1-1

Thomas, Jack Lyndon, 1944-
    Coyote Jack : drawing meaning from life and Vietnam :
a memoir / by Jack Lyndon Thomas.
    p. cm.
    Includes bibliographical references.
    LCCN 2005901061
    ISBN 0-9659843-1-1
    ISBN 0-9659843-2-X
    1. Thomas, Jack Lyndon, 1944- 2. Poets, American--
20th century--Biography. 3. Vietnamese Conflict, 1961-1975--Personal narratives, American. 4. Fathers and sons.   I. Title.

PS3570.H5635Z536 2005   811'.54'09
                                         QBI05-800228

lyndonjacks publications
506 West 19th Street #278
Houston, Texas 77008

w w w . l y n d o n j a c k s . c o m

Production Team

Rita Mills of The Book Connection — Project Manager
Shirin Wright — Conceptual Editing
Judy King — Line Editing
Cindy Guire — Cover Design and Map Illustrations

The paper used in this publication meets the requirements of the American National Standard for Permanence of Paper for Printed Library Materials Z39.48-1984.

Printed in the United States of America

Dedicated to: *Mobile Advisory Team III-56,*
a unit of Advisory Team 43

Shirley Cowen Thomas and
J. Lonnie Thomas

Summer Lynn Thomas

Allison Carter Thomas

TABLE OF CONTENTS

FOREWORD

Do love and hate, kindness and rage, forgiveness and bitterness, gentleness and violence, praise and sarcasm, optimism and cynicism, good and evil . . . all spew from the same fountain?

Inexorably the river roils beneath the surface, the discordance exacerbated by its subterranean confinement. Battering furiously against unforeseen barriers, the river churns with frustration as it tries to break free. To find its source, to understand the immensity of its strength, offers the only way to grasp the reasons for its turbulence—only then can a new path be slowly and imperceptibly carved.

I n June 1969, as a green, idealistic infantry lieutenant in the United States Army, I went to South Vietnam to serve on a Mobile Advisory Team (MAT) advising South Vietnamese militia units. Few Americans are familiar with this obscure and ill-defined assignment. Further, young Vietnamese today are seemingly unaware of South Vietnam's militia—called regional and popular forces—confusing them with the Army of the Republic of Vietnam (ARVN). For me, however, living one year among rice farmers in hamlets and villages spawned experiences that are woven into the fabric of my being. Their multifaceted hues saturate my soul.

No longer do I feel the need to deny, defend, or apologize

for my actions because they define who I have become. I have learned that if you have really lived, not only has your soul been wounded, but also other souls have been wounded by you.

The Vietnam experience constituted a microcosm that reflected the discord of my non-Vietnam life, a seething mass of inner conflicts and unresolved, unchecked turbulence. Before Vietnam, I held my three older brothers in awe, felt terrified of my father, and, while harboring the suffocated rage that accompanies a father's suppression and repression of his son, wanted my mother to save me. This baggage I carried both to and from the war.

Although white and upper middle class, I identified emotionally with the downtrodden, the oppressed. During the first fifteen to twenty years of my post-Vietnam life, I perceived from fellow citizens a stifling of expression and lack of caring, a mirroring of my youth. Nevertheless, while I attempted to fit life's mold as I had been taught, to live the way I thought life should be, I never squashed the rumbling discontent. I struggled to integrate what I felt into a harmonious whole that had at its center a dominant core that made sense and had purpose. Yet like an errant seed blown randomly by the wind, my search for enlightenment lacked direction and seemed fruitless. Life's light was fading.

In the early eighties, however, I wrote a collection of poems about my experiences in Vietnam, achieving clarity by accepting the myriad perspectives from which to view the engagement. Like a kaleidoscope, each turn produced a different view, each one valid. But poetry was a way of dancing around the issues—dashing and slashing, hinting and teasing at what was then still too difficult to put down in plain English. In prose I found nowhere to hide. Pain fueled the poetry. Need drove this narrative. Writing this book, I found the same intensity and emotion that I felt when actually going through the paces during that year of 1969/1970. In late October 1996 I sharpened those senses by returning to my operating area in Vietnam, where I also realized the value of my relationship with Jim Smith, my friend and fellow advisor. This is my story and the story of Mobile Advisory Team III-56, a unit of Advisory Team 43, as seen through my eyes.

JACK LYNDON THOMAS

I have used the following fictitious names for my ex-wife and for those soldiers whose versions of various incidents might differ from mine.

Alicia Thomas
Master Sergeant Louis R. Kerbow (deceased)
Staff Sergeant Ronald D. Adams (location unknown)
The Young Captain (location unknown)
Lieutenant George Shanklin (not consulted)

Mr. Loc and Mr. Phat, respectively our guide/interpreter and our driver, during the return trip to Vietnam, have also been assigned fictitious names. All other characters' names are real.

Italicized epigraphs introducing each chapter are by the author. The book opens with "Situation Report—A Fable," a fictional combat scene employing my brothers and nephew. My brothers served our country in the capacity indicated, but due to timing and circumstances, none faced combat. My nephew piloted an F-18 in both the Gulf War and Operation Iraqi Freedom.

SITUATION REPORT

—◆—

A FABLE

Slashing north through the murky Vam Co Dong River, the lead PBR Mark II, commanded by Navy Lieutenant Junior Grade (J.G.) Richard L. Thomas, races through the water in response to an alleged sighting of Vietcong off-loading supplies from sampans near where the river intersects Route 6A. Thomas's boat is armed with twin .50-caliber machine guns on the bow, an M-60 machine gun on each of the port and starboard sides, also a hand-cranked 40mm grenade launcher on the port side, and another .50-caliber machine gun at the stern. Two other PBRs are similarly armed, except that the stern of the second PBR houses an 81mm mortar instead of a .50-caliber machine gun.

Afternoon monsoon rains have pelted the brooding charcoal gray PBRs, whose camouflage-clad sailors peer off to port and starboard, anxiously awaiting further command. Roiling black clouds lift sparingly, allowing the late sun to erupt from the Parrot's Beak of eastern Cambodia, mockingly illuminating the Plain of Reeds while throwing crisp shadows. Off starboard, a deteriorating two-story French villa looms tauntingly, and more than one sailor conjures up an image of sharing a cocktail on the verandah with a beautiful Vietnamese girl. A rumor flows that the villa had once been a summer home of Madame Ngo Dinh Nhu, widow of Ngo Dinh Nhu, who had been assassinated along with his brother, President Ngo Dinh Diem, in the November 1963 coup. Just beyond the villa appears an abandoned sugar mill. Now, cloaked in silence, the sugar mill has died, mourning for the cane that has been hammered by the monsoons and blistered by the sun.

Remnants of civilization fade away, and Lieutenant J.G. Thomas becomes increasingly apprehensive as dusk encroaches. Intelligence reports document that the NVA are making more frequent forays into III Corps to bolster the sagging efforts of the Vietcong. The lieutenant's goal is to reach the objective before dark and make a quick search before securing a night defensive position on the east bank for the PBR triad. Suddenly intense small arms fire from AK47s peppers the starboard side. The sailors return fire from the bow and aft swivel-mounted .50-calibers and starboard-mounted M-60 machine guns while maneuvering to port, away from the contact. The ambush has been efficiently sprung, for waiting on the west bank is a dug-in platoon of NVA soldiers who simultaneously rock the PBRs with rounds from RPG grenade launchers and B40 rockets. Even though armor-plated, the PBRs are no match, for the range is close and repetition of enemy fire intense. All PBRs are in flames and sinking, the sailors killed or blown into the dark, cold waters of the Vam Co Dong. Before Lieutenant J.G. Thomas was blasted, unconscious, from the bow, he was able to transmit the approximate location of the contact.

At the 25th Infantry Division's Headquarters in Cu Chi, several kilometers east of the contact site, a radio message is received that naval PBRs have come under attack and are in serious need of support. As transmissions have been terminated, there is no way to assess and verify the severity of attack and whether the engagement is sustained. Night has fallen, and though there is no communication from the contact site, a decision is made to dispatch a reconnaissance sortie of two UH-1D Hueys from the 25th Aviation Battalion to appraise and report on the situation. Large enough to evacuate wounded if necessary, each Huey is armed with a 7.62mm minigun, a 40mm grenade launcher, and 2.75-inch rocket pods. Each crew consists of an aircraft co-pilot, door gunner, and medic. Major Harry L. Thomas, a qualified army ranger and career soldier, pilots the lead chopper. The weather is threatening, with visibility less than fifty meters. Gusting winds and lashing rain buffet the craft as they lift off, hover, then gain altitude before dipping their noses while striking a 280-degree azimuth from Cu Chi. Major Thomas, no stranger to flying in tight spots, will drop beneath the clouds to seek as a reference point the French villa near the village of Hiep Hoa, then streak north up the river. The boiling low clouds and rain are as brackish as the river water. Skimming low over the river to avoid detection and to gain an element of surprise, he has difficulty determining where the river ends and the shrouded sky begins. The Hueys dart past Route 7A and continue northward to where Route 6A bisects the river, but nothing can be seen. Too much time has passed. The PBRs have settled into their final, dismal resting place at the bottom of the forbidding river. Major Thomas radios to the other chopper, "Let's make one more run."

Close to hypothermia, Lieutenant J.G. Thomas clings to overhanging bamboo on the western bank before finally gathering enough strength to pull himself out of the river. Miraculously he sustained no bullet or shrapnel wounds, but suffers from what he figures is a concussion. Lieutenant J.G. Thomas had heard the choppers fly past, but had been too disoriented to try to raise anyone on his hand-sized radio. His radio is waterlogged, and he fears it has been rendered inoperable. Again he hears the thrusting rotors of the choppers come within range, at a slower pace, and he tries the radio once more.

Major Thomas hears a burst of static on his headset. It did not come from Cu Chi. Could it have come from the ground? He circles back. Both choppers, one more elevated than the other, now hover over the western bank of the river, and the other pilot thinks he sees a brief reflection of light off wet metal. Major Thomas goes in for a closer look, but a .51-caliber machine gun cuts loose and perforates the chopper's shell, severing the main fuel artery and decimating the base of the rotors. Major Thomas's bird gasps its last as it rolls over on its left side and tumbles into the river. The second chopper returns fire, using muzzle flashes as targets, and suppresses enemy fire while radioing for a Huey Cobra hunter-killer team to come on station ASAP. The second chopper has enough fuel and ammunition to stay on station for at least another twenty minutes until the fire-support team arrives. The monsoon rain has let up, a good sign for the pilots, but it is far too dark to see any targets other than muzzle flashes. The menacing Cobra gunships slice through the heavy atmosphere, but by the time they get on station, no more enemy fire is being received. It is suspected the NVA have pulled out, fleeing west toward their Cambodian sanctuary. Even though there is no communication with the ground, the three chopper pilots feel it is possible friendly WIAs may be somewhere nearby, so a decision is made. No indiscriminate firing.

Major Thomas was barely able to dive out of his craft before it hit the river. Treading water, he feels a sharp pain in his right leg, reaches down, and touches a three-inch piece of shrapnel protruding from his thigh. It is painful but not debilitating. Collecting his thoughts, he realizes he has lost his radio and emergency pack, probably all the crew, and has only a water-soaked .45-caliber pistol strapped to his waist. All is now quiet. Using breaststrokes, he swims silently toward the nearest bank, uncertain whether it is the east or west side. Reaching the riverbank, he gropes gingerly for a handhold to hoist himself up. He is startled to feel the firm grip of a hand.

At the 25th Division Headquarters, an operating plan is quickly put together. At first light, an infantry company from the 25th will be airlifted and dropped a couple of kilometers west of the contact site, then sweep their way eastward toward the river. Ever alert for any NVA, their primary mission will be to look for survivors. Augmenting the infantry company will be a platoon from the 65th Engineer Battalion, whose mission as combat engineers will be to locate, isolate, and neutralize any booby traps left by the NVA. The engineer platoon leader is Lieutenant Stephen L. Thomas, U.S. Army Engineer Command.

Just as dawn breaks, so does the weather, enabling the Eagle Flight to lift off. They will be on the ground, or rather in the swamps, shortly after sunup. The terrain is too wet and muddy for the choppers to land, so the soldiers rappel a few feet from the hovering craft to the muck below. The infantry company commander puts his troops in a staggered column with elements of the combat engineer platoon at point and on the flanks. They will proceed in this manner until they are approximately two hundred meters west of the river, then go on line in an effort to sweep up potential survivors. It is a dangerous patrol, primarily because of booby traps. Lieutenant Thomas chooses not to use dogs, speculating any scent would dissipate because of the water. He employs metal detectors but will mostly rely upon the experienced eyes of his men on point and flank. Lieutenant Thomas is uneasy. He has already lost one good point man to a pressure-activated Chicom 61mm mortar round. To be noiseless in the mud is impossible, for after each step the ground sucks back its own. The heavier Americans, not nearly as nimble as their wily adversaries, slosh clumsily through the water. The point man raises a hand, the patrol stops, and he stoops low to investigate more closely a thin wire stretched taut, one end tied to a small palm bush. He tracks the wire until he finds the other termination point. Nestled into another palm bush is a discolored Coca-Cola can, which contains one American fragmentation grenade, the pin already pulled. A normal step against the wire would have pulled the grenade from its housing, and it would have exploded within a few seconds, disabling or killing anyone within the effective radius. The best thing to do is to blow it in place, so a small plastic charge will be electrically detonated from a safe distance. A few meters farther a distinctive "ping" registers in the metal detector. Lieutenant Thomas probes the muck with a bayonet; it appears not to be booby-trapped and could be a cache of weapons or ammunition. They mark the spot for later investigation. There is a need to get to the river.

Now on line, the patrol reaches the river without further incident. Evidence of contact is strewn about. AK47 shell casings and flattened vegetation mark where North Vietnamese soldiers had lain in wait for the ill-fated patrol boats. There are no bodies. The enemy has carted away their dead and wounded, leaving only bloodstains soaked into the mud and bushes. A garbled sound is heard near the riverbank; Lieutenant Thomas cautiously moves forward to investigate the source, M-16 at the ready. What he finds rocks his soul! One navy Lieutenant J.G., drifting in and out of consciousness, and one army Major, bleeding profusely from a wound in his leg, are awaiting much-needed care.

As first aid is being administered, the three briefly glance skyward, gazing in awe at the squadron of F-4E Phantoms on the suspected route of enemy withdrawal. Soon their lethal M-61 Vulcans, 20mm multibarreled guns, will be uncorked and release napalm on any unfortunate NVA caught in the open. The squadron is under the command of Lt. Col. Gary A. Thomas, United States Marines, son of Harry L. Thomas.

Part I

~~~

LIFE AFTER THE WAR

1

THE BEGINNING

Anger and rage have been defined as unlived life. When you do not know how to, or choose not to, bear the discomfort of dealing with your inner pain and turmoil, you often inflict that pain on others, usually your family, wanting them to absorb your pain and do the healing for you.

⸺ ⸺

FRIDAY, 12 JUNE 1970

I was in a fog, my vision as blurry as the shimmering heat waves floating fitfully off the tarmac. All that had happened was now a sheltered memory, the end of a living nightmare . . . so I intended.

Mom, Dad, my brother Steve and his wife, and my friend Ron greeted me at the airport in Houston, Texas. I was dressed in wrinkled khakis, the shirt adorned with a few mementos pinned to my chest: the Bronze Star Medal for Heroism in Ground Combat, the Bronze Star Medal (First Oak Leaf Cluster) for Meritorious Achievement in Ground Operations against Hostile Forces, the Army Commendation Medal for Valor, the Combat Infantryman's Badge, and Vietnam Service Medal. One unknown woman at the airport approached and asked if I had just returned from Vietnam. I said yes, and she thanked me for our efforts. A gracious comment, one of the few times over the next twenty years anyone expressed that sentiment, yet I felt a paradoxical embarrassment for having survived but not having more medals pinned on my chest to justify my existence. I weighed one hundred forty pounds, twenty pounds less than when I had set out for war, but my body was intact.

Initially I felt no strong sense of exhilaration upon leaving war-torn South Vietnam, but rather a dominant though uncertain relief. Prior to my departure I had spent three days in Tan Son Nhut—euphemistically known as Pentagon East—where I turned in my tactical equipment and obtained orders authorizing a stateside return. Even in the relative security of the large, well-protected compound, I felt apprehensive that we might be infiltrated and taken out or that something else might occur to prevent my getting on that plane. But that did not happen, and I boarded an aircraft whose final destination was Travis Air Force Base near Oakland, California. Considering that I had played in the real game, I elected not to participate in future practice maneuvers and declined to join the reserves; consequently, it was at Travis that I mustered out of the Army.

Along with many other soldiers who served, I returned as I had left, alone. Since advisory units were small and personnel were constantly rotated into and out of the teams, there was no way to maintain unit cohesiveness when separating from Vietnam. The abrupt severance added to my sense of isolation and abandonment. While vaguely aware that unforeseen pressures were building, I was unprepared to deal with either the Vietnam aftermath or the unresolved conflicts from my youth. Like many men of my generation, I believed I could overcome the bubbling discontent through sheer will. The unresolved and the unexamined festered for a long time as I attempted to assimilate my existence back into society.

My effort to reconnect began with Ron. Our friendship, which had begun at age eleven in the golden age of Little League baseball, blossomed over the years, centering on sports and a gradual awakening to the mysteries of girls. Ron and I had gone off to college together to try out for basketball. Unfortunately we never got a serious look from the coach, so Ron transferred to another college the following year. We remained good friends, however, and talked straight with each other. The year before, as Ron was taking me to the Houston airport for my flight to Vietnam, I expressed to him my fear about dying. He said, "Thomas, you're not going to die over there."

A year later Ron expressed himself differently. "Thomas, you looked young and virile when you left. You look like death warmed over now."

"Death warmed over"! Perhaps that is the best description for the feeling of dragging around the remains of the worst that man can be—his brutality, his cruelty, and his arrogance. But there is more. In combat, all pretense is stripped away. Your full character is revealed. You see the best that man can be—his compassion, his sorrow, and his vulnerability. You see man. You see yourself.

Military service was ordained in our family. My father, who was born on 22 January 1898 in Whitewright Community, Hunt County, Texas, just northeast of Dallas, was a non-combatant in World War I. My three brothers, after completing the Reserve Officer Training Corps (ROTC) program at Rice University (formerly Rice Institute) in Houston, served as officers either at sea or overseas.

My mother's family contributed as well. Savannah Georgia Terry, my mother's paternal grandmother, at age thirteen married Lawrence Ludlow Cowen, Sr., twenty years her senior, and the son of a French mother and a half-Jewish German father. The original family name had been Cohen, but at some point was changed to Cowen. The senior Cowen served in an artillery unit in the Confederacy, either as a draftsman or as an artist, and reportedly went on to teach French, German, and art. And while no written documentation has been uncovered, oral family history proclaims that Savannah Georgia Terry was related to the brothers who formed the nucleus of Terry's Texas Rangers, a unit that fought for the Confederacy in the Civil War.

Ironically I had not wanted any part of the military, much less Vietnam, had not wanted to see man or myself at war. Upon finishing college, I had a job lined up with Ernst & Ernst, a "Big Eight" public accounting firm, and was looking forward to wearing pin-striped suits, button-down shirts, and polished cordovans. Uncle Sam, though, thinking I should wear different insignia, extended to me the irrevocable draft notice. These were the days before the lottery. I was not thrilled.

The world, now composed purely of shit, had dumped a load. Few of my contemporaries received similar invitations, as most of my friends went either to law school or medical school. Some got married and had children. Some got into the reserves. Generally any of the above activities provided a deferment. At the induction physical I was asked if I had any impairment that could hamper my ability to perform. I replied that I had lower back trouble—a disk improperly aligned. The examining orthopedist immediately looked upon me as a malingerer, a view I found amusing. I was simply following orders in reporting a previous diagnosis of a misaligned disk by a well-known Houston orthopedist. Both physicians would be happy to know that I suffered not one iota of back trouble during my three-year stint in the military.

Still, in 1967, if given an out, I would have taken it although I would never have dodged the draft because I severely feared the consequences of bucking society's conventional mores. Since I *had* to serve, I felt compelled to follow my brothers' footsteps and become an officer; only my route plodded through Officer Candidate School (OCS).

Now I was an ex-infantry lieutenant ready to get on with my life. My future looked bright and so it was—on paper. I was bright, single, handsome, and also a decorated military officer. With a professional career awaiting me at Ernst & Ernst, I would soon earn my CPA certificate. Before beginning work that summer of 1970, however, I rented an apartment, set up my treasured overseas purchases of stereo equipment, then took off for Big Bend National Park in a brand-new, dark blue Fiat 124 Spider.

The Big Bend landscape is wild, rugged, and lonesome. Towering vantage points afford sweeping views of dry arroyos, flat desert, and vast, jagged, rocky escarpments, with desert flora sprinkled throughout the landscape. Junipers, oaks, piñons, and big-tooth maples populate the high country. Twice during my childhood our family had vacationed in these Chisos Mountains. It was in the wilderness that my father and I best got along.

Hoping to tap into pleasant memories, I hiked through brush and cactus to the south rim, carrying my newly purchased .38-caliber revolver, a Smith and Wesson. A few hours later I reached the edge of the cliff that affords an unobstructed view deep into Mexico. I sat down with a tin of tuna, some crackers, and my canteen, recalling the time

Dad and I rode horseback to the Window as well as the hikes we took with Mom. But I could not find my father. I could not find myself. Instead something sharp and hot tried to pierce my consciousness. Though aware that something inside was smoldering, I dismissed the unwelcome probe.

Unsettled, I removed the revolver from my pack and thumbed the hammer to rotate the cylinder. I wanted to shoot at something . . . but at what? I just sat there, staring into space, then put the gun away and hiked back to the basin. The next day I drove to Boquillas Canyon, parked the Fiat, and walked to the bank of the Rio Grande. A large tunnel of reeds, wide enough to walk through, paralleled the river. I hesitated entering, then finally realized I was harboring irrational fears that Vietcong lay in ambush or that booby traps lay concealed alongside the path. The images were crystal clear for whenever a South Vietnamese militiaman had tripped a booby trap, the muffled, explosive puff ripping away part of his body, his empty scream trailing after what he had lost, I would look at my own body to confirm no pieces were missing. Although I had come back from Vietnam whole, I felt incomplete.

I drove away from the allure of Big Bend Basin and returned to the city to begin my work in public accounting. Jealous of those younger men who had not been to war and who had a three-year head start, I needed to make up lost ground. I was angry too. I was angry at having had to serve, I was angry at those who did not have to, and I was angry at not being welcomed home. I was angry with my father and at vague issues I could not define. Mine was a shotgun anger with no specific target. Nevertheless my daytime thoughts could be substantially controlled, much like we controlled the day in Vietnam, or so we thought. At night there was no controlling the subconscious. Again and again the Vietcong made their presence known—made me feel foolish. I was still at war.

～～～

It was the middle of the night. I was sound asleep at the family lake house in the Texas Hill Country when an electrical transformer exploded. Instantly alert, I assessed the situation. *Incoming from the northeast! Get to the radio. Call for artillery support. Any casualties?*

Using the first-floor intercom, I called downstairs to where my brother Harry and his wife were sleeping. "Are you all right? Are you all right?"

"Yeah! We're all right. Why are you waking us up?"

Oops . . . misfire! "Sorry."

I dreamed a lot . . . disturbing dreams . . . dreams about Vietnam.

Captain Wing orders Jim and me to occupy an ambush position. We comply, but stare curiously as he treks off to his bivouac with a woman. The evening is pleasant. Jim and I banter—until we reach the site. Where are the sergeants? They always fired the .50-calibers. Armed with our M-16s and a ridiculously large .50-caliber machine gun, a weapon almost impossible to carry by hand, Jim and I slither into position.

The foreign terrain dissolves into a familiar one, with the ambush site transformed into a concealed position under my boyhood home. Fields of fire become my neighbors' backyards. I set up the .50-caliber, ensuring that the ammo belt is stacked neatly in its can so the shells will feed properly. Each six-inch shell sucked through the chamber will leave the muzzle at a gut-wrenching velocity of 2,930 feet per second. I have a couple of hand grenades close by.

Suddenly there is movement to the west. Vietcong are clambering out of tunnels like scurrying ants—near the Abbotts' house. I do not want to fire. Vietcong see me peering at them. I see them peering at me. I raise my M-16. I fire. The rounds pop out of the muzzle in an impotent trajectory, like penises gone soft just before penetration. I will the rounds to reach their targets, where they plop softly into enemy chests. Yet blood is drawn and I see several soldiers fall.

But they keep pouring out of the tunnels, outflanking me on the right. Then an unarmed soldier in a regional force uniform materializes. I stand up and grab him by the arm. "Where are you going?" I demand.

> *Unafraid, the soldier stares at me contemptuously*
> *and says, "You will be sorry for what you do."*
> *"Man, I don't want to be here. I'm just doing my*
> *fucking job." I turn around. Hordes of Vietcong, some in*
> *British uniforms, are on line in assault, trying to overrun*
> *the position. I grab the .50-caliber. The barrel turns into*
> *a plastic hose, jerking spasmodically. The machine gun*
> *will not fire; rounds simply cook off. The regional force*
> *soldier has disappeared. I look for Jim. I cannot find*
> *him. I leave the machine gun, pick up my M-16, and*
> *run like hell. I pass a couple of sergeants and holler,*
> *"Beaucoup VC. Beaucoup VC." I continue sprinting and*
> *look for Captain Wing, who has disappeared too.*

As I lay in the chill of those nights, a tingling consciousness jangled my nerves, as if I should be doing something, but that something was vague, like trying to eradicate evil with evil. Over time, these apprehensions diminished in intensity, replaced by a shadowy sense that parts of me were missing and were floundering in the darkness, waiting for an appropriate blending of mutual acceptance and forgiveness between my former teammates and myself before I could reel in the lost pieces.

Although the plot of the dreams varied, the theme was invariably the same: anxiety, guilt, and fear. I was under assault. I would be running hither and yon trying in vain to find the PRC-25 field radio. I had my M-16 rifle but was unable to procure any loaded magazines. Or I found loaded magazines but no M-16. I would discover a box of hand grenades, only to find that they were all gone by the time I opened the box.

Complete uniforms were another curse. In the dreams there was this crazy, maddening awareness that I had an incomplete uniform. Therefore I drifted into a post exchange (px) and saw unlimited quantities of fatigues, but by the time I reached the racks all I found were either a fatigue shirt or fatigue pants, never a complete set. It was the same way with khakis.

Dreams about returning to Vietnam had a surreal quality, for in them I morphed into a detached and obscure state of presence.

> *After landing at Tan Son Nhut, I appear as an*
> *apparition in the middle of a rice field at night, alone. I*
> *search, encounter lights, but get confused and do not*
> *know which way to go. There is nothing tangible to hold*
> *on to. Ah, up ahead, I see Smith and the sergeants. Our*
> *spirits converse but drift apart before anything substan-*
> *tive is resolved.*

Time and again I dreamed myself going through OCS, dread-
ing the inevitable dawning of my next assignment: a return trip to
Vietnam. As time passed, the ending of these dreams began to change,
evolving to the delightful, liberating realization, "Wait a minute, I've
already done that and don't have to do it again."

I also felt a powerful, painful need to recapture lost camaraderie. With time and work, my subconscious began delivering more
tolerable messages, culminating in the most freeing dream of all, one
in which I was jogging, only to find my legs turning to lead, much as
they did in a February 1970 visit to the amputee ward in a Saigon
hospital.

> *I look to my left and see that I have come abreast of*
> *a Vietnamese man. He remains virtually impassive, but*
> *I offer an awkward smile and say something unintelli-*
> *gible, as if in explanation. He returns the favor. The next*
> *feeling I have is one of astonishment, for I move past*
> *him, and am again running freely.*

Thus, my dreams and subconscious trigger points—graphic remind-
ers of an unfinished world—festered behind a fortified barrier, and, like
floodwaters approaching the crest of an earthen dam, lay poised to pour
through the first break in defenses. I never knew when an unexpected
stimulus or poignant sensory experience would strike or what form it might
take. One incident might release a salve; another, a shudder.

In June 1996 on a trail ride in the San Juan Mountains in southwestern Colorado, my fellow riders and I were climbing alongside a
streambed among juniper, pine, and quaking aspen. A light, intermittent rain was freshening our ride, but as we were underneath a canopy of

trees, we were unable to see the boiling clouds that had been building above us.

My daughter Allison later told me she saw the flash of lightning from below, near the stables. We had no such warning. The clap of thunder was so close and so powerful that I jerked the reins back, injecting my fear into the horse. He reared but calmed quickly, as did I after realizing that my instinctive, instantaneous reaction of, "Goddamn, who in hell is shelling the mountain?" was patently wrong.

Two other riders, both hunters, commented that the booming thunder sounded like a shotgun blast. To me it sounded like an incoming 82mm mortar shell. But I could not explain the difference. One thing I have learned about mankind is that it is most difficult to empathize with something outside our realm of experience; if we are competitive, we have to be careful of one-upmanship. So I chose to remain silent about the thunderbolt. Besides, I carried my own built-in thunder.

2

DISCIPLINE

*Out of a haunting fog, a pattern of symmetry material-
izes. On the floor under the model-train platform in
my father's workshop, four bodies lay neatly on their
backs, side by side, feet toward the wall, with the heads
facing outward. Each body had a knife protruding from
the center of its skull.*

From a childhood dream.

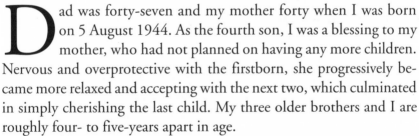

D
ad was forty-seven and my mother forty when I was born
on 5 August 1944. As the fourth son, I was a blessing to my
mother, who had not planned on having any more children.
Nervous and overprotective with the firstborn, she progressively became more relaxed and accepting with the next two, which culminated
in simply cherishing the last child. My three older brothers and I are
roughly four- to five-years apart in age.

All the brothers were cute babies, and I was no exception, with
long, curly blond hair and an infectious smile. "When you were three
months old," Mom told me, "and I was holding you, you arched your
neck and kissed me on the cheek. It's one of my fondest memories."
Mom's endearing name for me was "Lit'l Love," which she used lav-
ishly until I reached the age of two. Then she received a nonrescindable

order from my father, who, apparently afraid I might wind up a sissy, proclaimed that I was not to be coddled or babied and, most of all, I was no longer to be addressed in that loving manner. I suspect that she had also coined special words of endearment for her first three sons and that Dad might have discouraged her from expressing them as well.

In the last decade of her life, my mother also revealed that when they dropped me off at Sunday school (age two), I would not participate but take a chair, drag it to a corner, and sit silently until she came and got me. From birth I was trained to be a good soldier—to listen, obey, and not question. To dispute my father or question his commands incurred wrath. I feared him. I loathed him. And I loathed myself for not standing up to him. To remain silent was to remain safe. And, like my father and brothers before me, I was to tackle the road to manhood hard and tough. Yet Mom was to say that we were loved, that Dad used to bathe and play with us as children, activities in which he displayed affection. Still, in an undated letter written to my mother, probably in the mid-1940s, since he refers only to his first three sons, Dad expressed his view of discipline. From his hand, an excerpt:

> Richard, Harry, and Steve, this is addressed to
> you together as what I have to say applies equally to
> each of you. Daddy seems rather hard to you at times
> I know, trying hard to get you to do your jobs,
> fussing about this and that and yelling at you because
> you are out of sight or something, BUT all of that
> fussing, trying to make you work, talking to you
> about important things, calling you down when you
> get too loud and when you are quarreling, is not
> done just to hear my voice because I don't enjoy
> hearing it either, you see, it is done so that you might
> become used to working, used to controlling your
> voices, used to being polite to other people and used
> to being courteous at all times and to everybody. All
> this is done with the hope that you will grow into
> better men, stronger than most men, more polite and
> considerate than most men, more ready to take it on

the chin without crying than other men and so that you all three may become leaders of other men and so that they will like you well enough to want to follow your leadership and ways of life. You would be surprised how much you can get other folks to do for you IF they admire you and love you. They will help you get your job done if they have confidence in you and enjoy your presence.

And somehow, when Mother writes me that people on trains and in public places notice you and comment on how well behaved you are and how much personality each of you has and what little gentlemen you are and all the nice things we hear about you, I am glad that I yell at you at times and get a little tough with you because I believe that makes you realize that other people and their comfort and feelings are to be considered at all times and that you are not to conduct yourselves in such a manner as to excite bad remarks about your conduct like I have heard about some boys and girls at times.

You just keep up being gentlemen, leaving all bad habits to those who think it is smart and don't ever do anything just because some other boy does them but do things because you know they are right and that it helps make better boys out of you. You want to grow up strong in body and in character so that you can tackle any physical job and do it, finish it because you are strong and so that you can tackle any problem with your thinking (head) and finish that job too and finish it well, better than most can do.

You are good boys, we are very proud of you . . . We know you are not perfect and we know there is plenty of work to do on you. I will be making you work a long time I hope and will be fussing at you a lot more but will be doing it so that you will continue to grow stronger and better. We love you more than anything in the world every minute of our lives

and you don't really know just how very much we
love you and live for you.

So just keep it up, being little gentlemen and
work some every day, be polite to everybody, be
considerate, be kind, be unselfish, be helpful, be
careful and you will be surprised what it will bring
you when you get grown up and out among people.
Ask your Grand-daddy [I assume his father-in-law]
if I'm not right and ask him what he thinks it takes
to make a little boy grow into a man who leads all
other men to greater things and to do greater deeds
and leads them to win over things that get in your
way that are not right. You try it and see what it will
do for you.

Obviously he had high expectations for his sons. To this day I
am tempted to question whether what I perceived was real, tempted to
excuse my father's stern discipline as justified. When I was growing up,
Saturday was for yard work. We had a large lot to cultivate, and its
upkeep took most of the day. Yard responsibilities escalated commen-
surately with each son's increase in age, ascending from clipping grass
along the fence lines and curb, to sweeping, then to cutting grass with
a manual push mower, and finally to mowing grass with a power mower.
As our family prospered, we acquired a riding mower, and the ultimate
achievement was being given permission to operate that piece of equipment. I do not know any kid who would rather cut grass on a Saturday
than play ball, but it was the attitude, the environment in which we
sweltered, that made it ugly.

Since air conditioning was nascent, we were accustomed to the
heat and humidity, both of which were in the mid-nineties on a typical
Houston summer day. With his shirt off, his body glistening with perspiration, Dad barked his instructions. "Clip the fences, the curb, and
then sweep the walks and driveway. Do not miss any blades of grass.
Sweep the sidewalks and driveway clean. Sweep the cut grass into piles
and scoop it up."

"Yes, sir!"

"And come tell me when you are done. I'll inspect it. If it's not good enough, you'll do it again," Dad warned in his abrasive voice. Like being dragged naked over rough concrete, I felt his grating tone peel away my protective cover. For accompanying the admonishment that came forth for performing less than perfectly was a hateful message of nonacceptance. *I will love you upon your achieving perfection; if you do not achieve perfection, you are not worthy of being loved.*

Once Dad became tired, irritable, or frustrated, it was time to take cover. I would be clipping grass underneath a fence while out of the corner of my eye I would see a lawn mower sail ten feet across the lawn. I guess I was afraid he was going to throw me too. My older brothers began their training by slinging the manual push mower. We had to start with the basics and work up the chain before we could manhandle power equipment.

When I was nine years old, Harry, the second son, at age nineteen informed our parents that he had secretly married. Dad bellowed, "He couldn't have hurt me any worse than if he'd have stabbed me in the back." Those words and the wind on which they sailed socked me broadside. *Be careful. Do not get too close to the opposite sex for, if you make a mistake, you will incur my wrath.*

My perceptions of relating to Dad swung like a pendulum, from harsh delivery of disdainful, destructive messages aimed at the audacity of my existence to a tacit disavowal of my presence. I had been born with an extra finger on each hand and an extra toe on each foot, and often that's what I felt like in his presence—an unwelcome, useless appendage that may as well be discarded. Whenever he spoke in his vituperative tone, I trembled inside, literally shaking to the core, like one shivering uncontrollably from the cold. His silence also gave me a chill, for you never knew what might burst forth from the icy cavern.

Dad, essentially a foster child, was merely passing on a legacy. In his words: "After my mother's death, my father's sister Aunt Pal [Palestine E. Thomas Brown] took me to care for. The story is told that after some months Mr. Brown [Aunt Pal's husband], a mean old codger, wrote my father that he should come and get me or I would be thrown out. That must have been about a year after I was born as my father did go after me, and then after he got off the train from Fort Worth, he had to walk six or seven miles through snow and blizzard conditions, with me in his arms, to reach my grandparents' home." That incident occurred in late 1898 or early 1899.

Reared on rough, Spartan farms under the West Texas sun, Dad was a strong, wiry, sophisticated laborer whose physical toughness and stamina surpassed that of any man I ever knew. He was a classic example of pulling yourself up by the bootstraps. To support himself at college, no task was too menial—from waiting on tables to being a night attendant at parking lots to chauffeuring to grading papers to ushering at the Houston City Auditorium, where it was his duty to present flowers to the star of the opera or concert. Even though he majored in math and physics at Rice University, after graduation he wound up selling wholesale building materials for most of his adult life. The one time his primary employer by letter deemed his services no longer necessary, his customers grouped and canvassed the head office, resulting in a revocation of that dismissal. It is ironic that Dad, who turned down a job offer to become a geologist with the old Humble Oil and Refining Company because he had never had a stable home and did not want to travel, would end up traveling anyway as a salesman. During the weekdays for most of my youth he was out of town.

In contrast to Dad's upbringing, my mother grew up in a different environment. Her maternal grandmother, Emma Eliza Hawkins, came to Texas from Iowa while her maternal grandfather, Claude Asbury Arnold, came to Waxahachie, Texas, from Georgia. She describes her Grandpa Arnold as ". . . a delightful man, easy going, kind and loving. . . ." He directed a choir in a Methodist church. Her grandmother, however, became crippled at age thirty-five with "inflammatory rheumatism and . . . for the rest of her life she looked after her family and did all the necessary chores either on crutches or in a wheel chair. She had a remarkable ability to laugh at herself." She lived to be seventy-eight. Three children were born of that union, and one of them was named Effie May.

On the paternal side, Savannah Georgia Terry and Lawrence Ludlow Cowen, Sr. had eight children, one of whom was named Lawrence Ludlow Cowen, Jr. In grammar school he met Effie May Arnold, who would later become his wife, and described her as "the cutest little girl I ever saw." She replied, "I'm sorry I can't say the same for you." They married on 15 May 1902 and gave birth to my mother in Houston on 25 October 1904.

Mom's family moved around the South a lot, as ministers' families are wont to do. She lovingly describes her parents. Of her mother, "I was sick in bed with the measles and high fever. I can remember looking up to see her entering the room to minister to me and she was the most beautiful person I have ever seen. . . . Since his death [Mom's father] she has been an inspiration to all the family. Her cheerfulness has been remarkable. Her lonely, sad times have been well hidden. I always think of this line of poetry when I think of her, 'Hail to thee, blithe Spirit.'" Effie May lived ninety-four years.

Of Mom's father, "He was a man of strong convictions, absolute integrity, and had many talents. He was striking in appearance, voice, and manner. . . . Who could forget a father who brought a box of chocolates and a water spaniel (in his overcoat pocket) to his five-year-old daughter who just had her tonsils removed . . . and told spine-tingling ghost stories?" Having to quit school after the sixth grade to help support his parents and five younger siblings, he valued education and thus educated himself. Once apprenticed to a dentist, Granddad, who wanted to be a Shakespearean actor, instead wrote articles for the Houston Chronicle [early 1900s], sold life insurance, and eventually settled in as a Methodist minister.

Mom and Dad met at Rice University, which she entered at age seventeen. He courted her ardently. In a 13 December 1923 letter about their engagement to her parents, Dad wrote, "As to my [bad] habits I have few. As I said before I do not dance and have never in my life. I do not use tobacco in any form whatsoever . . . I do not drink any form of intoxicating liquor. I have never drunk a drop in my life. I do not gamble in any form. . . . I want to say now that I did not mean to be as abrupt in my letter as it seems I must have been. I only wanted to try to make you understand how much I really love and want her. . . . I want to give her everything in the world she wants and deserves and she deserves a lot. I want to make her perfectly happy . . ." My dad even had to provide references.

During that same time period my mother wrote her parents that "I didn't know it was humanly possible for two people to love each other as we do." She added this about my father, "He has changed wonderfully since I knew him [she had gone to SMU during an intervening year]—is so sweet and dear. He has always had wonderful ideals but used to be a little *hard-boiled*." They married on 26 December 1924. Mom went on to graduate "With Distinction" from Rice University. While she never really used her formal education in a compensatory manner, she read voraciously, worked and taught at the church, could knit and stitch like a pro, led book clubs, and mothered four sons.

Hard-boiled. Yes, he was. And I was on my way.

In the third grade I made the mistake of announcing I wanted to learn to play the cello. He scoffed. I never brought it up again.

Once, in my early teens, I was helping my father repair our roof. My job was to hand him nails that he relentlessly pounded into submission, securing any shingles that might ever want to go astray. I had to be at the ready because being a split second late, or not holding the nail at the bottom tip and at the proper angle so that he could snatch it with one swift sweep of his hand, was to incur his wrath. As the day wore on, the snatches became more impatient, more aggressive. For some reason I decided to hold one tightly, halfway up the stem, leaving him little room to snatch it. He swiped once, twice, three times, and the nail was still in my hand. He rose from his kneeling position, locked his eyes on mine, and cocked the hammer in his right hand, just above my head. His hand trembling, he wanted to strike, but he arrested the motion and lowered the weapon. I did not move a muscle and returned his stare with my own brand of hatred. *Strike me; I care not for you cannot hurt me anymore.* The confrontation over, I resumed handing him nails. He went back to hammering.

Another time I shot arrows through his beloved watertight tool shed. He had to have known who had done it, but he never brought up the issue. I expected to be punished, but was not, and never understood why not. On other occasions, for no reason or every reason, I would give Dad my crazy stare, a silent, defiant, taunting look that evoked the response, "Don't look at me like that."

My father never struck me, and, except for one incident in which my mother observed Dad kicking at my oldest brother when he was a child [she put a stop to it then and there], never struck the brothers. Dad just went underground. I learned well the traits of rage and silence. Silence, while seemingly an outward display of strength, carries with it a self-imposed sentence of stifling incarceration, a fertile breeding ground for rage. We were taught to kill, if not people, spirit.

So I carried my father's anger, my anger, and the stain from Vietnam into post-Vietnam life and into everything I touched. One of the first things I had to do to jump-start my interrupted career in public accounting was to take a standard battery of tests designed to measure, among other things, personality traits and intelligence or critical thinking ability. I did not want to take those tests. I felt angry and invaded and could not think straight—I am not sure I could have anyway, as I was still in the military's reactionary *nonthinking mode*—and my confidence was low. I resented every semblance of civilian life that either totally dismissed or significantly devalued the existence of the Vietnam experience. I remember clearly, however, the results of the tests as interpreted by an industrial psychologist.

"We're surprised you tested so low in verbal acuity and critical thinking areas." Translation: we didn't think you were that stupid. "Also, we're concerned that your personality profile indicates a strong need to tell people off." Translation: are you going to tell our clients to get fucked or come up here with an M-16 on automatic and spray the partners? In actuality I worried about my intellectual scores, and even though I knew I was angry, I treated the anger as if it belonged to someone else.

Prior to going into the military I felt connected to my college friends and would have preferred that that realm not be disrupted. Upon my return I felt severed from the simple, naïve world I had known. The visual form of things was the same as before, but my eyes saw them differently. I would see young men my age with no military experience and wonder how they might have performed in combat.

My Vietnam conflict was unresolved, the experience dangling in suspension as if floating in another dimension. I tried to absorb and integrate it but was unable to make the detached, disassociated experiences fit. I will never know how much my distaste for public accounting stemmed from my perception of the cold, competitive, and uncaring atmosphere in which rookie accountants were to accumulate billable hours, versus the restlessness within my own soul. But I hated public accounting—and I hated life. One reason I hated life was that my career choice had not been a courageous one designed to chart my own course but instead was based on the fact that two of my older brothers were making a good living as CPAs. Why not follow the pattern? I became one as well.

Everyone has to learn how to live, either by adapting to his environment or, failing this, by making the necessary adjustments to live with more integrity. Rather than trying to find out what was going on inside, however, I chose to live a life that attempted to wrap an accumulation of material possessions and achievements around my emptiness while further alienating myself with anesthetizing touches of alcohol and wildness.

I felt that if there were no trail or track, no witness to bouts of destructiveness, bursts of anger, or deceiving and self-deceiving acts of unfaithfulness, then, by sheltering the truth from others, I could hide it from myself. I became my own co-conspirator, a confirmed liar through denial, enmeshed in my own duplicitous web. I also chose to appropriate for my use the chip that had been on my father's shoulder. Now firmly entrenched in me, the chip was composed of a seething rage and burgeoning self-hatred.

3

FAMILY ASSAULT

All he ever wanted
was a beautiful and caring woman
to take him in her arms
hear his story
say it is okay
and make the pain go away.

"Savior—I." a poem.

ALICIA

In 1971 I met Alicia in a Sunday school class that my parents sponsored. I was twenty-seven and she was twenty-one. A recent graduate of Louisiana Tech, she had come to Houston to teach and broaden her life. I already knew her older sister, who, for some reason, shared with me a letter that a lay-minister friend had written about Alicia. The letter was so moving and poignant that I fell in love with Alicia before I even saw her. Several months later, when I met her, I thought she was the most beautiful woman I had ever seen. She wore little makeup and did not need it, for her face emanated a natural radiance. Alicia possessed a capacity to love that draped around those close to her. I fell instantly in love and courted her more ardently than anyone I ever had in my life.

Soon we became engaged. Was I crazy? Not much! After our engagement, I hopped in my Fiat and for a week cruised solo through Colorado, seeking escape through lust and excitement instead of working to build a life back home. Six months later we married, even though that same lay minister tried to talk Alicia out of the marriage, saying she was too young and not yet ready. Almost immediately I began to hit the bars, relishing the thrill of chasing women, trying to recreate the combat high. Inside I was screaming for someone to save me, not being able to or willing to do it myself.

Accompanying my anger, shame, and pain was a ludicrous lack of knowledge about relationships. I was a mess. To make it worse, early in the marriage Alicia said, "Jack, do you realize you bring up Vietnam every time we go someplace!"

That hurt, and I became even more frustrated, my anger escalating. Mostly though I was ashamed: ashamed for needing to talk about Vietnam, ashamed for wanting to talk about the war, and ashamed for not knowing how to talk about it. I felt a deep void that no one knew how to fill. I did not know how to fill the emptiness either since all I did was turn people off. No, I do not think Alicia was at all malicious for that is not in her being, but she, like the majority of people in the United States at that time, wanted little to do with Vietnam, yet I spoke about it in ways that she and others could not ignore.

When I went into my marriage, I was determined not to do as my father had done. Unfortunately I behaved exactly like my father, mirroring his behavior to the core. (I am referring here only to his rage because I am certain that neither my mother nor my father was ever unfaithful.) Like the Vietcong, I maintained a facade of normalcy during the workday, then went home and spread my terror at night. Like my father, I declared war on my family. It took me twelve years to destroy the marriage.

MESSAGES I

OVERTIME

On a Friday night in early spring 1972, public accounting year-end audits were in full swing. I left work around eight o'clock, having called to tell Alicia that I was on the way home. Instead I stopped at an all-night bar, where for eight hours I plied bargirls with cheap champagne. This was a seamy world, and the girls were rough and crude. Their job was to entice patrons with the lure of sex, never delivering but prolonging the encounters with promises to *engage* after "just one more bottle." Finally, after spending five hundred dollars, I decided enough was enough and headed for home in my new Triumph, a TR6. Barely avoiding a ditch, I continued weaving down the streets until stopped by the police.

"Get out of the car."

I complied.

"Where have you been?"

"Working late," I said.

One cop looked at me skeptically; the other seemed curious. "What kind of work?"

"Auditing."

"My brother-in-law is a CPA," the curious cop said. "Those guys work—"

"How many drinks?" the first cop asked.

I looked him straight in the eye. "A couple."

The discussion continued, but after observing me "walk the line," they let me go . . . without a ticket. By the time I arrived at our apartment, my audit manager and supervisor were there waiting with Alicia, who was beside herself with concern. They had been combing the roads, fearful I may have had an accident. Two hours later I was back at work in the client's office.

The Telephone and the Tire Tool

Whenever I was hurting, my rage ran the gamut from yelling at Alicia and the children to throwing a lawn mower as far as I could, trying to surpass the distance of my father's toss. Before my wife and I became homeowners, we were living in an apartment, and I do not recollect what triggered this incident. Using my hands as weapons, I assaulted a mounted wall phone simply because it was there, a hapless victim. For several minutes I grappled to rip the offending device off the wall, destroying the cover but failing to dislodge the base plate that was anchored to a stud. Yet I discharged sufficient anger and no longer had the need to display to the telephone, or to Alicia, who was in charge.

My temper was nothing new. As a teenager in high school, I had begun driving our '56 box Chevy, a pretty fair automobile with a standard V8 engine. The car rested in the garage on only three good legs; the fourth had gone lame. Dad instructed me to change the tire. I got all the lug nuts off but one, which was stuck tight. I had a four-pronged tire tool, the kind you could spin, as well as use to apply leverage. I could not loosen the last lug nut and got madder and madder. Taking hold one more time, simultaneously yelling and twisting, I snapped the lug nut clean off—sheared smooth just as if it had been sawed. It was common in those days to have a business relationship with a neighborhood service station, so my dad called them. A man came out, looked at the tire, looked at me, and said, "Wow! Who broke off that nut? Takes a powerful man to do that."

The Celtics

In the seventies the Boston Celtics, my favorite basketball team, were in the playoffs. It was the John Havlicek era and the game was not proceeding as I desired. In a futile attempt to remedy the situation and to express displeasure and contempt, I hurled a glass into the fireplace, where it shattered into bits and pieces, neatly severing long strands of ivy that my wife had lovingly cultivated.

Sins of the Son

After four years in public accounting I had left the profession and was working in industry. The company I worked for had divisions throughout the West, and often I tacked on some vacationing at the end of a business trip.

In the fall of 1979 I joined a weeklong photography workshop in Arizona. Ten photographers were present, including two young women, one blonde and the other brunette. It was the brunette who intrigued me. She was tall, slender, and well-tanned, with nice legs. We shared campgrounds, photo shoots, and peppermint schnapps . . . nothing else. I came closer to a friendship with a woman than ever before, not even aware of what it was I longed for, much less how to achieve it.

During our visit to the South Rim of the Grand Canyon, we were fortunate to stumble upon a piano concert being held at the canyon's edge. I had a sound movie camera and recorded the whole event. I felt euphoric.

Another stop was Monument Valley. It lies in northeastern Arizona and southeastern Utah and is dominated by magnificent red rock formations. Like the Texas Big Bend, it is untamed, an easy place in which to feel forsaken. The valley is quite dry and supports little vegetation.

On a family vacation in the mid-fifties, my father and I had gone hiking in the valley. We got caught in the open by a rare thunderstorm and took shelter under an overhanging rock. Soon a torrent of runoff water cascaded over us; it was one of those few, treasured moments that I felt connected to Dad.

Now, on this visit in 1979, it was night, the lodge was full, and I stayed by myself in a trailer, smoking a cigar while reading a paperback western. The two women had already left to return to the Grand Canyon. I stepped outside the trailer, looked at the stars, and yearned for my father. Overwhelmed by lonesomeness, I screamed to the heavens at the top of my lungs. No one heard me. Or did they? Did God? Shortly thereafter, things began to change, although ever so slowly.

In desperation I drove to the South Rim early the next morning, found the women's car in the parking lot, and waited all day for their return. When the brunette arrived, she was surprised to see me.

I stammered a bit, and then said, "I love you."

"What!" She looked at me as though I were nuts.

Humiliated, near despair, I left and drove to the Phoenix airport. There I wrote a long love letter but didn't mail it. Instead, on the return flight to Houston, I converted the longings into crude poetry, which I eventually made into a book of poems I dedicated to my first daughter Summer, who was then three.

When I arrived home, I called my brother Steve and complained about the inadequacies of my marriage. He suggested I call a psychiatrist, an old-fashioned psychotherapist whom I saw until he died, many years later. My first words to him were, "I want to be happy." He asked if I would settle for comfortable. I said yes, figuring the only problem was my sex life—I wanted more of it. Right! As if a woman I continued to bash emotionally wanted to make love with me.

I had little clue as to how much garbage I was going to unearth, and the therapy did not take right away. The incidents continued, my black moods festering like an active volcano, ever threatening to erupt and clouding our household.

SHUTTER AND ABBY

Alicia and I acquired a dog, a thoroughbred female boxer we named Shutter, a moniker I stole from my sister-in-law who had once called me that in reference to my interest in photography. Before long we acquired another dog, Abby, but this one was the unwanted offspring of an undesired union between our thoroughbred and a rapist. Four years after Summer's birth I proclaimed, in a self-deceiving tactic, that we needed a newer, bigger house, thereby creating a diversion from facing issues. In October 1980 we consummated the purchase and moved into a lovely new home on a cul-de-sac in the western suburbs. For a while there was no fence. During this time Shutter disappeared. She had either run away or been brutalized by the workmen building the house next door because she had barked ferociously at them. I speculated that the laborers buried her in concrete but could not prove anything.

We were left with our mutt. I did not want her; she was a half-breed, therefore imperfect.

Instead of accepting Abby's nuances and who she was, I attempted to coerce her to accept my will. I tried to keep her penned in by a five-foot-high solid wooden fence, the top of which I fortified with electrified wire intermingled with barbed wire, something analogous to trying to keep the Vietcong from penetrating our perimeter. In this case, though, I was trying to keep something in. Abby's will and athletic prowess were impressive. She consistently scaled the fence and jumped through the wire, cutting and shocking herself in the process. I would stand outside, catch her, and return her to the pen. When Abby yelped, I would yell, "SHUTUP!" at the top of my lungs. Then she would get that hangdog look in her eyes. I never hit her, but I hated her at those times. I felt something I could not describe but now know as rage.

Finally I gave up and took down all the barriers. In hindsight I think Abby merely wanted to be near those she loved. I do not think I was one of them. After the marriage ended, Alicia kept Abby for a while, then shipped her off to her parents' seventy acres in northern Louisiana. My understanding was that Abby released her pent-up anger toward her former master by aggressively chasing cows before retiring to a life of leisure and fattening up.

OBSTRUCTION

I was driving down a road under construction, having already ignored a warning sign that the street was closed to all through traffic. A man in a baseball cap and dark jacket positioned himself in a power stance in the middle of the street, raising a hand, palm forward, for me to stop. I stopped but did not want to, for I felt hateful and anonymous in the car. How dare this man impede my progress! After stopping, I inched the car forward and in the process intentionally nudged him with the front bumper. Quick as a panther, he sprinted around to the driver's window and flipped open his wallet, displaying his badge identifying him as a city of Houston police officer. It did not take me too long to realize I had made a serious error in judgment. He came within a hair of arresting me. I went back the next day, found him, and apologized.

THE LIE

In 1981, flying to El Paso on a business trip, I met a woman on the flight. She, in public relations, I, a CPA, and she, like me, married to someone else. It made no difference. With flaming libidos artificially fueled by the insidious tandem of alcohol and emptiness, we willingly seduced each other and agreed to meet in Houston upon our return. Courting disaster as well as each other, we met one time, and one time only, during lunch hour. The tryst began as a picnic on the bank of a bayou but ended up in a motel room.

Foreseeing the possibility of liking this woman and driven by guilt and fear, I chose not to pursue this illicit coupling further. Besides, as hypocritical as it sounds, I loved my wife. It was the thrill of the chase I sought, not the woman. When I *caught* one, I felt obligated to carry through. I was trying to emulate the adrenalin-induced combat high.

The problem with dancing along the edge of a precipice is that it is easy to fall off. Several months later, through morbid curiosity or perhaps divine intervention intended to hold me accountable, I called her place of employment.

"Is S—— there, please?"

"No, she doesn't work here anymore."

"Oh! Do you know what happened to her, where she went?"

"She had a baby."

As I hung up the phone, a chill crept through my being. I pulled out my calendar and fixed the point of our meeting. A calendar does not lie. A few days later I received a phone call.

"Jack?"

"Yes."

"My name is Charles. I believe you know my wife, S——."

I had no idea whether Charles wanted to kill me or talk to me, but, feeling that I had nothing to lose, I agreed to meet him. He would come to my office the next day.

When he arrived, I looked into the eyes of a man determined to set the record straight. Well dressed and articulate, he handled himself like a gentleman. Furthermore he had been a military officer with service in the Vietnam War.

After taking a seat on my sofa, Charles told me that S—— had spoken with a friend from her old company, and that the friend had mentioned my phone call. "That's when S—— broke down," he said, "and told me everything."

What could I say? I remained silent and waited.

"For nine months she carried all that worry and guilt." His tone indicated concern for her . . . directed no malice toward me.

He reached into his pocket and pulled out a packet of photographs. "Take a look at these."

I took the stack and riffled through it.

"The baby looks like you," I said.

"That's what I thought."

As it turned out, he had wanted this visit only to judge for himself whether the baby looked more like him or me. It was an easy call; it was his baby. That was the end of it, except that he admonished me never to see his wife again. The man's comportment impressed me. Had circumstances been different, I believe we could have become friends.

Thus, despite my intentions to speak to no one about the adulterous act, unanticipated consequences arose. My infidelity was a lie, an untruth, as well as a betrayal of the one to whom I had proclaimed commitment. Because consummation of the act had already been released and spread throughout the universe, my attempt to *bury* the event as if it had never occurred failed. Destructive messages and deeds not only spread but also leave a trail. Now, when I find myself faced with temptation, I remember that the man who slips a ring on a woman's finger is a potential friend.

～～

That was a turning point. I rededicated myself to therapy.

As Alicia and I began to talk more, she unburdened all the emotional pain she had absorbed like a sponge, and I began to learn that a man does not lose his masculinity by expressing tenderness. As a way of trying to rebuild the marriage, all lies had to be exposed, so I confessed my unfaithfulness. This disclosure almost crushed her, but she was so strong, so loving and forgiving, that she was willing to give our marriage another chance. One significant problem still had not been adequately addressed, however, despite extended time in therapy, because I had not begun to accept the depth of my rage. There is a thin but complicated volume by Allen Wheelis entitled *How People Change,* in which he describes change as a sequence of necessary steps, beginning with suffering; proceeding through insight, will, and action; and culminating ultimately in change. Each step must be faced and worked through; the work is tedious, requires effort, and progress is slow. My idea of suffering was to make other people do it, to have them suffer for me.

Nevertheless, through therapy Alicia and I made some progress on our marriage. We even decided to have another child. Allison, a beautiful and feisty baby girl, was born in 1983.

To try to cement the family, Alicia suggested we take a Bible-study course. At first I resolutely refused but later relented, hopeful that this search might lead to that elusive peace. Also it was something we could do together. The first course was a ten-week overview of the Old Testament. For reasons of her own Alicia dropped out, but I continued in my quest. Though reared in the Methodist Church, I had rejected Christ or, more appropriately, I had never grasped what his presence and saving grace were all about. As I continued my study of the Old Testament, I felt worse, seeing no possible way for forgiveness or salvation. What did me in were the Ten Commandments, for in my mind I had broken them all. I felt irretrievably lost, hopeless, and unsalvageable. The only book in which I found solace was Solomon's Ecclesiastes, for there was a man who had everything yet constantly searched for the meaning of life. But it was not enough.

There was also my guilt. In addition to the general horrors of war, three specific incidents that occurred in Vietnam haunted me: the girl on the bicycle, the baby in the box, and the near-miss with a grenade. My daughters never understood why I badgered them to wear protective gear when riding their bicycles. Babies' cries of anguish unsettled me. As for the grenade, a scent in the wind, the rustling of tree leaves, or an unexpected shout could trigger a flooding memory. My emotions were raw, I suspect, because only recently had I written poems about all three. I just refused to talk about them.

Soap Bath

Late one night Alicia and I were having a discussion, if you could call it that, and it quickly turned into an argument. She invited me to talk, to discuss my feelings and our relationship. I rejected the invitation, choosing self-destruction instead.

We were in the master bathroom. I took a plastic bottle of soft soap and squeezed the life out of it, whereupon the contents spurted all over me. Alicia laughed. Humiliated, I wanted to die at that instant. But by the time I retrieved my fully loaded .38-caliber Smith and Wesson revolver, cocked the hammer, and placed the barrel of the weapon on my temple, I had lost my will to pull the trigger, yet I kept the gun barrel pressed against my temple until Alicia screamed, "What are you doing?" It was emotional blackmail at its worst.

Sickness

We were nearing the end. It came when I chased down a woman in a bar in Corpus Christi. No sex was involved, but I hated myself.

When I returned home from the business trip, two-year-old daughter Allison was sick, and I spanked her for crying in the middle of the night. To become sick in our family was never okay. It was a sign of imperfection. As a child, my violent fits of coughing also occurred at night. My father's response—it does not matter that I do not remember whether I heard it once or repetitively—is indelibly imprinted on my memory. Spat out like venom, his words, "JACK, SHUT UP!" trumpeted from my parents' bedroom like an airborne virus.

Mom, who had inherited from the women on her side of the family the stoic ability to absorb, endure, and remain silent about their pain, said pleadingly, "Don't yell at him." She and I—perhaps my brothers as well—shared an unspoken acknowledgment that it was our lot to endure Dad's wrath silently. So I buried my mouth in a pillow, trying to muffle and suppress any sounds that might escape. Still I had caught the airborne virus, and now I was passing it on to my family. Did Allison too bury her mouth in a pillow?

The tension was so thick in the household that Summer, then age nine, could not bring a dinner fork to her mouth without flinching. Alicia refused to contain her silence any longer and spoke up. She had endured twelve years of hell; the children were suffering, she was suffering, and she no longer was going to make any effort to save me. She needed to save herself and the children.

"Jack, I want you to leave."

4

REPARATION

Cresting the foaming rapids
  I anticipate with exhilaration
  the energetic thunder
  of my forthcoming plummet.

Downriver
  the roiling subsides
  clear water
  clear vision
    phase in.

Peace has come.
Real work begins.

       "White Water Therapy," a poem.

A fter Alicia's declaration I was bitter and felt I had lost everything, but for reasons I cannot explain, I pursued my study of religion. I asked a local Methodist minister what being a Christian meant. He responded, "Jack, I don't know what else to tell you but that you have not yet experienced God's grace." I had no idea what he was talking about.

The New Testament study covered almost all of the synoptic gospels, and I began to like what I was reading, hungering for and soaking up the messages that Christ delivered on Earth two thousand years ago. I began to feel better and to feel hope that it was possible to be forgiven for the mediocrity of my youth, my actions in war, and my unfaithfulness in marriage. I went to Bible study meetings, read voraciously in my one-bedroom cave, and was fortunate to be around loving people.

The blow struck during my study of Acts. I was jogging, reflecting on the description of Christ's ascension, when I felt totally engulfed by an overwhelming sense of peace and forgiveness. I just stopped and started crying, believing I had undergone a born-again experience. Later I intellectualized that if Christ could forgive me, then who was I not to forgive myself? At that time I still wanted the marriage, telling Alicia I had become a Christian. It had little effect, for too much damage had been done. I think she believed that I was trying to manipulate her again, and I do not blame her. She also said she thought I was already a Christian. Lesson there.

Is there a God? Is Christ real? Does prayer work? I had begun praying, and one prayer being offered was that Alicia not file for divorce.

It was Sunday. I had taken the children back to the home that we had lived in as a family. Spring had come, displaying the fresh, richly saturated greens that are vibrant in Houston. The day was wonderfully clear, with cotton clouds lingering lazily in the sky. I was standing in the driveway. Alicia asked me if I was okay. I said that I was and then felt a shudder ripple through my whole body—it pierced my soul and every part inside me moved. God had answered my prayer; it just wasn't the answer I wanted.

Years later, when I reflected on the events surrounding the divorce, I realized that I had not acted responsibly again because, at that time, I knew I was in turmoil and I needed a separation to clear my soul. Instead I created the environment to be fired through divorce, and Alicia accommodated me. She also disclosed that my *black moods* were a big reason for her decision.

C. S. Lewis, in his book, *The Problem of Pain*, states:

> The human spirit will not even begin to try to

surrender self-will as long as all seems to be well with it. . . .

Until the evil man finds evil unmistakably present in his existence, in the form of pain, he is enclosed in illusion. Once pain has roused him, he knows that he is in some way or other "up against" the real universe: he either rebels (with the possibility of a clearer issue and deeper repentance at some later stage) or else makes some attempt at an adjustment, which, if pursued, will lead him to religion. . . .

Everyone has noticed how hard it is to turn our thoughts to God when everything is going well for us.

New houses, motorcycles, women, and alcohol do not work. They never have and never will. Yet, for me, Christianity was not a cure-all, for even though I quieted my rage, I did not eliminate it.

THE MECHANIC

Several years later during spring break, my daughters and I went skiing in Breckenridge, Colorado, a town that has retained its rustic nature despite being overrun by skiers. On one cold, starlit evening we wandered the streets of Breckenridge in search of a restaurant. The aura was festive, invigorating, but my mind was elsewhere. I had been reading Neil Sheehan's book, *A Bright Shining Lie - John Paul Vann and America in Vietnam.* A maverick both in his military career and in his civilian capacity as a principal leader in America's advisory effort, John Paul Vann seemed to have had credible solutions, but no one listened. Sensing Vann's frustration, my own ignited once again, rekindling not-so-dormant embers. And the peace with Vietnam I thought was mine melted within its fragile shell.

As the three of us walked, our boots crunched through crusted snow, the winter equivalent of cowboy boots displacing gravel. These are nostalgic, earthy sounds. Summer and I were side by side, and Allie trailed a few yards behind. I should have been content. Instead my face conveyed the rage I felt. We encountered a young Vietnamese man coming from the opposite direction. He had on the same mask. We read each other well, exchanging vicious glares but passed without incident. I turned my head slightly. Out of the corner of my eye I saw that he and Allie had come abreast. He swiped at her but did not connect. Others noticed and were startled. I yelled, "Hey!" and started to charge but stopped short. My blood boiling, we continued on our way.

The last day of the trip we skied down the mountain, reaching the bottom thirty minutes before our bus was to depart for Denver. I went into the men's room to change clothes. It had a one-stall latrine, and I hung a set of clothes on the stall door. A husky maintenance man came in, looked at me, looked at the clothes, then looked at me again, not knowing what to do. Needing to use the stall, he took hold of my clothes and handed them to me. I snatched the clothes from his hand and threw them on the floor.

"You got a problem?" he asked, not too gently.

"Yeah, I got a problem. I didn't like the way you handed me my clothes."

We exchanged more words, then he went into the stall and shut the door.

"Go fuck yourself," I yelled.

He charged out of that stall like a bull out of a chute and we were nose to nose. What had I done! We did not come to blows, but it was the closest I have ever been to a fistfight.

"You know, we don't need guests like you around here. Leave and don't come back."

The bus was scheduled to depart in ten minutes, and I was in the lobby with the girls, trying to act as if nothing had happened. I was stewing but started to think. I wanted to make excuses, but they did not stick. Then it hit me. I did not want to leave that evil debris in my wake. I got up and went back to where the maintenance man was working. He was lying flat on his back under a watercooler, and his anxious look told me he was wondering what this crazed man was going to do next. Before he moved or spoke, I blurted out, "I was completely wrong. I'm sorry." He stood, took off his glove, and shook my hand. Then he put his right arm around my shoulder and gave me a gentle squeeze.

Vietnam was neither the reason for my divorce nor an excuse for destructive behavior, yet I wonder what life would have been like without the Vietnam debacle. That divorce is painful for everyone involved has been substantiated time and again. Occasionally on Sunday nights when I brought two-year-old Allison back to her mother's, Allie would put one arm around one of my legs and her other arm around one of Alicia's and try to pull us together. Nevertheless a positive result from the divorce has been that the children were exposed less to my hovering, suppressive anger.

Even though we do it to ourselves, for many displaced fathers the pain of separation from their children, particularly when they are young, never goes away. It just diminishes in intensity as the children grow older. Sharp pain is replaced by a dull ache. You are always saying goodbye: goodbye after an alternate weekend, goodbye after a week's vacation, and goodbye to the mythical, healthy family unit that never was but you wished could have been.

That I damaged Summer and Allie is a given. And like my father, who, in an undated letter, clearly recited his years of abandonment, danced around his pain at not having been loved, and in a roundabout fashion apologized for his behavior and asked for my forgiveness, I have made clumsy efforts to apologize. Children have a remarkable resiliency and ability to forgive, and from them I have learned something about loving. Also, through their will, I have learned that certain of my fathering attempts can only be described as ridiculous.

MESSAGES II

THE HILLBILLY DOLL

During a motorcycle trip to the Ozarks I purchased a hillbilly doll for Allison, who was about four at the time. The doll's face was disguised with a fierce, long red beard; the head featured a backwoods cap; and the hands held a corncob pipe and a miniature jug of whiskey. I thought it was cute. The next weekend that Allison and I were together, I asked politely but manipulatively if she would like to sleep with the doll. She remained completely silent and pointed to what I thought was the floor. I asked her if that was what she wanted. With all the courage she could muster, she pointed again, this time bolstering her gesture with a verbal, "No, in the closet."

A Slightly Disoriented Bird

We were at Brazos Bend State Park southwest of Houston. A picnic! Summer, Allison, and I were walking the perimeter, searching for sightings of the inimical alligator. I was standing slightly behind the girls, who were fifteen and eight. A bird scurried in to land on a lily pad, stumbling over one like Snoopy's friend Woodstock before coming to rest on another lily pad in a clumsy landing. My first thought was that the dumb bird had violated the laws of grace in flight with an imperfect landing. I was disappointed, disgusted. Summer, on the other hand, saw humor in the irony of life's imperfections, giggled, and accepted with grace the awkward touchdown. I looked at her in awe and wonder. She even thought the baby alligators were cute.

The Polaroid

Every fall the community of Magnolia, just north of Houston, hosts an event called the Renaissance Festival, an elaborate re-enactment of costumes, customs, comedies, melodrama, and jousting. A variety of foods similar to those consumed during that period are made available, as are sundry arts and crafts. Jugglers, magicians, and actors intermingle with the crowds and on occasion parade through. Allison brought along a Polaroid camera she had purchased with money she had saved. I simultaneously encouraged and discouraged her shooting, verbalizing one message but emotionally and physically sending another by positioning her and the camera, for nothing but clear, sharp, and well-composed images should emerge from this, her first effort at photography. She became disheartened because I shut down her natural spontaneity and expression.

Once Upon a Rock

North of Kingsland, Texas, just off Ranch Road 1431, the Llano River, en route to Lake LBJ, cuts a wide swath through low-slung hills permeated with variegated limestone. From a low-water crossing you can wade upstream or downstream for hundreds of yards, sliding on rock polished slippery smooth or displacing grains of sand that tickle the toes. An adequate water level provides opportunities for short, energetic bursts of rapid inner-tube rides. And it was at one of those natural entertainment centers that I admonished the girls not to run or skip—whereupon I immediately slid off the slippery pulpit from which I had just preached my short sermon, cracking my right shin on the rocks below. I tore off a strip of towel and tied it tightly around my shin to stem the flow of blood. We skimmed the water on inner tubes for a couple of hours, then went to the Kingsland clinic, where I had five sutures sewn in my leg.

Wisdom and the Grand River

In the early summer of 1990 Summer and I journeyed to the south rim of the Grand Canyon. There we joined a group for an eight-day raft trip. I was forty-five and she almost fourteen. What a wonderful opportunity to honor her with the benefit of my wisdom gleaned from mistakes in life! So at the trail's edge I sermonized, talking really good stuff. Less than enthralled, Summer stood with her right foot slightly in front of her left, stabilizing her stand, locked her left hand firmly around her right wrist, strengthening her defensive posture even more, and completed the fortress with a slight upward tilt of her head. Rolling her eyes to ward off any possible invasion, she said, "Dad, let me learn from my own mistakes."

We descended the winding trail to the water's edge, where the Colorado River displayed its awesome unharnessed power. If you tumbled into the river without a life preserver, it would mean goodbye. The rapids, while not frequent in number, are rated differently from other rivers because water level and intensity vary directly with the volume released from Lake Powell. When snow-fed tributaries join forces with the Colorado, the resulting confluence charges wildly downriver like a running of the bulls. The river's depth and pace therefore vary significantly, resulting in rapids rated from one to ten compared with one to five for true whitewater rivers.

After the nine-mile descent into the heart of a world wonder, I was out of control, having completed the hike on a severely sprained ankle—injured two weeks earlier while trying to maintain masculine identity playing coed softball—encased in an air splint. In addition, because of my anxiety, I had neither slept nor had a bowel movement for two days prior to the trip. To top it off, I did not drink enough water on the jaunt down. This resulted in body spasms and cramps, followed by a day and a half of severe diarrhea, culminating in a coup de grâce whereby I was excreting body waste on the riverbank when another load of rafters floated by, exuberantly waving their arms and yelling in honor of this exhibition.

With this glorious history, I once more enlightened Summer as to how to live her life and what she should do on this trip. She again assumed the aforementioned power stance, only this time her eyes were not rolling. They were glaring, boring into me like lasers. I was afraid she might turn into concrete.

It was apparent to the women on the trip that not only were my efforts of no avail, but they were also inhibiting Summer's riverine experience. They admonished me, saying, "Jack, leave her alone!" I did, and thereafter we had a soul-enriching journey, one of the best I have ever been on. Summer handled herself with grace, strength, and dignity and won the hearts of all on the trip. I was one proud papa. The river guides baked a birthday cake for her.

Dye Your Egg

My daughters and I spent one Easter at our family lake house in the Texas Hill Country. I had not been involved in the business of dyeing Easter eggs in years and decided to remedy that omission, so we went into Marble Falls to buy eggs and assorted dyes. Back at the production line in the kitchen, I became irritated with younger daugh-

42   JACK LYNDON THOMAS

ter Allison while trying to instruct her in the delicate art of perfectly dyeing an egg. No cracks. Deep colors. She was becoming nervous. Summer did not like the scene and spoke up, "Dad, leave her alone." I listened. I turned loose and the day evolved into spontaneous fun. I accepted the cracked eggs and again received instruction that life is not about unattainable perfection but companionship and sharing.

THE HAIRCUT

Allison was seven years old. Her mother was remarrying the following week.

"Dad, would you cut my bangs?" she asked in a matter-of-fact voice.

"I guess so."

She had never asked me to cut her bangs before. It could not be that difficult. So I went to the kitchen, retrieved the kitchen shears, and began to operate. With a brush I smoothed out her bangs and made one deliberate cut. The bangs that were left popped way back on her forehead. It did not look right, the bangs appearing like uneven teeth on a saw blade. I stopped there, deciding enough damage had been done.

Summer walked in. "Allison, I can't believe you let Dad cut your bangs. You know Mom wanted them long for her wedding."

THE SNOWMOBILE RUN

During spring break of 1994 ten-year-old Allison and I were skiing the slopes of Alta, Utah. Her seventeen-year-old sister was unable to join us since she was at home in Houston recovering from a gallbladder extraction. We stayed at the Goldminer's Daughter, an enchanting lodge that boasts a dining environment where families intermingle, sharing tables. Allie was one of the few children. She more than held her own, participating in conversations, clearly articulating her point of view, and listening attentively when spoken to by others. I was proud of Allie, but even more so when two adult men, independent of each other, complimented her on her presence and poise.

Allie and I skipped skiing one day and embarked on a guided snowmobile tour to frolic through the wilderness—an inviting, invigorating wilderness that sparkled beneath a crystalline sky. Narrow, twisting trails serpentined among gentle, undulating hills dotted with rhythmic clusters of towering aspens, whose snow-encrusted spindly limbs, like warped, whitewashed fence pickets, shimmered in the glistening sunlight. We were the last ones, and Allie hung on to my backside as we abruptly ascended a steep hill. The trail turned left at the crest of the slope and, to make up time, I cut the turn short, positioning the snowmobile at a precarious angle. The snowmobile did not like this maneuver and wound up perched delicately on its left runner, about to tip over. As with motorcycling or rafting, there are times to clamber to the high side for counterbalance. While riding the right edge of the seat, I shouted to Allie to do the same, but it was not enough and the snowmobile was on its way over. At the last second I whipped the bars completely to the left, and the snowmobile responded favorably, regaining balance, only now we charged downhill and out of sight of the pack that had left us behind. I, of course, acted as if nothing was wrong, and Allie, in her youthful, wonderful innocence, asked, "Daddy, why are you going this way? Everybody else is going the other way."

ANOTHER BACKSLIDE

Spring break of 1996 found the three of us in Park City, Utah, skiing through tree trails and intermediate slopes. Summer fell, got tickled with herself, and could not get up. Allie went over to help her; she got tickled, fell on top of Summer, and neither one could get up. They continued to laugh and giggle, their limbs and skis so intertwined that it would have taken a master puzzle solver to unravel their web. I was impatient, unable to take pleasure in my own skiing or what my daughters were experiencing, and I dampened their spontaneous joy.

Later in the week we were crossing the main street of Park City with the light in our favor. Disregarding the light, a van came round the corner, turned directly in my path, and slammed on the brakes just before depositing its right front tire on my foot. I did not move and slammed my glove-enclosed fist on the window, yelling a "Goddamn" in the process. I took pleasure in observing the passenger's mortified look before the van left the scene. Summer said, "Dad, that was uncalled for." What made things worse is that I affected Allison. Her lips contorted in a silent look of pain until she could hold it in no longer and burst into tears. I hated myself, but not as much as she hated me at that moment, considering that once more I was infecting her.

Have they caught it? Have I passed on the virus? I hope not. I pray not. We have talked about these things. They have witnessed the folly and destructiveness of unfettered anger, and I believe that they do not want any part of it, that they do not want to live their lives that way, and that they have both embraced and been embraced by an aura of love strong enough to ward off the demon of rage. Ultimately only time will tell how they play out their lives. I believe that a *rageaholic*, like an alcoholic, is never completely cured, that even though the flash point becomes less volatile, the risk of explosion is always present. Much like keeping watch while on patrol, you must constantly watch over yourself, lest your poisonous venom spew on innocent victims.

MESSAGES III

Just before Summer turned sixteen, she was diagnosed with Crohn's disease, an inflammatory bowel disorder of the same family as ulcerative colitis. It is nonfatal but chronic, and the degree of severity in attacks varies from patient to patient. There is no known cause or cure; gastroenterologists continue their search for both.

Stress! How much of it is stress? Summer was a very sick teenager. Being stoic like her mother, she managed it like a trooper, perhaps too much so.

For several years I dragged the children to church, hopeful that the infusion of the Christian message would negate my destructive ones. The minister possessed a gift for taking complex theological issues and boiling them down to simple layman's terms for application in everyday life. The sermon that day was on David's battle against Goliath, a metaphor for the times we face seemingly insurmountable obstacles or hardships in our lives.

"Summer, what did you think of the sermon?" I asked on the way home.

Before she could answer, Allison, who had become a charming dancer and an excellent student, piped up from the back seat, "Yeah, Summer, you might be fighting your Goliath right now."

"Allie, I didn't know you were listening."

"Yeah, I was listening while I was coloring, Daddy."

So, despite the backslides, things gradually were getting better, but Vietnam still called.

5

Follow Me

We want people to see us as we wish them to, ignoring our dark side, denying the ugliness that resides within. By disregarding the impact of destructive behavior, we blur the line between the acceptable and unacceptable. Unacceptable behavior becomes tolerated and, therefore, becomes acceptable by default because we do not talk about it, challenge, or confront it. It exists, but we relegate the unspeakable to another world as if it is not ours.

Shame and guilt are most effective suppressants, coming packaged in their own cylindrical vaults complete with an integral, complex combination lock. Rolling around within are self-perpetuating, destructive patterns of abuse and silence, protected and buried secrets that inhibit our becoming what we could be.

From 1982 through 1995, on journeys from two to five weeks in length, I lashed out at the back roads of the Texas Hill Country, Big Bend, the Ozarks, the Blue Ridge, New Mexico, and southwestern Colorado, covering some sixty thousand miles in fourteen states. Whether it was to flee the corporate world or escape into the past, I was never sure, but motorcycling offered a channel for understanding and developing my life. On each journey I pursued lifelong dreams of writing and photography, making a serious effort to develop that part of me which was intrinsically sanctioned but not ordained.

I have always loved to read maps, to study them, to peer intently into their depths to find that unique road that few have traveled upon. It took me years to realize that I was searching for vestiges of my father in small, remote, enchanting roads and towns. Though he had been dead for more than fifteen years, and I had not taken a trip with him for more than thirty, those were the times we shared. He showed a warm, compassionate side during those excursions. I watched him see and feel nature. I learned to do it too. My amateur career in photography began at the age of nine when I received from Dad a small camera with a foldout bellows. Ever since then, in every photograph of a wildflower or distant landscape, the part of his being, his presence, that I so desperately needed to be meshed with mine, found its way onto the final image.

Motorcycling in our family was off the chosen path, a dare early on, even though I think my father would have fallen in love with the experience had he ever taken the plunge. Brother Harry was the first to take up the two-wheel thunder as a symbolic defiance of our father's harsh repression and an indirect flaunting of his will. It was while riding with two of my brothers, when we camped, smoked cigars, and talked, that I realized I was not alone, that they too experienced our father similarly. Mostly, though, I rode the miles in solitude, using speed to whisk away the clutter and free my mind. I sought wide, enticing views that swept in and expanded my soul—places where I could settle down and reflect. I thought about my aborted efforts in athletics where, had I been successful, I still would not have earned my father's love and acceptance. I reflected on my career and my dreams—dreams of the future, unfulfilled dreams of the past, and, of course, dreams of the Vietnam War. It was a war, by the way. It was a war.

When the fall of 1995 marked the end of my three-year stint as chief financial officer of Slick 50, an engine treatment company that sold out to Quaker State, I launched another motorcycle run in search of myself. On a burgundy BMW K1100RS I chased rainbows through the Ozarks, fought headwinds through the rolling farmlands of western Missouri, then demolished the romantic illusion behind the *Bridges of Madison County* in Iowa. The exhilarating crispness of autumn sharpened my senses, and ideas that had been germinating began to crystallize. Returning to the corporate world was not one of them.

One dream involved the purchase in Germany of a glacier green 1996 BMW R1100RT, then breaking it in by touring through the European Alps, which I accomplished in early summer of 1996. The trip was a watershed event, the mix of riders a blessing, and I chronicled it all on a laptop computer carried in the chase van. I photographed with abandon the breath-taking, stimulating scenery so startlingly different from my Houston flatland home.

The walls of my home are adorned with enlargements of photographs, remembrances of charming places I have seen, which represent my quest for meaning. Thousands of slides, the majority of which will forever remain encapsulated within tin boxes, reside in a closet.

Also tucked away in a closet is a set of polished jungle boots, a set of camouflage jungle fatigues adorned with military insignia including first lieutenant's bars (the insignia blackened so as not to broadcast officer status to a sniper), and a set of dress greens. Staring at the jungle fatigues always triggered the same reaction—unsettledness. Would the feeling ever go away? I made a decision: return to Vietnam and revisit the one year at war I spent in that foreign land.

Next I placed a phone call. "Jim, this is Jack, your former teammate. I'm going back to Vietnam."

"What for?"

"To confront my ghosts." I took a deep breath. "How about coming along?"

Through his silence I felt his hesitancy.

"I'd dearly love for us to do it together," I said, hoping to sway him. "Are you interested?"

"Let me think about it."

Even though we had remained in contact over the years, we had never really discussed the war. The next day I sent Jim a copy of an audiotape he did not know I had, a recording of two attacks we had undergone at the An Dinh outpost. Live combat—our combat.

A few days later Jim called. "I'm hooked," he said.

Jim needed to be in Atlanta in September for a technical trade show for business security systems. He extended an invitation. "Why don't you come to Atlanta for a long weekend? We'll go down to Fort Benning, visit our old stomping grounds of OCS."

"Great idea. What a warm-up! We'll be prepping ourselves for the return."

It had been twenty-eight years since Jim and I departed Columbus, Georgia. We began to bring memories alive: first, of battling through OCS, and second, of serving as tactical officers in OCS where we did to others what had been done to us. Speciously alluring, Fort Benning's grand entryway is separated by a manicured median, where pines stand ramrod straight throughout, like silent sentinels guarding the fort, the swaying branches serving as a conduit for the wind's whispered, soothing messages from infantry soldiers of other wars saying, "It's okay, it's okay, we understand."

Inside the post, any country-club trappings trail away as the whitewashed stucco homes of colonels, lieutenant colonels, and captains give way to barracks housing for NCOs and trainees. For this is the "Infantry School," where its one hundred eighty-two thousand acres accommodate airborne and ranger training as well as basic infantry doctrine and tactics.

The post looks the same now, but it is not. Only one OCS company—and it is coed—is undergoing training, and its fourteen-week cycle is nearly complete. The new OCS graduates will not even be around to harass basic candidates when a new training cycle begins. During Jim's and my tenure, twelve to fifteen OCS companies were engaged at some stage of the cycle in the six-month course, with basic candidates being constantly harangued by senior candidates. When not in class, OCS candidates were marching, double-timing, performing calisthenics, parading, yelling, being yelled at, and singing in cadence. Electricity was in the air, the atmosphere charged, partly from the pure numbers of candidates, partly from the spreading Vietnam cloud.

In the 1996 program, newly commissioned officers are channeled into sixteen branches of the Army. Each officer will then undergo another sixteen weeks of training in that specific branch. The current OCS battalion commander, Lt. Col. Scott Ambrister, points out that OCS candidates receive thirty weeks of training compared with twenty-four in our era. Was ours harder and tougher, is theirs, or is it the same? Who knows? It just feels different.

A senior officer candidate takes us to see the refurbished OCS Hall of Fame. Neither Jim nor I had made the cut as you had to have attained the rank of a general officer, been awarded the Medal of Honor, or contributed something of significance to this nation, such as being elected a congressman. Over America's war years several OCS graduates have been awarded the Medal of Honor, and Jim and I sense this young man's pride in the work his company has performed in sprucing up this testimonial to service. We sense a strong combination of work ethic and values ingrained in this soon-to-be lieutenant in the Signal Corps, who hopes to study electronics and management information systems after graduation.

Fort Benning is also the home of the National Infantry Museum, an attestation to the role the infantry soldier has played in battle. Housed in a three-story complex that used to be the post hospital, the museum's array of weapons encompasses the archaic as well as the most modern. A section of one wing is dedicated to the Vietnam period, and we revisit several weapons with which we had become intimately familiar during our tours. Before leaving the post, we observe two platoons of airborne trainees who have just completed jump school.

When I reflect upon the history of sacrifices the American soldier has endured to preserve the rights of this country, a feeling of pride wells up once again. But for me the message has been tempered with reality for, as I ruminate on one of the missions of a small unit infantry leader, which is to exhort his men to lay down their lives for their mission, the words seem out of date, almost hollow.

9 OCTOBER 1996

Sebastopol, California—Jim's home for the last several years. We drive into San Francisco to meet our trip coordinator at Noey's Bar and Grill, at the corner of Twenty-fourth and Church Streets. We review final details: passports with visa stamps, itinerary, and name of our primary contact in Vietnam. Our preventive inoculations are up to date. Satisfied with our preparations, we are ready to depart, protected against everything except emotion.

6

SAIGON TO TAY NINH

Old soldiers
standing precariously at attention
on weathered
withering frames.

Old soldiers
surrendering to the wind
their silvery hair mirroring
the day's waning incandescence.

Old soldiers
grieving their frailty
their wisdom tossed aside
as the lessons of war.

Old soldiers . . .
going to seed.

"Old Soldiers," a poem inspired by
a photograph of backlit cattails.

2100 Hours, 12 October 1996

"Well, it's sure as hell as humid as it was twenty-seven years ago," Jim comments as we disembark the Vietnam Air flight that has transported us from Hong Kong.

"It's hard to believe that Tan Son Nhut was the busiest airport in the world during the late sixties. There's nobody here now. Where is everyone?"

Sensuous young Vietnamese stewardesses, adorned in rich pink *ao dais*, had provided in-flight services on the last leg of our journey. A saying in Vietnam, "The *ao dai* covers everything but hides nothing," is a testament to the rippling, sensual, and provocative fantasies that accompany the swirl and flow of that decorous garment. But those images are quickly subjugated once we reenter the sweltering, steaming world.

Noticeably absent this time, however, are the green Army buses, their windows covered with screening to ward off uninvited grenades, that had taken us to the processing center. Instead, there to greet us is a young Vietnamese man, Mr. Lo Van Loc, our tour guide and interpreter, who is dwarfed by Jim's six-foot two-inch frame. Mr. Loc's build and soft manner remind me of Sergeant Thanh, our former interpreter.

Walking toward a van, I observe flickering lightning and hear reverberating thunder as a monsoon shower tapers off in the west. Soon the rainy season will end and the dry season will begin, which was the period when American mechanized units unleashed their tanks and armored personnel carriers. The tracked vehicles were more effective then because they were less susceptible to bogging down.

The slashing lightning and rumbling thunder kindle an odd thought. "You know, I remember the relentless rain. I don't remember the lightning and thunder."

"Yeah, well, maybe you slept through it all," Jim says.

Right—as recollection of sleep deprivation comes into consciousness.

After checking in at the Saigon Star Hotel, we eat a bite, then trudge to our room and hit the sack. It has been a long journey.

Sunday morning Jim and I rise early and take a walk. The streets of Saigon—it will always be Saigon to me—are more congested and congealed than ever, as they now field traffic for more than five million inhabitants in Saigon proper and another two million on the periphery. The city is a quivering mass of street flesh, small cc motorcycles, cyclos, bicycles, small automobiles, lambrettas, and trucks. On rare occasions refurbished jeeps and two-and-a-half-ton trucks appear, any U.S. military insignia long since obliterated.

Motorcycles predominate. The cycles are so close together that a passenger can place her hand on an adjacent passenger's shoulder. Observing this tangled mass negotiating lane changes and turns is like watching an out-of-step marching band cross ranks. Even though there is a scarcity of street signals to regulate the throng, riders slip in between and around each other, miraculously avoiding collision.

There are a few policemen about, some of whom appear to be in plainclothes. Vietnamese citizens are not allowed to own or possess weapons. Interestingly even armed policemen have to turn in their weapons at the end of their shift. Horns blare incessantly. Crossing a street as a pedestrian is an art form, best accomplished at a sauntering pace that does not impair the swirling masses' ability to avoid impact. If you run, you will throw the riders out of sync and be nailed.

Like a tide, memories come flooding back, particularly the harsh impact in 1969 with the girl on the bicycle. Another war-worn image of the South Vietnamese manifests itself—their grace and elegance. The farmers didn't walk—they glided. Using a rocking, flowing gait, they carried produce in baskets hanging from the ends of long bamboo poles that were balanced on their shoulders and pulsated with the rhythm of weight transferring like the swing of a pendulum, only up and down.

These people are agile, wiry, and persistent. Oh, are they persistent. Cyclo drivers follow us for blocks, imploring us to travel in their foot-pedaled taxis.

"Hey, you! I show you Saigon."

Side streets, chock-full of *authorized* vendors cohabiting with mama-sans cooking over small fires, are also clogged with street urchins hawking everything from T-shirts to gum, and with beggars. The beggars get to me, their touches from behind like the clammy feel of death, as if they had emerged from gravesites for a day of solicitation.

Families live above intimate, intricate shops displaying for sale almost every piece of ware imaginable, their technological offerings only a generation or two behind the latest advances. Evidence of new construction exists, primarily in the form of hotels and office buildings, but less so in the city proper, due to limited space.

"I don't think Saigon's changed very much. It seems engagingly familiar."

I nod. Not that we knew it that well, however, because we seldom made it into the city. Still, it is the aura, the feel of the place.

We continue our stroll. A man urinates against a wall, not an uncommon sight off main thoroughfares. Among the sidewalk vendors and foot traffic lay human feces.

Allegedly the average monthly wage in Saigon is equivalent to eighty-five dollars, compared to a monthly wage of sixty-five dollars in the field. That is the official line. Jim and I see evidence to the contrary. The official currency is the dong, but everyone freely accepts U.S. dollars. Black market capitalism reigns supreme in Communist Saigon.

"Did you see that?" Jim asks, shaking his head in astonishment. "She had a roll of hundred-dollar bills."

"Makes sense. If a new motor scooter costs three thousand dollars, that's equivalent to three years' salary. I doubt if their credit is that good. They're making money somehow."

I can buy a T-shirt in a store for fifteen dollars. I can buy the same style on the street for a dollar fifty. Receipts are available only upon asking, even in the few department stores.

We meet Mr. Loc and have lunch at the Rex Garden, which is adjacent to the Rex Hotel. Behind it looms a large, white-columned building, now known as the Revolutionary Museum. After lunch we pile into the van, Loc beside the driver, Jim and I taking seats in the back.

Loc escorts us into Cholon, the Chinese district, allegedly the most prosperous one in the city. Buyers haggle with textile vendors. Robed monks walk among old men clacking mah-jongg tiles on game boards. The poignant aroma of incense permeates the air.

Even though Cholon means "big market," the prosperity is not apparent, but then, all of Saigon is full of paradoxes, of mystery, of misunderstanding. TV antennas are omnipresent, motorcycles abundant, technology evident (a phone call to the States from our Saigon Star Hotel room resulted in an instantaneous ring), but it is as if the Vietnamese have leapfrogged over the development of basic human services, such as sanitation and healthcare. I would hate to become sick here. And I wonder where they are going to put all their children. They are replenishing what was lost in the war, their workforce. The population in all of Vietnam approximates seventy-two million, of whom forty-five percent are under age twenty, and were not even around in the war years. They have a bi-daily school system, with one set of children attending in the morning, another in the afternoon.

We continue our expedition, weaving through throngs of children on bicycles that further clog street arteries.

"Jim, recognize that building?"

"Yep. The Reunification Palace. Used to be called Independence Palace. Two renegade South Vietnamese Air Force pilots bombed it in 'sixty-two."

I had forgotten Jim is an amateur historian.

"Let's take a look."

And that we do, beginning with the basement that showcases accessible escape tunnels. Operating maps, used during the war by South Vietnamese intelligence and communication specialists, are plastered on the walls. Red overlays denote areas that were dominated or contested by Communist, NVA, and Vietcong activity. A tidy little red rectangle hovers over our operating district.

We scrutinize the maps intently, emotionally inserting ourselves, casting sidelong glances westward toward the Cambodian border. The picture is falling into place, coming together again. We are getting closer to our war.

In addition to the ground floor, the Reunification Palace contains three main floors, two mezzanine levels, and a terrace with a helicopter landing pad. There are reception rooms, conference rooms, study rooms, banquet rooms, and living quarters. The palace is open, so the environment can work itself in, but the building reeks of coldness and sterility. It is while we are standing on the highest balcony, the one facing the palace gates, that the realization sinks in.

"Can you imagine watching NVA T-54 tanks crashing through the gates, demanding that you give up your country?"

Saigon was not our primary realm of experience during the war but a specious way station, a perverted contrast to life in the field. The motive for returning to South Vietnam is to revisit our operating sector and recapture the part of our souls still searching for purpose among the rice fields of Duc Hue District. Headquarters for this irregularly shaped district plat lay fifty-five kilometers northwest of Saigon. Duc Hue was part of Hau Nghia Province, which was formed in October 1963 by appropriating districts from contiguous provinces already in existence. The province was roughly pentagonal in shape; the reasons for its boundaries were dictated more by politics than by natural lines of demarcation. The focus was strategic for it was a major link—or impediment, depending on your point of view—between eastern Cambodia and the coveted Saigon arena. Also the province's rice production provided a convenient source of supply for the Vietcong through contributions—voluntary or otherwise.

The waning sun casts a shadow over these recollections as we leave the Reunification Palace. Close to sensory overload, we have absorbed enough for the day and decide to return to the hotel.

Monday morning finds us driving northwest along Highway 1 and then continuing on Highway 22 to Nui Ba Den (Black Virgin Mountain). During the war the 3,225-foot-high mountain was laced by an enemy tunnel network, where Jim had participated in an operation to root out the well-entrenched Vietcong. The mission failed. South of Nui Ba Den lies Tay Ninh city, the birthplace of the Cao Dai, a minority religious sect. They, much like the Catholics, had been more favorably disposed to America's cause than were the Buddhists. During the Indochina War, the Cao Dai had their own private Army and fought alongside the French against the Vietminh.

Ornate, the Cao Dai temple runs the approximate length of a football field. Twin towers frame their religious icon, the omniscient eye. The Cao Dai blend four religions: Buddhism, Taoism, Confucianism, and Christianity.

We arrive in time for the noon ceremony. The priests bow and rise in unison while a choir chants a mind-numbing hymn, its reverence emphasized by a series of gong beats. Spiraling serpents, their grotesque heads just above an intricate tile floor, wrap around pink columns supporting a ceiling of blue sky and white clouds. Shades of turquoise combine with varying hues of green, blue, black, and gold to garnish the temple's sandy walls. Exterior columns support multitiered balconies and a rambling tile roof. The sharp angles, rounded shapes, and disparate colors blend in harmony. It is an impressive sight.

Next we double back and pay a visit to Cu Chi, which from March 1966 through December 1970 served as headquarters for the United States Army's 25th Infantry Division. The location has been transformed into a training site for the People's Army of Vietnam. We try to get in but are refused admission. It seems as if, by obliterating all vestiges of American presence, the Communist government can more easily deny our occupation.

One area we are allowed to enter, however, includes a bizarre booby trap exhibit as well as access to the infamous tunnels of Cu Chi. Reflections on these guerrilla-warfare devices are covered in the final chapter of this book.

Consumed again with emotion, we return to Saigon for dinner and a good night's sleep. After breakfast the next morning we check out from the Saigon Star, then continue the search for traces of ourselves.

In Bao Trai, the former provincial capital of Hau Nghia located seventeen kilometers southwest of Cu Chi, we look for what had constituted province headquarters, but no structures stand out that match those clearly etched in our memory. Bao Trai village houses a small café at an intersection, and there we stop to partake of a Vietnamese lunch. Although other former American soldiers probably have preceded our return to the area, I speculate that the number would be few, so I am surprised when I hear the English language.

"How da ya do?"

"Huh?"

"My name is Antran. I lived in Houston for eight years and now I live in Las Vegas. I gamble for a living."

Obviously Vietnamese, he belies his origin with a dark but thin mustache, difficult for many Vietnamese to grow. "What are you doing here?" I ask.

His response is simple and direct. "I am visiting relatives."

Antran, the only name he gave us, had been a boat person, but Vietnamese expatriates are now free to return to visit their former country. This is ironic. The country has been purged of Amerasian children, remnants of American presence essentially have been eliminated, former South Vietnamese soldiers we served with were either killed or reeducated and taught to disavow any prior association with us, or, if fortunate, were allowed to leave the country.

Our outstanding guide and interpreter, Mr. Loc, had three brothers who became refugees, fleeing to Australia, where they still live. After Loc warmed up to us, he dropped the party line, confiding that he too is interested in moving abroad some day.

"My father was a commissioned officer in the Army of the Republic of Vietnam," Loc says. "He spent two years in a reeducation camp. If he had spent three years, our whole family would have been free to emigrate to America."

Mr. Loc has talked to his brothers and, of course, sees Caucasians in his line of work. But there is still a lot of fear, a lot of repression; to express how you really feel is not something a Vietnamese can do publicly and be looked upon with favor.

Loc says in good English, "There are few books on the Vietnam war in Vietnam bookstores. And they are not objective, I think. I would like to know more about the war, about America. Would you send me some books? I think they would be more objective."

"You betcha!" I reply.

Mr. Phat, Chief of Guiding Department & Car Team for a tourism company, joins us. Obviously not shy, he insists on piling additional quantities of food on my plate. Phat does not speak English, but we are told he is familiar with this section of reconstructed Long An Province.

Jim has a mission. "I want to see if we can find remnants of the airstrip, where you and I were dropped off."

"Roger. Let's do it."

After finishing lunch, we five set off in the van to peruse the area around Bao Trai, once a Vietcong stronghold, then a province capital of South Vietnam during the latter stages of the war, and now current party line Communist village. Five minutes later Jim points to an area beside the road. "That could be it," he says, "but I can't be sure. The stretch is long enough for an airstrip, but I hadn't thought about vegetation growth over the years. I wonder how old those bamboo and palm trees are."

Our driver pulls over and the four of us trudge one hundred meters toward a hedgerow. Again an old familiar feeling pops up like a slap in the face. The humidity is suffocating, our bodies quickly excreting perspiration that sucks our clothes to our skin. Curious villagers emerging from the hedgerows soon surround and observe us, the round-eyed strangers, an occurrence to be repeated at every stop in the field. The farther inland we go, the more remote the places we visit, the more the villagers and farmers flock to us. Loc speaks to an elderly woman.

"What does she say?"

"She says this was the airstrip. She remembers the perforated steel planking laid down for the runway. She also says she lost two children in the war. They were not soldiers, and she is not sure which side killed them."

This is not the only time I doubt the veracity of Loc's comments when potentially inflammatory issues surface, as if he were trying to protect one side or the other regarding responsibility for death—in this case, the old woman's two children. But Jim and I sense no hostility at all from these villagers. In fact, when I transfer from my video camera to 35mm, they find it amusing, peering into the lens and laughing at the number of my electronic gadgets. The most important thing is that the existence of the airstrip has been confirmed; we have found our first field link, a manifestation of our earlier presence.[1]

7

DUC HUE DISTRICT

The old man,
a carpenter by trade,
lived in the village
of Hiep Hoa.

We spoke little of his language.
He spoke none of ours,
so we took our interpreter.
Jim and I each wanted a table.

His home was small, Spartan too.
We shared a pot of tea,
which seemed common to me.

We visited a while, exchanged nothing profound.
Nor did we speak of the enemy,
whoever that might be.

A pleasant little old man—
he seemed eager to please.
Jim and I each got our table—
made of hand-polished teak.

That was a long time ago.
But I wonder—
was he left alone?
He could even have been one of them.

I still have the table.
Good luck, old man.

"The Table," a poem.

❦

From Bao Trai we head north on old Route 10, turn left on Route 7A at Tan My, then head southwest to the villages of Hiep Hoa and Duc Hue, home of the old Sugar Mill, tantalizingly close to the old French villa.

The road has been resurfaced, but it is extremely rough and slows us down. Then we hit water. Several kilometers of the road are inundated, which means that the houses fronting the canals—and, farther on, lining the riverbanks—will be flooded as well. The water level is the highest in eighteen years. Modern utility poles have petered out, the scant availability of electricity evidenced by wavering bamboo poles, whose wiring and proximity to groundwater make them seem extremely precarious and potentially dangerous. TV antennas, secured to bamboo poles, still pop up, but generators, not utility lines, power most of them. The primary source of illumination in the rice fields of Duc Hue District comes from oil lamps, just as it did twenty-seven years ago, or perhaps even twenty-seven hundred years ago.

The rice fields are another irony in a land full of contrasts. Although situated about twenty degrees latitude farther north, Houston, the only home I had ever known other than Vietnam, is also well known for its thunderous rainstorms and is as flat and low as the land I am treading upon now. Before Houston's urbanizing tentacles spread westward, overrunning what used to be verdant rice fields, the two lands experienced a tenuous, distant kinship, bound together by a common purpose. I will always feel a sense of brotherhood with Vietnam's land and its people for part of me will always be there.

As our van churns through swollen waters, we scan the terrain to our right in search of the road threading into the interior and terminating at the mysterious hamlet of Rung-Tre, the site that represented our initiation into Duc Hue District.

"That must be it. There weren't any other roads splintering off this one."

"Yeah, but it's a quagmire. We'd never make it."

Disappointed, we maintain course and reach another intersection that would take us to the river, the site of the villa, but the water appears too deep to traverse.

"Mr. Loc, we've got to get there. What can we do?"

In what turns out to be characteristic of Loc's resourcefulness and creativity, he responds, "I will make arrangements for you to go by boat—in two days."

Jim and I gaze skeptically at the wooden sampans. Bleached by the sun and worn smooth by time, the wood reflects bursts of sunlight as if in warning not to climb aboard. The sampans, some powered by single-cylinder engines with an extended shaft and small propeller affixed to the other end, others propelled by muscle power, carry the same people and culture now as then.

It is the middle of the day and time for the next step. Still dripping with perspiration, I extract from my camera backpack a three-inch-thick bundle of photographs. Several Hiep Hoa villagers excitedly gather round to peer curiously at the pictures, rapidly flipping through the stack before passing them on to other hands. We are filled with apprehension as to how they will react, but when bursts of giggles and laughter emanate from the gathering, our fears are dispelled. No definitive link with any of those we knew has been acknowledged, but we have bridged another gap.

After completing arrangements to float down the canal to the river two days hence, we pile back into the van and plow forward to see if floodwaters have receded sufficiently to allow access to the Sugar Mill. They have, barely. As we hydroplane down old Route 7A, the wake from the van fans outward and gently laps at the ankles of villagers gazing intently at our vehicle, wondering who these Caucasians are.

We arrive. The Sugar Mill is being refurbished and remodeled, this time in concert with Cuban partners, not French. We look for signs of familiarity, such as structures, concrete walls, or people.

I stand quietly, scanning for definition, as a fickle wind breathes into my consciousness vague vestiges that have long lain dormant and are gradually gathering both shape and meaning. What is significant is what is not here as well as what is. I feel as though I have arrived at a long-ago movie set, whereby I received pay for playing a bit part in an action movie. Except it was real; neither side fired blanks.

The armed guards stationed at the entrance gate represent a different government now, and they refuse us access to the mill's sacred workings.

"Why?" I ask Loc.

"They [Sugar Mill security] say they are afraid local police would not approve of our visit."

At least they are consistent for we had already been denied our request to visit with former North Vietnamese Army officers.

A security guard speaks to Loc. He translates. "Put your camera away."

I do, but not before snapping a couple of photos from the hip. Big deal. A Communist flag flies above a government building.

"The tower's gone. It was distinctive. Stood out like a beacon. Remember the red and white checkerboard pattern?"

"Yeah. It reminded me of Ralston Purina, a comforting landmark for the choppers."

Staring at the exterior walls, I wonder if all the bullet holes have been patched. (A description of the structure as it was is covered later in the book.) It is a shame we are not allowed to see the new version.[2] Nonetheless time edges forward, and so must we.

"Mr. Loc, does the villa still exist?"

Loc inquires and then shakes his head.

Allegedly it has been destroyed. If so, it is a major setback for it had been our escape from the field, a haven where some semblance of civilization and civility was made available.

Swallowing another lump of disappointment, we decide to loop around the villa, taking the road that formed the southern perimeter of our operating area. Fortunately it is navigable to the river's edge.

There, to our surprise, we see a bridge spanning the Vam Co Dong. During the war, either helicopters or river patrol boats ferried us across.

"We must stop here," Loc says.

Jim raises his eyebrows. "How come?"

"Too close to Cambodia," Loc replies, offering no further explanation.

The Cambodian border lies roughly sixteen kilometers due west. After all this time, it seems to me the Vietnamese are taking an unreasonable stance, and I wonder if there is something they do not want us to see.

The five of us exit the van. Walking across the bridge, we peer north in search of the villa site, but a protrusion of wooded land frustrates any sighting and precludes confirmation. Jim and I are more determined than ever to sail upriver and see for ourselves whether the former district headquarters might still stand.

A woman from the west side spots us and approaches Loc. They share a brief conversation.

"What was that all about?"

"She wants to know if you are Russian. She wants to sell a baby."

Then, as if embarrassed by this disclosure, Loc says she was only kidding, but I do not think so.

Leaving the Vam Co Dong for now, we head to Tan An, a city approximately forty kilometers southwest of Saigon. Smaller and less active than the mother city, Tan An fronts the Vam Co Tay River. Here, sampans and Chinese junks crowd the waterway. Once night falls, the tide gropes through the town like a black phantom, baptizing all in its path, as if there's a continuing need for renewal. For the locals, rising water is nothing out of the ordinary as pedestrians wade and bicyclists pedal unconcerned through the swollen river.

Wednesday morning begins with a clamor. At 0530 hours the Communists broadcast over community loudspeakers *the news*—thirty minutes of it. I find this melancholic. Regardless of what is being transmitted, however, I know that real news of the outside world travels along the grapevine, via expatriates such as Antran who return to visit, not to live, and spread the word of available opportunities in America, Canada, and Australia. Seeds of capitalism are becoming more widely dispersed and planted every day.

Jim interrupts my thoughts.

"I don't think I can go today. I felt fine when I first got up, but now my stomach's about to explode."

This is bad news, but I am not surprised because he will eat almost anything. Disappointed, I try to offer words of understanding, but in actuality prod him to go. "We can always stop on the roadside, just like before."

"No, I'd better stay here. You go on. I'm going to rest up and hope I can go tomorrow."

"Okay. Anything you need?"

"Ask them to send up some steamed rice at noon."

Hence, I set out as the lone American, with Loc, the guide Phat, and our driver. We retrace the previous day's route as far as Tan My, only this time we do not make a left turn but instead continue northwest on Route 10 toward the village of An Ninh. The stretch of road from the Tan My intersection to the link with Route 6A runs nine kilometers. Excitement and anticipation are welling up inside for the memory of the An Dinh outpost—the shell of a house, the almost square hedgerow surrounding it—is as vivid as yesterday. Stored images had already been resurrected and crystallized from studying twenty-seven-year-old aerial and ground photos. For me the outpost is my primary objective, and I stare anxiously and intently out the left window.

A hedgerow looms to my left front. Silent thunder reverberates within, churning my stomach, my chest, my soul; feelings want to cry out from their silence, to release themselves through my mouth and eyes in mixed cries of recognition, relief, joy—and sorrow. I want to scream, to proclaim, "That's it; that's where it all happened." It is as if amidst all the mortar shells that had fallen and all the rounds that had spewed from the muzzles of rifles and machine guns at the An Dinh outpost, I had emerged from the hedgerow and greeted myself.

Yet I squash the feelings, thinking this site too soon up the road for it to be *my place of birth*, but my gut instinct refuses to be quieted for only a short distance farther north emerges An Ninh Village. No other hedgerow had stimulated such emotion, so I file away the image, then issue another request.

"I need to see where this road meets the river traffic," I say to Loc, "where the Vietcong had come across."

We turn left. The northern boundary of our primary operating area was Route 6A, a road essentially running east-west that I had traveled a portion of, but never taken to its terminus at the Vam Co Dong. Composed primarily of laterite—a reddish clay—the pathway has not been resurfaced. Dodging chuckholes full of mud, we cover four kilometers and stop just before the crumpled road dives into the watery tentacles of the Vam Co Dong. Am I the first American to return to this site? If not the first, I am one of the few. Again villagers stare curiously as Loc makes arrangements to rent a manually propelled sampan, one that will take us a couple of hundred meters to the river, where we will encircle the village, then pole back through the flooded, thatch-roof, bamboo homes of An Ninh West.

The stifling humidity, a combination of steam bath and dry sauna, envelops us, yet the oppressive heat instills a sense of belonging. And once I have squatted in the small wooden sampan, sharing space with two young Vietnamese girls, a small boy, two boatmen, and my guide, I accept with fervor that my experiences were real, that no one can ever, ever take them away. Along with my perspiration I feel my shame evaporating. I feel the depth into which Jim and I immersed ourselves twenty-seven years ago and hear again Sergeant Kerbow's courageous words of admonishment that helped me stay alive.

Forging over the river, I see children wading waist deep, school books slung over their shoulders as they slosh to their homes. When they lay their heads down for the night, it will be on wooden slats mere inches above water level or on ancient hammocks hovering just out of water's reach. The young girls in the sampan adroitly adjust their position, causing but an imperceptible ripple in the water over which we glide. They stare at me with a detached curiosity. Expressionless faces, stiff lips—even the camera lens moves them not. As the sampan glides silently through the bamboo and palm, I visualize the deft Vietcong ferrying weapons and supplies from across the river, a staging area for underground caches farther inland. The hamlet had been abandoned during the war, relinquished to men and women of the night—the Vietcong. Now the farmers are back, content to plow their fields and harvest rice, and consciously rearing children to do the same. Not many will break from the mold.

After reaching the river, we pole south a short distance before shifting east on a canal, a natural artery. Brushing away palm fronds, crouching low as we tunnel under a weathered wooden footbridge, I sense the farmers' tranquility flowing as easily as the tide. They do not fight the elements but move with them, savoring the longest peace-time in generations. Sampans emerge from under tree-lined canopies, carrying home fresh produce from market. Clothes are suspended from makeshift clotheslines, their drying retarded by the sweltering humidity. Women pluck them off the lines while standing ankle-deep in water. Electricity has yet to make a significant impact. Oil lamps will illumine the night. This is their way of life in this silent, watery world. Upon reaching dry land, I hop from the boat and amble through the village marketplace, where once again I am met with curious stares, smiles of wonderment, and occasional laughter.

I think about my father's comment during that mid-fifties family vacation in Monument Valley. Senses alerted by a Navaho baby's cry, my father had said, "All babies cry in the same language." The corollary, "All people laugh in the same language," rings a sweeter bell.

We depart An Ninh West. Clattering back down the broken road, we pass rural schoolchildren who have been released from the first session. Most of the children are riding bicycles, but one girl, perhaps four or five years old, is skipping along the road. She is in a world of her own, oblivious to the turmoil that engulfed this land for so long. And I cannot help but think, if she is skipping, she must be content. If content, she must have enough to eat, and she must have enough love. And perhaps that's enough. She does not need me to tell her how to live.

We turn the corner and are now heading south on old Route 10. The image I had filed away earlier comes alive.

"Mr. Loc, I want to stop at that hedgerow I pointed out." I need to get my sense of it.

Shortly we roll to a stop beside the trail that leads to the hedgerow. Full of anticipation, I pull out my dog-eared packet of pictures and go search for my South Vietnamese home. The outpost had been near An Dinh hamlet, one of the many hamlets that made up An Ninh Village, and though twenty-seven years of vegetation growth clouds perspective, the shape is intimately familiar. But upon penetrating the hedgerow's interior, my heart sinks, for the shell of the house that once stood stands no more. A different house! I look for the well, the outhouse we constructed. Nothing. Walking beyond the hedgerow, scanning former fields of fire to the south and the west, I search for the small graveyard that Jim remembered as being nearby. Again, nothing. I feel crestfallen.

"Mr. Loc, how long have these people lived here?"

"She says . . . forty-two years."

"Forty-two years! That's impossible. Show them the pictures."

Loc hands over the photographs. They look for signs of recognition. There are none. No, they have never seen that house. No, they do not recognize any regional force soldiers with whom MAT III-56 shared time and space. No, there was never an outpost here, not on this side of the road. Then I know. Then I know. I never felt safe in An Ninh Village, never got to know the people as I did in Hiep Hoa. There was an air of deceit and treachery then; there's an air of denial now. It does not matter, for I have been here—I was here, and I am here again.

I slip the packet of photographs back in my pack. We hop in the van and return to Tan An.

"Jim, how are you feeling?"

"Ah, better. I slept most of the day. Ate the steamed rice and was able to keep it down. How was it?"

"You must see for yourself." I refuse to tell him more because I don't want to taint his perspective.

The next day at 0530 the Tan An community loudspeaker again drills through our subconscious, the shrill tone jarring us awake with not-so-subliminal messages as to the latest news. It is a modulated truth, like masking rubbish with wrapping paper to hide the real substance.

Jim's stomach has settled—that's the good news—so we decide to try to access the site of the old French villa. Thus, the first leg into our operating quadrant repeats a previous day's route, toward the village of Hiep Hoa. Traffic in Tan An, while significantly less congested than in Saigon, is still a microcosm of its parent but begins to thin, with fewer motorcycles, bicycles, and ubiquitous water buffalo, as we delve deeper into the heart of the rice fields. Overflowing canals and flooded homes line the path, and while the aura is similar to that experienced when departing Saigon, the feeling is like driving through a different neighborhood in your hometown several years after you have left it. The sensation is familiar but not nearly as poignant as that which comes from your own. By the time we reach Tan My, however, a pervasive intimacy washes through us as we recognize land that we once trod upon.

Just before the La Cua hamlet, that splinter of a road—the winding, muddy, gutted pathway leading to the interior hamlet of Rung-Tre—beckons our indulgence. We can still hear the grinding groans of first and second gear while piloting our jeep through the monsoon muck.

In 1969 Rung-Tre, which in Vietnamese means "bamboo forest," was the home of a small military outpost constructed not too long before my arrival. The enclave was a typical, well-fortified, company-sized garrison with protective sandbag bunkers on the perimeter and a command post bunker in the center. Soldiers assigned to the American infantry company that established and manned the outpost felt they were in a remote spot, which they were, and the arrival of advisors surprised them.

"Jack, you should've seen these guys. They'd been airlifted in, and the troops knew little about their surroundings. Here they were, thinking they were out in the middle of nowhere, when one of my sergeants and I drove up in our jeep. We came out of the hedgerows, sloshing through mud in first gear, and they're sitting on tops of bunkers wondering, 'Where in the fuck did these guys come from?'"

Regardless of the mud, we are determined to infiltrate the hedgerow, our resolve strengthening as the darting memories bond together in a coherent image of continuity and permanence. Although we saw little action there, many a night was spent on the ground or in hammocks, and that was where we became entwined with Trung-Uy Hot.

Jim wants to complete a mission. "Jack, I want to find out if anyone in the hamlet knows what happened to the girl."

"What girl?" I ask, and he tells me this tale.

An old man, bleeding from a stab wound to his chest and seeking help, had come to the Rung-Tre outpost, which was manned by an infantry company from the 25th Infantry Division. He stated that the VC had stabbed him and his daughter, seriously wounding her. Jim suggested to the American commanding officer that he redirect the night ambush position to cover the old man's farmhouse. Jim, along with Sergeant Adams, an interpreter, and a squad of Americans, set out for the farmer's home, estimated to be one kilometer from the outpost. When the ambush patrol reached the farmhouse, Jim set up an ambush line, leaving the American lieutenant in charge. Adams stayed with the American radio operator in case Jim needed to communicate with them. He never really trusted Adams, feeling he was trigger-happy. Then the old man, the interpreter, and Jim proceeded to the front of the farmhouse. There they found the farmer's daughter lying motionless on the ground. Jim picked up the wounded girl, who was bleeding profusely from her stab wounds, and put her on his shoulder. He carried his M-16 over his other shoulder with his finger lightly squeezing the trigger.

Jim had wanted to move the girl to another location to see if he could determine the nature of her wounds and apply first aid, but as he stood, the father of the girl shouted, "VC, VC." Turning around, Jim found himself face-to-face with an astonished adversary clad in black pajamas. He shoved the muzzle end of his M-16 under the startled man's chin, almost pulling the trigger at the same time, but as the VC appeared not to be armed, Jim made a humane decision not to shoot and waved the fellow away. Then he called in a dust-off to come in, pick up the girl and her father, and take them to safety. He had no idea whether she survived the attack.

Again Loc comes through; he makes arrangements with the police in the La Cua hamlet. Done. We will ride on the backseats of 125cc motorcycles that will be operated by local Vietnamese policemen. Not a problem, except a good portion of our anatomies, especially Jim's, protrudes over the narrow seats. Hands on the operator's shoulders, we embark into the interior once more, initially bypassing the buffalo-cart route. The bikes slide and groan as they ferry the extra weight over the slippery crowns of rice paddy dikes. Once my operator loses control of his bike, which flings me off the backseat. I land on my feet in a puddle of muck, and my feeling of return is further confirmed. Everyone laughs. It is good to hear this.

After zigzagging along the maze of dikes, we intersect a cart track where we bounce along until arriving at the former outpost site. As we have come to expect, no remnants of the outpost exist. Rung-Tre is a dispersed hamlet, made up almost totally of farmers.

We dismount. An old man and a child wander over. I step back to begin photographing with the video camera, positioning my body to film an unimpeded 360-degree sweep, and what intrigues me most is how knowledge of our presence is spreading. Two more farmers emerge from a hedgerow to the east, a few more from the west, until as many as thirty, perhaps forty, have come to see who has come to see them. All are friendly, and there are no hassles.

Jim asks Loc to inquire about the wounded girl.

Loc does, then assembles responses from the gathering and translates. "The young girl was brought back to the hamlet area. She lives nearby."

"She is okay, then?"

"Yes, she is okay."

Jim feels a sense of completion, a sense of having helped someone, that all was not in vain. I hope this is true, but I remain skeptical. During the war a high risk existed that our interpreters would tell us what we wanted to hear as opposed to the truth. With this in mind I distribute the photographs. As before, villagers pore over the pictures, exclaiming with delight when recognizing civilians or objects of interest. Another pattern develops—the face of denial—for when the villagers thumb through the photographs, pictures of the Vietnamese militia we served with are met with telling blank stares, the price of recognition and acknowledgment too fearful to contemplate.

A farmer speaks up.

"He says he was a Vietcong."

"How does he feel now?"

"He says he was just doing his job, like you. Also did you know that there were tunnels in the area?"

No! That we had not heard, but I believe him. Now all appears to be forgiven, both sides sad for damaging the other. As we prepare to depart, the farmers tell us how glad they are that we have come. We have made them feel good, and they have made us feel good. The Vietnamese clasp our outstretched hands with both of theirs, a more intimate gesture, and we feel their flowing warmth.

Afterward we climb aboard the scooters and take the country lane back to the Duc Hue road. En route we see a Communist flag waving ominously above the hedgerows. It flies over a seemingly abandoned government building, the colorless facade a testament to the legacy of neglect after the impact of war. The scene reminds me of untended French villages perched atop obscure alpine passes I traversed during my European motorcycle journey.

At La Cua we break for lunch, savoring a simple meal of bread, cheese, and bottled water. Once again I distribute the photographs. One woman smiles when she sees Jim, says she recognizes him from when she was a young girl, then plucks from the packet a picture of him from three decades ago. Jim is doubtful at first but becomes convinced, particularly when she comments, "You are much heavier now." Another woman recognizes the photograph I have of a local schoolteacher in Hiep Hoa, says she lives nearby, and asks if she may have the photograph to give to her. I gladly hand it over. (After returning to Houston, I found in my notes that I had given a copy of that same picture to the teacher herself in 1969, and I wondered what she felt upon receiving another in 1996.) Another woman recognizes a picture of the Rung-Tre outpost. We give her that photo.

To the river!

We travel by van as far as we can, then leave the vehicle to clamber aboard a sampan, which is powered by a single-cylinder engine. The boatman skillfully navigates through throngs of other watercraft, adroitly leveraging the propeller blade out of the water so as not to clog it when encountering vines and other debris. I have no fear of tipping over for the Vietnamese excel in balance, and I am again amazed at the loads carried along the waterways in these timeless contrivances—pigs trussed up in cone-shaped bamboo baskets, indigenous fruits and vegetables, even lightweight motorcycles. We are continually gawked at, the reactions ranging from polite waves and smiles to exuberant shouts. Another sampan carries a gaggle of Vietnamese schoolgirls, one of whom spontaneously bursts out laughing, clasping her hand to her mouth in wonder, as though saying, "Who are these white, round-eyed strangers?" Her laugh is infectious, transcending boundaries of race.

"I think she's laughing at you, Jim."

We skim down the arterial canal for forty minutes, then grow serious for the Vam Co Dong is near. Reaching the river, we turn north. Jim and I become quiet, each lost in his own thoughts, scanning the east riverbank for sights familiar. In another twenty minutes we round the bend that we could not peer past from the bridge two days before. The Sugar Mill comes into view, telling us we have gone too far and must turn back.

The boatman cuts the motor; we drift into a village under water.

Poling deeper into the village's belly, our boatman pokes around before bringing the dugout to a halt. Villagers come by sampan and bicycle or on foot, wading on trails obscured by the murky, swollen river. I hand out the pictures. A uniformed policeman pedals up, leaving a small wake in his path, looks at us curiously, then joins in to look at the pictures. He too bursts out laughing.

"What is he laughing about?"

"He says you have a picture of his grandmother."

"Is she alive? Is she near?"

"She died several years ago."

And there lies a connection. Seemingly an old woman then, the photograph shows her squatting in the marketplace surrounded by her baskets. Again I wonder. I wonder how I would feel if someone from another race came to me out of the blue and handed me a picture of my grandmother.

"Jack, that's Co Duc. Co Duc?"

I join in, "Co Duc? Co Duc?"

The woman looks familiar, but she is not Co Duc. We are disappointed. One of the cooks who attended to the Americans at district, Co Duc was the mama-san around whom things flowed, the woman I tried to seduce one late, lonesome night at district with nothing on but a towel around my waist. Imbued with integrity, she would have none of it. We pass out pictures of all three Vietnamese women who worked at district: Co Duc, Co Hanh, and Co My. All of them are recognized. They do not live here anymore. A niece of the sisters Co Hanh and Co My tells of their moving away, but we are unable to glean more detailed information. I show a picture of myself in camouflage jungle fatigues, cradling my M-16, appearing, I think, similar in the present to the picture then, except that my mustache was dark. A woman laughs.

"Mr. Loc, why is she laughing?"

"She says you were young and handsome. Now you are old."

Jim and I disembark from the dugout, leave the throng, and wade in water one foot deep. A concrete gun bunker looms in front. This is the spot, but no villa.

Loc translates what the villagers say. "It burned down two months ago. The gate was washed out by the flood."

Did it really burn? That's hard to believe for other than the concrete gun placement and a concrete wall, no vestiges remain. Perhaps the villagers completed the destruction that was started by fire. Perhaps it was destroyed a long time ago. It does not matter. It is not there. Oh, how I wanted it to be. I yearned for it, as if the life that I felt then could flow back into me now. We wade around the grounds, pointing out to each other what was where—the water supply, the veranda, the radio room, the dock, our room, the bar—the haven away from the rice fields, where we pondered our dreams of the future. I try to will the villa to reconstruct itself, but I am not powerful enough and have to rely on the images burned indelibly in my soul.

With mixed feelings we climb back in the sampan for our return cruise through the lush tropical vegetation. Now on the last leg of the day, our van cruises slowly north on old, pockmarked Route 10, from Tan My Village toward An Ninh Village. Not wanting to influence Jim in any manner whatsoever, I keep my lips sealed. I watch him as he plaintively and reflectively studies the emerald green rice fields and hedgerows to the west.

"Jack, I think that's it!"

Yeah! It is the same hedgerow. An Dinh. So we delve into its grip one last time. Jim and I—along with two young Vietnamese boys who express a bemused curiosity, as if to say this land has always been their land, the land of their fathers and of their fathers' fathers—ramble over the dikes and through the silent rice fields, gathering and bundling our refreshed, swirling reminiscences to take with us. Breaking the silence, however, is a sound noticeably absent twenty-seven years ago or, if not absent, had been filtered from our senses. Squeals and laughter from young boys at play, like the butterflies dancing in the late afternoon sun, ripple across the fields, gently touching rice stalks swaying in the breeze. I feel as if I have recovered the detached part of my soul that has been drifting in the winds, waiting patiently for my return.

"Where are the gravestones?" Jim asks. "There were gravestones less than a hundred meters from the outpost. They're gone. That doesn't make sense."

"I don't know, Jim."[3]

We feel as complete as the circumstances permit for the shell of the An Dinh house—the bunkers, the well, the outhouse—will remain forever destroyed, and acknowledgment of South Vietnamese militia we served with, painfully denied.

This day, our last in the field, is fading. As our return route takes us through Duc Hoa, we make one more effort to find the small Cao Dai temple where Jim had served before transferring to Duc Hue. We reach the village where, on three separate occasions, we had persuaded Loc to inquire as to whether the shrine still existed. No luck. This time we try a different tactic and simply drive at random. We turn onto a smaller, intricate road that meanders down a country path shielded by a canopy of trees. It feels as if we have entered a private domain and are driving through a farmer's backyard. Our driver kills the engine and we exit the van. A reverent aura envelops us as we plod along the trail. In a quiet settling down, the shade of dusk descends, exacerbating pungent countryside scents which congeal into a composite intimacy, an intimacy that in 1969 evoked romantic fantasies.

We round a bend. I watch as Jim enters once again the portals of that small Cao Dai temple, keeping his thoughts and feelings to himself. We have found his temple—older, weathered, but still intact—and Jim claims a remnant of his past.

"What happened here during your assignment?" I ask him.

He rubs his chin before speaking. "About a month after I'd been in country, I heard these bloody screams in the middle of the night. The Cao Dai priest came up from a hamlet outside Duc Hoa Village and approached our barbed wire and concertina wire (coiled barbed wire). He said a lady was suffering and he couldn't stop the pain. She was delivering a baby. There was a lot of fear about going in there because we thought it might have been a setup. But prior to that time I had promised the priest that we would never shoot at his temple as long as he would let us know what was going on and cooperated with us, so I felt that he was sincere with what was being said. I brought the medic out and asked him if he wanted to go in.

"Even though reluctant, we went anyway. Sure enough, we got into the middle of the hamlet—just a square with a temple on one side, a couple of stores and houses, maybe about fifteen structures altogether. There was a lady squatting in the middle of the square, two other ladies were rubbing her, and she had needles in the back of her head and she was screaming. I approached her with the medic, as I recall, and I was nervous, fearful actually. The medic pulled the needles out of the back of her neck and had her lie down. He said something about a breech birth and he had to do some stuff; for whatever reason they trusted him completely. At that point I walked to the temple that was about fifty feet away. I just had a feeling that there was something else going on and I wanted a barrier behind me. But the medic delivered the baby. It was the most horrible thing I have ever seen; it was bloody, but it was almost as if it was a miraculous happening. I mean it was just the most fantastic thing one moment and the most horrible the next because I had never witnessed anything like that. Then the mama-sans, they went and took over right after that. I think they took the new mother and her baby into the temple. That was on a Friday because two days later they had a big party honoring the medic and myself, which I shouldn't have had any part in. I think we gained a lot of respect that night by coming out."

Thus Duc Hoa and a local Cao Dai sect were responsible for Jim's spiritual awakening in Vietnam. Who knows what impact the local priest had on his salvation, and whether the word ever spread to Duc Hue! "I'm sure you did earn respect," I tell Jim. "See any more action?"

"A couple of weeks later we took a couple of rockets from the temple, and the South Vietnamese actually wanted to shoot and blow up the temple, which we could have done easily. We didn't shoot at them at all that night and the priest, who was influential, appreciated it. Another night we were in an ambush position and we detected movement and opened up; we wasted a water buffalo and had to compensate the farmer.

"The last big event occurred just before I left Duc Hoa. We had built an additional room on to the local schoolhouse. The villagers had a party for us. The morning of the big parade some kids were marching along the canal road and one of them tripped a mine the Vietcong had set. As I recall, about ten or twelve of the kids got injured, but I don't recall any deaths so I don't think it was a bomb or anything. It was probably a homemade grenade that they had set up. But from my perspective, they wanted to warn the people of the village not to cooperate with the Americans. And if they did, they were going to pay. The Vietcong knew Americans were taught that if children were in the area, we could presume it to be relatively safe."

No rule was inviolate to some guerrillas, and on rare occasions, even if inadvertently, children wound up as decoys. During a night ambush, a young Vietnamese girl, a hapless victim of being in the wrong place at the wrong time, took six rounds in the leg. At night it was extremely difficult to tell who or what might be the enemy, and decisions were made based on what was not supposed to be there. Nothing was safe, including the venerable water buffalo that wandered into the field of fire.

Jim had not been afraid to act in 1969. At Duc Hoa he relieved his second-in-command, sending him to the rear because he did not like the junior's insolence and his reluctance to risk field exposure. Jim had also contracted food poisoning in that district and spent one week in the hospital, where he was packed in ice to bring down his fever.

Now, after suffering his brief stomach ailment in Tan An and revisiting this Cao Dai temple, Jim has completed his cycle.

All in all, the return trip was more than I had hoped for. I felt a sharp, painful disappointment, however, upon discovering that our outpost and the villa, two key structures from that lost world, had been destroyed, eliminating forever any possibility of physical reconciliation. The need to embrace emotionally, to touch physically, to walk through, to feel the presence of comrades, to have another chance at redemption, will remain unfulfilled. A 5 October 1981 *Time* magazine editorial, "Downsizing an American Dream" by Lance Morrow, best expresses the longing. "We all drive past the house where we grew up and stare at it oddly, with a strange ache, as if to extract some meaning from it that has been irrecoverably lost." They denied us even that. Not only had the two structures been annihilated but also, in a fitting irony, Hau Nghia Province no longer exists, having been struck from the map and absorbed into Long An as part of the Communists' design to deny and obliterate evidence of an American presence.

As a further discounting of the whole experience, I felt at a loss in discerning any acknowledgment of the South Vietnamese soldiers with whom Jim and I had served. It was as if our counterparts too had never existed. Realistically they had either been killed or reeducated and relocated. And while most villagers remained silent out of necessity, I realize we had an impact, then and now, and it was not all destructive. Trung-Uy Hot and Sergeant Thanh, where are you?

In retrospect, my association with Jim made the Vietnam experience more tolerable. Unknowingly he helped me make it through, as did the sergeants, from whom I learned a vast amount. I also learned a lot from Jim, who was not afraid to step where I was afraid to. What we went through during the war and intervening years constituted a unique blend of circumstances that have culminated into feelings I no longer am ashamed to express. I love Jim like a brother— for who he was, who he is. I am grateful that my journey led me to such a person as he, a person who judged me not, a person who accepted me as I was, as I am.

Something else becomes abundantly clear. As that year of 1969-1970 in Vietnam was the defining year of my life, the early morning of 9 November 1969 was the defining day of that year, where everything came together and where everything fell apart, the time when the futility of war began to make itself known. I am grateful for that year, for that day, for the experiences opened within me a deeper, broader view and understanding of the world and its people than I ever could have achieved otherwise. I hang on to a fervent prayer that, amid the turmoil and destruction, scattered seeds planted in Duc Hue District by MAT III-56 gave some cause for hope and will be remembered with compassion. And maybe, just maybe, some of our ruff-puffs survived the juggernaut that overran them, survived the reeducation camps, and have found a new life in Canada, America, Australia, or France. And maybe, just maybe, they will remember that we went through it together. Because in spite of our cultural differences, in spite of the conflicts, in spite of a lost cause, we stood side by side.

Part II

MAPS
AND PICTURES

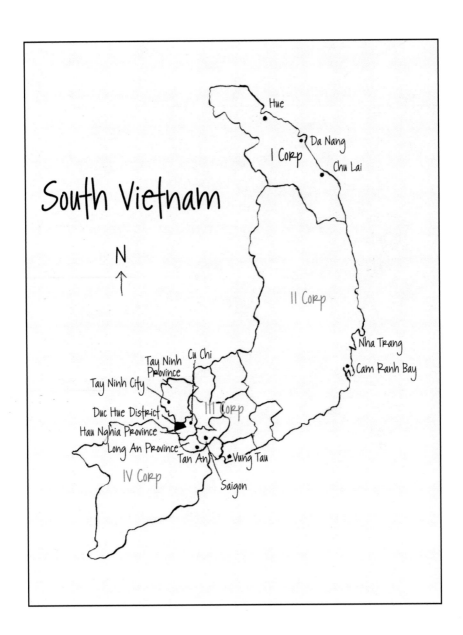

South Vietnam

N
↑

Hue

Da Nang

I Corp

Chu Lai

II Corp

Nha Trang

Cam Ranh Bay

Tay Ninh Province

Cu Chi

Tay Ninh City

Duc Hue District

III Corp

Hau Nghia Province

Long An Province

Tan An

Vung Tau

IV Corp

Saigon

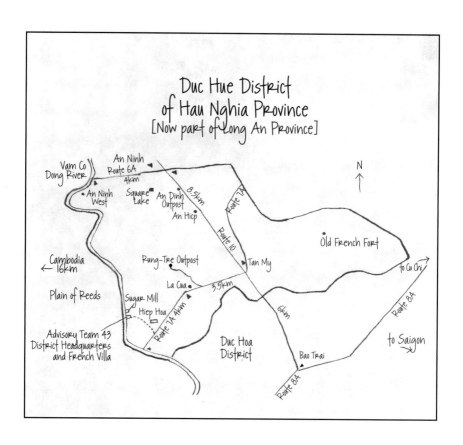

Duc Hue District
of Hau Nghia Province
[Now part of Long An Province]

N

Vam Co
Dong River

An Ninh
Route 6A
4km

An Ninh
West

Square
Lake

An Dinh
Outpost

An Hiep

8.5km

Route 7A

Route 10

Old French Fort

Cambodia
← 16km

Rung-Tre Outpost

Tan My

to Cu Chi

La Cua

3.5km

Plain of Reeds

Sugar Mill

Hiep Hoa

Route 7A 4km

6km

Route 8A

to Saigon

Advisory Team 43
District Headquarters
and French Villa

Duc Hoa
District

Bao Trai

Route 8A

Tết Việt Nam
1970

Left, handing out candy during Tet; *below*, dinner during Tet, author seated second from end on right.

Left, Hiep Hoa schoolchildren and *below*, their teacher.

Lieutenant Jim Smith, seated, with popular force platoon.

Hiep Hoa marketplace, 1969.

Mama-san in Hiep Hoa marketplace.

Sergeant Thanh standing on dock behind the district villa; river is the Vam Co Dong. The Cambodian border looms sixteen kilometers west. Thanh, our beloved interpreter, was later seriously wounded in a booby-trap explosion.

River patrol boat on Vam Co Dong.

Regional forces dining
in the outpost.

Cockfighting at the An Dinh
outpost, an exercise not
condoned by MAT III-56.

Counterpart's wife at the
An Dinh outpost.

Above, mortar position at popular force outpost
(Photo by Jim Smith); *below,* Lieutenant Smith
and author at Rung-Tre.

Shirley Cowen Thomas pinning second lieutenant's bars on author after his graduation from Officer Candidate School.

Co Duc in district kitchen.

Thanksgiving celebration at district. *Left to right*: Co Hanh, Co Duc, Co My, unidentified, and Captain Ray Wing.

Author and MATMOBILE at district headquarters.

Above, left to right: unidentified NCO, Lieutenant Bob Trifiletti, and Sergeant Isaac Charleston. Dogs are Lit'l Shit on right and Snowball on left; *left*, author at district headquarters wearing popular force beret, which was unauthorized headgear for U.S. forces.

Vietnamese youth guiding water buffalo in shallow canal
outside Hiep Hoa Village.

Canal along eastern boundary of Hiep Hoa Village; scene was
similar during return trip to Vietnam in 1996.

JACK LYNDON THOMAS

"Water-skiing" on the Vam Co Dong; participants alternated roles with third person taking photos and carrying M-16 for protection. Surfboard was cut from hull of abandoned vessel. Later Captain Wing ordered water-skis from Sears, but occasional sniping from west side of the river discouraged this activity.

District villa as seen from the rear, Vam Co Dong River behind the camera; allegedly the villa had once been the home of a director of the Sugar Mill. There were gun emplacements at the two corners facing the river, an 81mm mortar pit to left of center in the backyard. A concrete ammo dump, kitchen, and billets lay to the far left, out of sight. Regional and popular forces provided security.

Sunset photo overlooking the Vam Co Dong River, taken from
second floor of villa; the Sugar Mill lay just north.

Protective wire at Rung-Tre outpost.

JACK LYNDON THOMAS

Above, popular force platoon; *below*, regional forces questioning farmer.

Trung-Uy Nguyen Ngoc Hot at Rung-Tre outpost; Hot, the able commander of 494 Regional Force Company, was a forty-year-old soldier who had gone to military school to become an officer.

RF soldiers making adobe for use in constructing new oven at Rung-Tre.

Outside the Rung-Tre outpost; *left to right*: unidentified soldier, Trung-Uy Hot, Lieutenant Smith, and Sergeant Thanh.

Outpost wives filling sandbags.

JACK LYNDON THOMAS

Author and
Lieutenant
Smith at
Rung-Tre.

Above, Sergeant O'Hare with regional force soldiers at company
outpost; *below*, Lieutenant Ward on operation west of the Vam Co
Dong. (Photo by Richard O'Hare, courtesy of David Ward.)

COYOTE JACK

Above, aerial view of An Dinh outpost alongside Route 10,
1969; *below*, An Dinh hedgerow as it appeared in 1996.

JACK LYNDON THOMAS

An Dinh outpost—manned first by 158 Regional Force
Company and then by 221 Regional Force Company during
author's tour.

An Dinh outpost—house shell was used as MAT III-56 headquarters until command bunker could be completed; RFs in foreground are repairing fire arrow, which is upside down. If radio contact was lost at night, this emergency device was used to indicate direction of attack to supporting aircraft. When operative, arrow was mounted on spindle, and flammable substance placed in cans positioned along the prongs of the arrow was lit.

Left, regional force barber at An Dinh; *below*, well and bathhouse. Sergeants constructed bathhouse from scrounged materials to provide privacy for both regional force soldiers and their wives as well as for the advisors.

Author preparing to leave An Dinh outpost on operation (Photo by Jim Smith).

.50-caliber machine gun position at An Dinh.

Sergeant Louis Kerbow and Trung-Uy Thom, commanding officer of 158 Regional Force Company.

A casual moment for MAT III-56 at the An Dinh outpost; *left to right:* Lieutenant Jim Smith, Sergeant Ronald Adams, Sergeant George Brevaldo, and author.

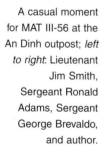

Regional force soldiers could be resourceful as well. In addition to being worn for protection, the "steel pot" was also used for cooking and bathing—a common practice in many armies.

Above, author wielding a sledge on engineer stake during
construction of An Dinh command bunker; *right*, Sergeant
Adams; *center*, Sergeant Kerbow; *below*, completed bunker.

Left, the little boy at the An Dinh outpost, 1969; *below*, girl in sampan on a canal near An Ninh West Village alongside Vam Co Dong, 1996.

Left and below, regional force soldiers crossing water-filled bomb craters.

The Buddhist monk.

Sergeant Brevaldo, during an operation in the Square Lake area, marking position for an element from the 2nd Battalion (Mechanized), 22nd Infantry, 3rd Brigade, 25th Infantry Division.

Smoke break.

Shaving mirrors
were scarce.

Above, author receiving
Bronze Star Medal from
Captain Wing for action
on 9 November 1969,
Sergeant Adams to his
right; *right, left to right*: RF
soldier with Army
Commendation Medal,
Sergeant Khanh (our
second interpreter),
Sergeant Brevaldo,
author, and RF company
commander, all with
Bronze Stars.

Counterpart, inside completed command bunker at An Dinh.

Underground bunker at old French fort, east of Route 10 and northeast of Tan My Village.

Eagle Flight, en route to insert a regional force company, author, and Sergeant Kerbow for a combat sweep operation.

Above and below, medevac approaches to pick up wounded
regional force soldier who tripped a booby trap.

Trung-Uy Hot and
company on PBR
cruising Vam Co Dong
prior to insertion for
ground patrol, on the last
operation in which author
had personal contact
with this impressive
counterpart.

Vietnamese policeman near villa site, 1996; he recognized a picture of his grandmother in Hiep Hoa marketplace from packet of 1969-1970 photographs taken by author and distributed during return trip.

Author on back of motorcycle near Rung-Tre Hamlet during 1996 return to Vietnam (Photo by Jim Smith).

Right top, former lieutenant Jim Smith at Rung-Tre Hamlet; *right bottom*, Jim Smith standing on site of destroyed villa, 1996.

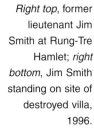

Jim Smith at Rung-Tre, 1996.

Schoolchildren on the "walk" home, An Ninh West Village, 1996.

Scene on Route 10, just outside the An Dinh hedgerow, 1996.

Above, Hiep Hoa villagers on flooded road, 1996; *below,* mother and child near An Dinh hedgerow on Route 10, 1996.

Above, *w*omen alongside flooded Route 7A near La
Cua Hamlet, 1996; *below*, young woman washing on
canal behind Hiep Hoa Village, 1996.

Left, Cao Dai Temple in Tay Ninh City, Tay Ninh Province, during return visit in 1996. Note all-seeing eye in top center. The religion blends Buddhism, Confucianism, Taoism, and Christianity; *below*, the chapel near Angel Fire, New Mexico.

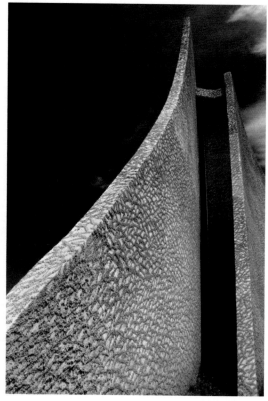

Jack Lyndon Thomas

Above, standing, left to right: Jim Smith, author, David Ward, Richard O'Hare, and Clifford Simmons, *seated, left to right*: Dorsey Holsinger and Ray Wing during Florida reunion, 1998; *right clockwise*: author, Jim Smith, Richard O'Hare, and Ray Wing during California reunion, 2003.

Left to right: Ken Rose, David Ward, John Bennett, Richard O'Hare, author, George Diggs, and Jim Smith. Author and Jim Smith served on MAT III-56; the others on District Advisory Team 43. Reunion held September 2004.

Nicole, as she appeared in Acapulco early summer 1967; tragically, she died on 1 January 1968 in Paris, France, due to a skull fracture sustained in an auto-pedestrian accident.

Left, Shirley Cowen Thomas on her 99th birthday; below, left to right: sons Harry, author, Steve, and Richard.

John R. and Jennie Thomas,
author's paternal grandparents.

Lawrence Ludlow Cowen, Jr.,
author's maternal grandfather.

Effie May Arnold, author's
maternal grandmother.

Above, Shirley Cowen and J. Lonnie Thomas, author's parents; *left,* J. Lonnie Thomas.

JACK LYNDON THOMAS

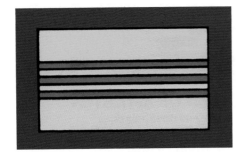

South Vietnamese flag.

Regional force insignia.

Popular force insignia.

MACV, United States Military
Assistance Command, Vietnam.

Combat
Infantryman's
Badge (CIB).

THE UNITED STATES OF AMERICA

TO ALL WHO SHALL SEE THESE PRESENTS, GREETING:

THIS IS TO CERTIFY THAT
THE PRESIDENT OF THE UNITED STATES OF AMERICA
AUTHORIZED BY EXECUTIVE ORDER, FEBRUARY 4, 1944
HAS AWARDED

THE BRONZE STAR MEDAL

TO

FIRST LIEUTENANT JACK L. THOMAS, INFANTRY, UNITED STATES ARMY
FOR
HEROISM IN GROUND COMBAT
IN THE REPUBLIC OF VIETNAM ON 9 NOVEMBER 1969

GIVEN UNDER MY HAND IN THE CITY OF WASHINGTON
THIS   19th   DAY OF   DECEMBER   1969

CREIGHTON W. ABRAMS
General, United States Army

SECRETARY OF THE ARMY

Bronze Star for Heroism in Ground Combat.

HEADQUARTERS
UNITED STATES MILITARY ASSISTANCE COMMAND, VIETNAM
APO San Francisco 96222

GENERAL ORDERS
NUMBER   7363

19 December 1969

AWARD OF THE BRONZE STAR MEDAL

1. TC 439. The following AWARD is announced.

THOMAS, JACK L.   457-22-5997   1LT   INF   USA   Adv Tm 43, III CTZ, APO 96225

    Awarded: Bronze Star Medal with "V" Device
    Date of service: 9 November 1969
    Theater: Repblic of Vietnam
    Authority: By direction of the President under the provisions of Execu-
              tive Order 11046, 24 August 1962
    Reason: For heroism in connection with military operations against
            a hostile force: First Lieutenant Thomas distinguished
            himself by heroic action on 9 November 1969 while serving
            as Assistant Senior Advisor to the 221 Regional Forces
            Company, Duc Hue District, Hau Nghia Province, Republic of
            Vietnam. On this date, the company was assigned the
            defense of An Dinh Outpost in Hau Nghia Province. Suddenly,
            the unit began receiving extremely intense mortar and
            automatic weapons fire from a Viet Cong force. Lieutenant
            Thomas fearlessly exposed himself to the enemy fire as he
            directed artillery fire and United States air strikes
            against the enemy positions. Inspired by Lieutenant Thomas'
            personal bravery and gallant example in the face of heavy
            enemy fire, his Vietnamese comrades rallied and repulsed the
            Viet Cong attack. First Lieutenant Thomas' heroic actions
            were in keeping with the highest traditions of the United
            States Army and reflect great credit upon himself and the
            military service.

FOR THE COMMANDER:

OFFICIAL:

LOUIS J. PROST
Colonel, USA
Adjutant General

ELIAS C. TOWNSEND
Major General, USA
Chief of Staff

DISTRIBUTION:
    Special

JACK LYNDON THOMAS

THE UNITED STATES OF AMERICA

TO ALL WHO SHALL SEE THESE PRESENTS, GREETING:

THIS IS TO CERTIFY THAT
THE PRESIDENT OF THE UNITED STATES OF AMERICA
AUTHORIZED BY EXECUTIVE ORDER, 24 AUGUST 1962
HAS AWARDED

THE BRONZE STAR MEDAL
(FIRST OAK LEAF CLUSTER)

TO

FIRST LIEUTENANT JACK L. THOMAS, INFANTRY, UNITED STATES ARMY

FOR

MERITORIOUS ACHIEVEMENT
IN GROUND OPERATIONS AGAINST HOSTILE FORCES

IN THE REPUBLIC OF VIETNAM FROM JUNE 1969 TO MAY 1970
GIVEN UNDER MY HAND IN THE CITY OF WASHINGTON
THIS 15th DAY OF MAY 19 70

CREIGHTON W. ABRAMS
General, United States Army

Stanley R. Resor
SECRETARY OF THE ARMY

Bronze Star for Meritorious Service.

UNITED STATES MILITARY ASSISTANCE COMMAND

By direction of the President

THE BRONZE STAR MEDAL
(First Oak Leaf Cluster)

Is presented to

FIRST LIEUTENANT JACK L. THOMAS

United States Army

For distinguishing himself by meritorious service in connection with military operations against a hostile force during the period June 1969 to May 1970 while serving as Senior Advisor, Mobile Advisory Team III-56, Advisory Team 43, United States Army Advisory Group, III Corps Tactical Zone, United States Military Assistance Command, Vietnam. Throughout this assignment Lieutenant THOMAS displayed outstanding professional competence and uncommon resourcefulness in his demanding advisory duties. He worked closely with his Vietnamese counterparts and succeeded in the difficult tasks of training Vietnamese Regional and Popular Forces in all phases of offensive and defensive infantry tactics as well as proper maintenance procedures for individual weapons. Those newly acquired skills greatly enhanced the fighting ability of the territorial forces and proved decisive during frequent encounters with the enemy. Exhibiting sound judgment, ingenuity, and courage under difficult and perilous conditions, he gained the trust and confidence of the Vietnamese soldiers and significantly increased their morale. First Lieutenant THOMAS' performance of duty was in keeping with the highest traditions of the United States Army and reflects great credit upon himself and the military service.

DEPARTMENT OF THE ARMY
Headquarters, 3d Brigade, 25th Infantry Division
APO San Francisco 96225

Mr. & Mrs. J. Lonnie Thomas   6 January 1970
6438 Vanderbilt
Houston, Tex. 77005

Dear Mr. & Mrs. Thomas

The enclosed picture of your son was taken the other day when General Camp,
the Assistant Division Commander, visited his unit to present him with the
Army Commendation Medal for Valor. 1LT Thomas was well and in fine spirits,
and his superiors informed me that he is doing an excellent job in MAT III.

As an Infantry Brigade Commander here in Vietnam, I consider it a gratifying
experience and a personal pleasure to work with young soldiers like your son.
He is a most valuable asset to this command in the performance of its mission
and his efforts are greatly appreciated by the United States Army and the 3d
Brigade, 25th Infantry Division.

                        Sincerely,

                        OLIN E. SMITH
                        Colonel, Infantry
                        Commanding

Army Commendation Medal

JACK LYNDON THOMAS

Part III

~

MY WAR

1

PASSING THROUGH

It is my first night in the Army, you see,
and I am a draftee.

Filling out forms in the middle of the night,
I do believe it is a ridiculous sight.

My head glistens with the absence of hair;
somehow it just does not seem fair.

I look to the left and look to the right;
who is it that started this fight?

We all have to pull fire watch I am told,
so we march out and about where it is frightfully cold.

My army cap slips down over my ears;
would not have happened if not for the shears.

I look up and down and feel dumbfounded;
three years I am to be hounded.

Ah, but I have a specialty degree,
for it is a CPA I plan to be.

So put me in finance, safe and sound,
and I will not have to duck all those rounds.

My eyes are not blessed with perfect vision,
but this is greeted with perfect derision.

The sergeant gleefully says with esprit:
you are best fit for the infantry.

"First Night," a poem.

~ ~

MONDAY, 12 SEPTEMBER 1967

"Aw right, you shit birds and scumbags, you are mine. I own you. You will do what I tell you, when I tell you," the drill sergeant barked gleefully.

"John, what have we gotten into?" I asked my new comrade, whom I had met on the flight from Houston. John, a college graduate, featured sweeteners in his repertoire: a law school diploma, successful marks on the bar exam, and a black belt in karate.

"They go to a special Neanderthal school," he said. John, less than six feet tall, of average weight, with dark brown hair and matching glasses, had run track in college but could not outrun the draft. And neither could our other friend John, who, like John the First, hailed from Baytown, a small community east of Houston overlooking Galveston Bay. When our plane lifted off from Houston, Little John, who packed power in his wiry five-foot six-inch frame, asked me, "How can you be so calm?" It was numbness, not calmness, I felt.

The drill instructor's (DI) tender greeting—the genesis of Army life for many trainees at Fort Dix, New Jersey— set the tone on that metamorphic Monday as we began four months of basic and advanced infantry training (AIT). Feelings of bemusement, apprehension, and wonder—wonder at how quickly you could lose your freedom—dominated this gaggle of recruits.

JACK LYNDON THOMAS

We trainees began the process by filling out paperwork; they needed to know where to send your body. Loss of dignity followed. A sardonic supply clerk asked our hat sizes, then slung across the counter the correct, non-adjustable, Army-green baseball caps. Immediately barbers shaved our heads, rendering the caps one size too large, and once carefree, confident young men with the world at their fingertips assumed new roles as circus clowns.

"Thomas, you look like shit in that hat," said a young Alabaman with a wide smile.

Supply clerks issued the rest of our military field gear—fatigues, web belts, canteens, shoulder harnesses, boots, helmets, and bedding—which we stuffed into olive drab (OD) duffel bags. Except for the stoutest men who effortlessly carried their equipment, the rest of us awkwardly hoisted the duffel bags to our shoulders, staggering under the load, while trying to maintain some semblance of control.

Inoculations, injected by air guns, completed the transformation. The shots were painless, but not the anticipation, particularly when a timid trainee flinched and pulled his arm away at injection point zero, emerging from the booth with blood trailing down his arm.

I did not experience the physical training in basic or AIT as difficult. What proved difficult was adjusting to the displacement from home. There were few rights and no privileges. If you had a girlfriend and the drill instructors found out about it, you were singled out for ridicule.

"Hey, Bronco! Who's screwing your lady now?"

While not subtle, it was psychological indoctrination at its best. If you were not married, the chances of your relationship lasting were slim for most of us were going to Vietnam in some capacity. And whether you were married or not, whether you liked it or not, the DIs used grassroots psychology to prepare us for the pain of separation. Nothing was sacred. Basic Training was about doing what you were told, no questions asked.

"Thomas, you move once more in formation, I'll have you pushing the ground all the way to China," bellowed Sergeant Avery.

"Yes, sergeant."

We were being weaned from civilian comforts and assimilated into a subculture with its own structure. What evolved, however, was the cherished by-product of military life—friendship! Lonesomeness, foreign environment, shared miseries, fears, and hopes formed the ingredients for developing camaraderie.

The DIs taught us survival skills—to roll with the punches and develop a sense of humor. Humility was an asset.

"I'm a college graduate. I don't have to do kitchen police (KP) duty," one draftee told the mess sergeant.

The mess sergeant could not believe his good fortune. He attempted to sound vicious, but his elation shone through as he shouted, "You what! Get in there and start washing pots and pans, you scumbag!" The rest of us covertly chortled at the arrogant recruit's misfortune, knowing his time in servitude meant less scalding water for us.

Basic Training was also about conformity, marching, weapons, and attention to detail. Training provided a link to the past—flashbacks to virile images depicted by post-World War II movies that embodied saving the free world, movies glorifying war. I looked for connecting threads to that glory. Learning about weapons, marching in step, and witnessing the evolution of undisciplined civilians into a cohesive unit whose survival depended upon interdependence was gratifying.

Feeling the awesome power created by a simple trigger pull was exhilarating. The first time I ever fired an M-14, my military-supplied glasses cracked from the recoil. A good lesson because from then on I carried an extra pair.

I was always sensitive about my eyes, having been saddled early on with the moniker, "Four Eyes." When I started first grade, I did not earn praise for academic excellence, my performance being less than stellar. Tipping the chart with straight Cs, I did not find out till third grade that I was 20/200 in each eye. Teachers placed us alphabetically in those days, and I sat in the last row. I do not remember if I could see what was written on the blackboard. What I do remember is my brother Steve admonishing, "What do you mean by making all Cs?" Even with glasses my scholarly performance did not improve a great deal. In fifth grade I failed to keep my grades up and got kicked off hall patrol. But I learned to take care of my glasses. In Vietnam I carried two extra pair and cleaned the lenses several times a day, which drove Jim Smith crazy. Today we laugh about it.

In Basic I felt a patriotic if naïve pride to be called upon to perpetuate what our brothers and fathers accomplished before us—the ingraining of a universal sense of worth and significance, the opportunity to contribute value to our country—which necessitated subordinating self-indulgence to a grander purpose. Unfortunately ingested emotionalism is a powerful weapon not always well guided.

The majority of us shrugged off the ridiculous, like the military dentist who threatened court-martial for anyone failing to disclose tooth abnormalities, or our rookie company commander recently graduated from ROTC, who had majored in geography and who, in reality, was almost as green as we were. The lieutenant yelled, the drill sergeants yelled, and the dentist yelled, but in contrast to the disparaging attitude of my father, whose yelling seemed vengeful, theirs packed no punch.

"Jack, you'll never amount to a hill of beans!" he'd say to me.

Was that the legacy bequeathed to my father? Shuttled about as he was, it is hard to know. Tired of the nomadic life, which during his childhood included one-hundred-mile covered-wagon jaunts to visit relatives, Dad dropped out of high school to support World War I. Because he was cursed with flat feet, both the Navy and the Marines rejected him. Finally, in El Paso, he found acceptance from the U.S. Army, where he was assigned to the 17th Cavalry. "Pancho Villa was active across the border, and it was rumored he was going to invade El Paso, so we were called in and issued rifles even though we were not qualified," Dad wrote in the abbreviated narrative of his life. Subsequently he was ordered to Fort Barrancas, Florida. When his unit deployed overseas, Dad was confined to the hospital with the flu.

"The flu was deadly that winter of 1918. There were so many cases we were put to bed on Army cots with just a blanket. The only attention we received was a visit once or twice a day from a doctor or an aide who administered a dose of iron, quinine, and strychnine. Bodies were hauled away from the hospital in trucks."

Later Dad became a supply sergeant and for a while was "put in command of a company." How did he feel about not shipping out with his unit? His grandfather, Daniel Esquerige Thomas, father of John Richard Thomas, enlisted in the Confederate Army in 1861 and was captured by the Union Army near Vicksburg on 4 July 1863. Even though he was paroled seven days later, how did he feel about having been a POW? Apathy, relief, guilt, or shame?

As my summer of 1967 metamorphosed into autumn, the trees took on bleak expressions, and, as if a portent of things to come, an ominous chill crept into my soul. Fort Dix, with its red brick classrooms and barracks, seemed a hybrid of school and prison camp, the red brick reminiscent of innocent childhood schooldays—betrayed by the stark reality of confinement. It was the time of *To Sir, with Love* and *Valley of the Dolls*, and every time the messages of unrequited love and depravity slipped into my consciousness, I felt a dreary yearning to be somewhere else. It was that perennial conflict—I wanted to go through it and I did not want to go through it.

In AIT, I thought I saw a way out.

"Anybody out there with a background in accounting?" our drill sergeant asked.

"Yes, sergeant, I do," I replied lamely, knowing that one of the unwritten rules was never to volunteer for anything in the Army.

"What is it?" he bellowed.

"Sergeant, I've got a BBA degree, a major in accounting, and have passed three parts of the CPA exam."

"Outstanding, Thomas. Fall in over there."

I spent the rest of the day collating and stapling papers, apparently a task for which I was eminently qualified.

Fall turned into winter. On our post-Christmas-leave bivouac, snow flurries dusted our food, and the nights were so cold we marched around a pathetic stove and sang songs. The daytime temperature hovered at zero degrees, and for a week we planted our vulnerable, naked butts on ice-covered cutouts in the outdoor latrine. It snowed so much that final firing qualification on the M-60 machine gun was held during a blinding storm. One adapted. Great training for the tropics.

At the end of eight weeks of AIT I received our training company's outstanding eleven-bravo award—the infantry designation destined to become my Primary Military Occupation Specialty (PMOS)—for the highest combined score of physical training and academic achievement in our company. It was dated 26 January 1968.

Those of us going to OCS looked forward to it with a considerable degree of trepidation. The world we once had known slipped further into a distant realm.

OFFICER CANDIDATE SCHOOL

Fort Benning lies adjacent to Columbus, Georgia, a stone's throw from the Chattahoochee River on its relentless journey to the Gulf of Mexico. After a short leave in Houston, John the First and I whipped my new white Volkswagen bug into the land of deprivation. The unsavory reputation accompanying small military towns is attributable to the extraordinary imbalance between excess testosterone and the available supply of estrogen. You can smell it in the air.

We breached the perimeter of the hallowed infantry school and abandoned the bug in the parking lot, where it suffered inconsolable periods of solitude for that was the last we saw of it for a while. The feeling upon entering OCS was different from basic or AIT. Apprehension and anxiety were higher; the training would be more difficult, the harassment incessant, yet it was more than that, as a subtle realization sank in that most of us were going to war. Our hopes and dreams of carving out a niche in the business or academic world were put at risk, or at least deferred. Even though all of us volunteered or had been talked into going through OCS, for the majority of our group the beginning of this endeavor was the draft notice.

"Well, candidates, welcome to Infantry OCS. Your day begins at five a.m. Lights out at ten p.m. There won't be enough time to get everything done. You'll always be behind. If you drag too much, you'll never make it. We'll wash you out." With that introduction from our soft-spoken company commander, Captain John E. Connor III—a West Point graduate and Vietnam combat veteran—Class 507, 61st Company, 6th Student Battalion, got under way.

The tactical officers under Captain Connor ran life in the barracks. Led by Senior Tactical Officer First Lieutenant Gary Carter, also a Vietnam veteran and excellent screamer in his own right, tactical officers pushed, berated, challenged, mocked, and rated us. How well would we stand up under pressure? How well would we lead? My platoon tactical officer was First Lieutenant Les Smith, a man I respected and admired. Lieutenant Smith may have kept me from getting kicked out of OCS late in the program.

On a rare weekend leave I was chugging the bug back to the

barracks when an overzealous military policeman (MP) stopped me and wrote me up for following a car too closely. I was two minutes late to formation.

"Thomas, where were you?" Lieutenant Smith and Lieutenant Carter asked in not-so-gentle tones.

"Sir! The MP was out of line. I was not following too closely. I was not speeding."

I believe that while Carter wanted to kick me out, Smith talked him out of it. I would have another run-in with an MP before my military career ended.

Each training day lasted longer than seventeen hours. After lights out, beneath our woolen blankets, under flashlights, we polished boots and brass, studied, and wrote letters home. The mission of the intense, six-month school was to turn out disciplined second lieutenants deemed qualified to command small units, usually as an infantry platoon leader.

Both officers and noncommissioned officers ran the infantry school. Drilled into us were infantry tactics, weaponry, map reading, logistics, leadership, creativity, and other subjects selected to prepare us for the tasks ahead. Without fail, the best training came from combat veterans, be they officers or noncommissioned officers or graduates of West Point or high school.

On several occasions Captain Connor and his tactical officers designed additional combat training exercises utilizing infantry skills being taught in the classroom. These weekend war games instilled in us a pinch of reality. (Because of Captain Connor and his commitment to excellence beyond the call of duty, I believe more of us lived than would have otherwise.)

Two hundred and twenty young men started in this company; one hundred graduated. Most went to Vietnam. Three were killed. Ellis was one. I do not know the circumstances of his death, but I felt guilty for what had transpired in OCS. Leadership roles were rotated so that each of us received a good look relative to our tactical knowledge and leadership ability. Ellis's assignment was acting platoon leader, and he issued a command. I have no recollection of what it was.

"Ellis, that's stupid I'm not going to do it," I replied insubordinately.

I turned my back and walked away. Ellis lost his composure, jumped me from behind, got a choke hold around my throat, and said, "You take that back, you take that back."

It took three classmates to pull him off. I apologized but had wounded Ellis's heart. Even so, he put his arm around me and said, "Jack's my buddy. Jack's my buddy."

(I will never be able to say how sorry I was for his heart was big and he was only trying to do what he thought best. He did not even write me up.)

Some candidates tolerated the physical hazing better than others. I found it a challenge to see how long I could remain in the front-leaning rest position (push-ups) in relation to the rest of the candidates. It was a game. Until we reached senior status, we double-timed everywhere. Double-timing was more arduous when we carried the ten-pound M-14 rifle at port position (cradling the weapon at a forty-five-degree angle across the chest, arms extended at the elbows). I loved the outdoor obstacle course. Here you could run, jump, climb, or crawl to your heart's content.

What most of us did not like was "breaking starch," the minimum of twice-a-day change of fatigues, which were so heavily starched that trying to slip your leg through was like prying apart two boards glued together. The fatigue shirts came from the cleaners with the mandatory ten staples affixing the laundry tag to the front bottom of the shirt. The folded, securing portion of the staples faced inward, and it took no genius to discover these were best removed for when we marched, the stapled portion of the fatigue shirt invariably maneuvered its way through the slit in your OD shorts, resulting in the staples pricking your penis.

Occasionally the reality of our future sank in deeper. One crisp, clear spring day, when birds were singing, we spent our leisure time cradling our M-14s and low crawling on our backs in man-made mud under foot-high horizontal steel bars. I was almost through the course when Captain Connor materialized suddenly, with legs spread wide and hands on hips.

His gentle tone belying the intensity and purpose of his mission, he asked, "How do you like that, Thomas? You are going to be doing it for a year!"

I felt at a disadvantage since I was on my back, gazing upward into his steady gaze, and I replied silently, "Oh no, not me."

OCS fostered initiative, a welcome relief from my repressive home environment. At times that attitude encouraged a tacit bending of the rules. During certain training exercises, for example, the rifles became caked with mud, which necessitated an alternative approach to conventional arduous and time-consuming cleaning methods. Lookouts sounded a password if it appeared that an outsider might intrude upon those of us who, naked, hand-washed rifles in the shower under hot water. The hot water dissolved mud fast and evaporated quickly, leaving no damaging residue. Dab on a light coat of oil and you were done.

Academically I breezed along in OCS with a low A average. Then I received the letter, and my heart sank like a stone tossed in a well. In the early summer of 1967 I had taken a week's vacation to Mexico where, in a fanciful effort to deny my inevitable military stint, I fell in love, a feat easily accomplished when your feet are planted firmly in mid-air.

In a hotel lobby in Acapulco, a sensuously attractive young woman, with dusty brown hair and milky smooth complexion, walked up and inquired in French if I spoke the language. Fortunately she was fluent in English, and we spent the next two days together. Nicole was from Besançon, France, southeast of Paris, not far from the Swiss border. She saw our interlude for what it was—a pleasing but fleeting encounter with a most doubtful future for no solid connection existed. I, however, wanted to be saved from whatever fate awaited me and made the decision to hold on to the fantasy. I conjured up a dream in which I would be commissioned in finance and sent to Europe; there I would find her. (Even today, when I stumble across her picture and gaze into her sultry smile, I feel a longing for her presence.)

Dated March 14, 1968, the letter was from Nicole's sister—who lived in Montreal—and was a translation of a February 2, 1968, letter written in French that I had received from their mother.

Dear Mr. Thomas,
    You will probably be shocked to know what
happened to Nicole, as we have all been. Nicole was
hit by a car in Paris and died of skull fracture wounds

on January 1st. I am Nicole's sister and it is with
mixed emotions that I read your letter—deep sadness
because you were reminding me of those terrible days
we went through—but also happiness, knowing that
everywhere she went, Nicole made friends. . . .

Beautiful and full of life, Nicole possessed an air of innocence
and trust approaching invulnerability—no doubt like that of many
young men dying across the pond. With the disclosure of her death I
lost my fortitude for a while, and there came a grudging acceptance
that my fantasy of getting commissioned in finance and assigned to
Europe was also dying. I finished with a low B average.

I composed a letter of my pain to my parents with news of Nicole's
death. To my surprise, I received a letter from my father, which, contrary
to his characteristic acerbity, poured out sympathy and compassion.

Hi Fellow,
We enjoyed your letter so much but were stunned
to hear of the tragic death of your friend Nicole in
Paris. She was real cute in the pictures and I am sure
she was an intelligent and interesting person. It is sad
that her parents were trying to tell you in French and
could not get through because of the language
barrier. At any rate we are saddened by the tragedy;
we know you are hurt because of it. One doesn't meet
interesting people on every corner but then, perhaps
all of them are interesting in some manner.
You seem so mature to us now, you have grown
into a man of whom we are proud, to say the least,
and your attitude toward the loss of a friend and what
to do about it shows that you have arrived in so many
ways. Your seeking out a minister in this case was wise
and I think his advice was wise also. You don't hesitate
to seek help when you feel that you need it—spiritual
that is—and the right person is a man of God. There
simply is no other source from which one can get the
strength and wisdom to handle certain problems.
"God is my refuge and my strength, of whom shall I

be afraid," is one of my favorite Bible passages. Show me the person who believes in God and practices his belief in God by his daily living and I'll show you a person who is not afraid.

A good effort, the letter helped assuage my loss.

Humor also helped. Once, as we were being marched to the barbershop for the shaved-head ritual, a couple of tactical officers were jacking with us. I was in charge of the squad, and, after getting our heads shaved, one tac split the unit, having one half march off while the remaining half remained stationary but facing the other way. I received the order to reunite the column.

"Well, what are you going to do, Thomas?"

"Leftovers, about face, forward, march." The tacs doubled up in laughter.

Another candidate incident occurred during mealtime, which took place in the company dining room at tables placed on polished floors. Captain Connor and other officers sat at long rectangular tables facing the candidates. I was sitting with John the First and some other candidates when Captain Connor asked me for John's middle name. Hell, I did not know his middle name, so I made something up.

"Sir, Candidate John's middle name is Snidely, sir."

"Snidely! Are you serious?"

"Sir, no sir."

The quirky humor too I learned from my father. At Rice University he used to pilfer surplus Blue Goose oranges from a bowl on the professors' dining table. The ones not eaten were used as missiles and chucked from a fifth-floor dorm room at unsuspecting professors. Also Dad told how, in a hardware store a long time ago, salesclerks rang up sales and collected the proceeds, depositing same in a cup, which was then transported by rope and pulley to an upper-level cage wherein resided the cashier. Change was made, put in the cup, and rerouted back to the salesclerk. She would flip the cup over in her hand, enveloping the change before giving it to the customer. Imagine the salesclerk flipping over the cup as she had done hundreds of times before, only to find contained within her hand one small frog.

On occasion the tactical officers liked to play, and one of the senior tac's favorite games was ping-pong. The barracks' long hallway played a prominent role. Whenever Lieutenant Carter called us together, you never knew what was coming next.

"Half of you idiots line up with your backs and heels plastered to one side of the wall, you other idiots get on the other side. Stagger yourselves, so that no one is directly across from another. When I say 'ping,' you jump forward, turn in midair, and squarely plant your heels against the other side of the wall. When I say 'pong,' you are to reclaim the space from which you originally came. Are there any questions?"

"Sir, no sir!"

The game began slowly and accelerated rapidly until we were all tangles of arms and legs laughing at our absurdity.

OCS afforded me challenges that enabled me to feel better about myself. It felt good to have to stretch and to want to achieve. In addition to OCS classroom training was the sanctioned physical training, which consisted of a series of physical training tests conducted throughout the six-month course. There were five standard events. Although these events could not be classified as athletics, they represented physical expression, an important measuring stick in our family.

After World War I, my father went back to Abilene and finished high school. One of Dad's double first cousins was enrolled at Rice University in Houston and ran track. This was the connection, the outlet my father needed. He entered Rice, where he lettered on the track team two years, participating in the 440, the mile relay, and the javelin throw. Athletics seemed to have been his real love, the umbilical cord in his search for significance and acceptance. One of his proudest statements was, "Several times I beat The University of Texas javelin man."

In the seventh grade I played second-string quarterback on the B team. I was small, could not see without my glasses, and never played in a game. In the tenth grade I almost worked up the guts to go out for high school football. I went into the locker room late; only dregs of the equipment remained. Discouraged, I went home. I was too good for the dregs. To justify not trying, I lied to myself. In actuality I was perpetuating a self-fulfilling prophecy.

In baseball I was a pretty good fielder and fair batter, but I gave up baseball my junior year of high school. Bellaire won the state championship two of the three years I was there. I got a shot on the junior varsity team, and there was always the chance of moving up to the varsity. Six of us tried out for shortstop. The coach, who later became the head baseball coach at a major college, said anyone who fielded six grounders in a row would start the next junior varsity game. I was the only one who succeeded. I fielded six in a row, cleanly, and my competitors acknowledged the feat.

"Coach, I thought you said anyone who fielded six grounders in a row would start."

"Thomas, all I can say is that I wish you were a sophomore."

I never set foot on the playing field.

Taking up basketball late, I grew to love it best. In high school gym class I developed a fine shooting touch and caught the eye of the basketball coach. One day my gym class was scheduled to go outside and play touch football, but the coach kindly asked if I would like to stay in to play basketball. I was flattered and my heart was ringing with hope, but, filled with self-destructiveness and fear of failure, I rejected the opportunity, vaguely aware that I was bursting my own bubbles of life.

So in high school I maintained a B grade point average but basically shunned all other activities. My total number of dates could be counted on one hand . . . without need of the extra digit. The poignant ache for the fulfillment I believed would have come had I been a star athlete and active high schooler has been diminished by my Vietnam pain. The sports pain was more about not being true to myself, not giving 100 percent effort, versus giving my all and risking failure. Not testing my capability, I left myself with open wounds.

Yet it was more than that. At some point it would not matter what my talent level was—whether I was good enough to make this team or that team. For eventually there would have been a team I could not make. What mattered was that I did not have a sense of perspective of where I fit, a sense of security that behind my efforts was a supportive father. Once I overheard Dad tell Mom that Stevie—who at Bellaire High School had not only lettered in football, basketball, and baseball, in his senior year he was also named to Houston's all-city football team—was the only one who cared about sports. The cut ran deep. It was not only that I failed my soul by not trying, but also salting the wound was that the father did not know the son.

At Southwestern University, a liberal arts college of approximately 1200 students located in Georgetown, Texas, I participated in all intramural sports except swimming. Tackle football was a nine-man game in pads and I loved it. When several teammates asked me where I had played in high school, I glowed. For while those compliments failed to fill my ache at never having played for a *real* team, those innocent, almost cavalier, questions began to instill in me confidence.

OCS afforded another opportunity. Away from home, where no family member could measure me, I made up my mind to do my physical best.

The first event was a forty-yard low crawl that had to be scooted in twenty-three seconds or less, while maintaining constant ground contact with chest and hip, in order to achieve the maximum score. Another was the run, dodge, and jump, with a ditch and four hurdles that had to be negotiated four times in twenty-one seconds or less for a max score. A third was the horizontal ladder whereby a candidate suspended himself from each bar, never placing more than one hand on any bar, and traversed as many bars as he could within a one-minute time limit. To achieve the maximum score, seventy-six bars had to be negotiated. The horizontal ladder had thirteen rungs; each participant had to turn five times, again never putting more than one hand on any bar. You were most vulnerable to falling while executing a turn.

A fourth event was the dummy grenade throw. To achieve a max score you had to lob five throws at a target ninety feet away. The target consisted of a series of concentric circles; higher scores were awarded for center shots. Then there was the one-mile run, which had to be completed in combat boots in six minutes or less, the only event I never maxed. John the First mastered it. The best I ever did was during the final test, as I wanted to achieve a total score of 500 points, the highest possible. I was not close on the mile, completing it in six minutes, forty-five seconds, but it was good enough for a total score of 487 points, the highest in our company. I was proud of that. Many of my classmates were surprised since I wore big, thick-rimmed glasses—having forsaken the Army glasses at that point—and looked more like an intellectual than an athlete.

I also liked map reading for I cherished landscape, my *sensors* stimulated by the love of nature. The red hills of Georgia with the fresh scent of pine were a poultice to my soul. Navigating by compass and reading contour lines on maps was an exciting challenge as each achieved objective represented another accomplishment. Along with those successes I continued to build confidence.

After six months of physical, mental, and emotional challenges, it was over. This group of officer candidates was one of the best to go through the program. Several co-graduates made the Army a career, reaching the rank of colonel or lieutenant colonel, and a few became helicopter pilots, flying medical evacuations, combat support, or combat missions in Vietnam. Our OCS Company had performed well in the classroom, in tactics, and on the parade field. I learned a lot from my classmates and respected their ability to take command. (Owing to the dispersion of our assignments, we did not, with rare exception, see each other for twenty-five years. Then, in 1993, thirty of us met in Chicago for a heart-warming reunion.)

Mom and Dad came to graduation and I was pleased they did. All one hundred graduates relished the successful completion. I will never forget a comment John the First—law school grad and black belt—made upon graduation, "I am more proud of this than of my diplomas." So was I.

I told one co-graduate, "If I stay in the Army, I'll become a general."

He looked at me quizzically and with a tone of incredulity asked, "How can you say that?"

The initial assignments of the one hundred were as follows: sixty-four commissioned in Infantry, twenty in the Signal Corps, and sixteen in Armor. A few had subsequent transfers to other branches. The three who lost their lives in Vietnam were infantry.

ANOTHER RUNG ON THE LADDER

Infantry! I was both proud and apprehensive. My ten-month assignment, the one I wanted least, was to serve as a tactical officer—doing what was done to me, harassing and weeding out undesirable officer candidates. As a tac, I could yell and scream with impunity, and did. I think they must have thought I was crazy. Nevertheless I developed an affinity for the job.

In early 1969 I wrote a short essay.

THE MEANING OF DISCIPLINE
AND OBEDIENCE TO
THE NON-CAREER MAN

Americans in the past have had to fight for their freedom just as Americans in the future will have to fight for theirs. We Americans simply could not have obtained the privileges of education, advancement, and potential luxuries without the protection from the armed services.

This brings us to you, the officer candidate. Some of you will not make it but some will. Why are you here? Some of you are here because you want to make the Army a career. Some of you are here because you feel that being an officer is commensurate with your educational level. Some of you have no clue why you are here. Nearly all of you want to enjoy the money, prestige, respect, and potential advancement that being an officer offers. But let us look beyond the materiality of the situation. Let us look at the man—the man who has the potential or he would not be here. A man who has the ability to lead has an obligation to himself and his fellow men to fulfill his obligation. God did not give you ability for it to be wasted, nor was this country made by people shirking their obligation. Sure, some of us would rather be working in civilian life with no immediate danger from combat, and making more money. But a man is one who faces a distasteful task for the intrinsic value of it. This man accomplishes this task for the benefit of others if not for himself.

If this man decides not to make the Army a career, he can go back to civilian life knowing he did his part. He is satisfied; he is proud of his peace of mind. Now he can more fully appreciate the luxuries of life—what it means to work for something. He does not take so many things for granted.

So let us get closer to you, candidate. At times you feel picked on and harassed for no apparent reason. We bring pressures on you to see if you can take the stress. A leader has to stand under pressure. The Army works on strict discipline; if one cannot follow, he cannot lead. A leader is one who may disagree with the procedures employed in a certain situation, but he has the discipline and obedience to look beyond his own reason. The man above has his own, and it is your job to carry them out.

Jack L. Thomas
Second Lieutenant, Infantry
1969

As the days waned, I played ping-pong and pool, shot archery, and photographed. I fell asleep in the Volkswagen driving to Calloway Gardens and woke up chugging along a wide, shallow ditch off the opposite lane. Drivers passed by, mouths agape, but nothing was going to keep me from my appointed destiny.

When I think of my inexorable march toward Vietnam, I think of a childhood nightmare. Our sprawling home on Vanderbilt Street in West University Place, a pleasant Houston neighborhood near Rice University, was built mostly by Dad. A long, narrow hallway leading from a small alcove housed an enchanting built-in hutch containing books and a rotary dial phone. Nearby was a blackboard on which family messages were inscribed or children's ramblings scrawled. The hallway led directly east, terminating at the living room that flared off to the left, with an unobstructed view to the front door. The nightmare was always the same.

Feet suspended above the floor, I am being sucked down the hallway toward the front door, unable to resist the pull. A feeling of dread begins to materialize as the unseen but indomitable power draws me on this unwanted journey. In horror I now see that the front door is open, where stands a shrouded figure beckoning me

onward, and I am trembling at the core of my soul. My
body has been pulled free of the hallway, the foreboding
intensifying as I am drawn closer to this menacing dark
figure, whom I can only feel as evil. I glance to my left. I
feel hope, a chance to be saved. My mother is sitting in a
chair in the northwest corner of the room, the one
farthest away. I want her to come get me. I try to speak,
but no words come. I am not sure if she is smiling or
desperate. She sees me but does not get up, gestures for me
to come to her. I cannot and I am drawn silently scream-
ing toward a world of terror.

What was shadowy and sinister in my youth took on a new definition. It became an adult world, real, one of our making. My orders
arrived. Stateside military service was finished. I said goodbye to a
woman I had been dating—a friend from high school—accepting, but
refusing to take to Vietnam, her gift charm of Saint Christopher, the
patron saint of travelers. Nor would I take photographs of loved ones
or any other item that if lost might create an insidious worry that "my
time was up." In Houston for a brief leave I visited with my mother,
who said, "Don't be a hero." Deep down, however, I saw a chance for
redemption, a chance to go where no member of my family had gone
before.

2

ANOTHER DIMENSION

Who was the most courageous: one who took the oath of allegiance, a conscientious objector who served alternatively, or one who dodged the draft and went to Canada?

❧

1200 HOURS, TUESDAY, 17 JUNE 1969

I stepped off a chartered Braniff flight spiced with the cruel allure of unavailable, trim-figured stewardesses, and felt a vague sense of betrayal as the no-longer attainable winged their way safely stateside. After eighteen hours, with stops in Honolulu and the Philippines, we were dropped into a foreign world to be parceled off into a realm few bargained for. Tan Son Nhut Air Base, or "Pentagon East"— a maze—contained appendages for everything military, plus basketball courts, swimming pools, tennis courts, and movie theaters. It was also headquarters for U.S. Military Assistance Command, Vietnam (MACV), and the gateway for descent into the unknown.

Unit cohesiveness did not exist. Navigating through the labyrinth, we tumbled out of individual tunnels into every job imaginable in the United States Army—platoon leaders, advisors, communications personnel, logistics, intelligence, and public relations—all part of a self-regulating culture.

I drew the straw I expected, participation on a Mobile Advisory Team (MAT) as advisor to South Vietnamese Regional and Popular Force units (local militia). The MAT concept began as early as 1964 with the authorization of fifty five-man teams to work primarily as splinter elements of regular American units, advising Vietnamese militia and upgrading their effectiveness. In 1967 the concept was modified to have mobile units operate autonomously, independent of standard American combat units.

A buck sergeant tossed a basic issue of field gear—helmet, flak jacket, web gear, collapsible two-quart canteen, jungle hammock, and other sundries—across the counter. From the armory I acquired an M-16. The next leg began roughly fifteen kilometers northeast of Saigon at Di An, home of the U.S. First Infantry Division, also home of the U.S. Army Vietnam Advisory School (USARV) where, for fourteen days, I received further indoctrination. Essentially the school was an adjunct to the six-week MATA Sector Unit course I had completed at Fort Bragg, North Carolina, where we had been introduced to the language, customs, religions, culture, geography, and history of Vietnam. At Bragg we had also slogged over low-slung sand hills on a daily two-and-a-half mile run in combat boots, a prelude to patrolling in muck.

New recruits joining regional and popular forces also underwent training at Di An. Rumors clogged the pipeline that on more than one occasion trainees at the rifle range had received live fire in return. I was ever closer to crossing over a murky threshold into a morass that only man can create.

A cadre of officers and NCOs taught the classes. They passed along valuable tips—tips that, if utilized and combined with fate or luck, might enable one to go home in one piece. That the war effort was full of contradictions and fuzzy objectives was reinforced by an unofficial but specific doctrine, DEROS (date eligible for return from overseas), that had little to do with winning a war. I viewed the instructors with both awe and envy. They had made it, whereas our cluster of impending encounters was packaged deep inside the unknown, to be revealed only through the passage of time. In nightly card games in the barracks, no amount of speculation assuaged the uncertainties.

Training completed, we said our goodbyes and trickled off to individual assignments.

ADVISORY TEAM 43,
DUC HUE DISTRICT, HAU NGHIA PROVINCE,
III CORPS TACTICAL ZONE

Embarking from Bien Hoa, which I had reached by truck from Di An, a four-seater single-engine plane transported me, the only passenger, to provincial headquarters in Bao Trai. The official designation of the transport was Air America, reportedly a civilian-run airline but controlled by the CIA.

The pilot relayed through the headset, "I'm not sure if we can land. There were reports of incoming earlier in the day."

"What am I getting into?" I wondered as the first bubbles of fear began to ripple through my chest. I did not know if the pilot was pulling my chain, but it was another rung on the ladder of reality. The fear was multidimensional: fear of being maimed, fear of death, and fear of incompetence—the last, perhaps, the strongest fear of all. Would I measure up? Or would Vietnam be my nightmare come true? The next eleven months would tell.

After landing at Bao Trai, the pilot lingered not, leaving the prop running, then quickly lifting away. Nothing unfriendly dropped out of the sky during my brief stay. Two days later, on Saturday, 12 July 1969, I boarded a helicopter for Duc Hue District—my home for the next eleven months.

As the fluttering UH-1 Huey approached its destination, I saw villagers scurrying like ants in a hurried but deliberate rhythm. Beyond the hamlets and villages, block-shaped rice paddies, delineated by a network of dikes, consumed the majority of the landscape. Arterial canals tangential to the Vam Co Dong River provided access into the interior. The village of Hiep Hoa itself seemed deceptively quiet and peaceful, but in a derisive simulation of events as they were, the chopper stirred up a maelstrom among unsecured items as it landed.

Duc Hue District was wedge-shaped, appearing as though it had been rough-cut from flint, like an Indian arrowhead. The western boundary was the river, and the arrowhead's jagged tip extended east to within four kilometers of the Cu Chi area. District headquarters, a commandeered two-story French villa, sat pinned on the east riverbank at the southwestern edge of the district. The rumor that the villa had once been the home of Madame Ngo Dinh Nhu was just that, a rumor; in actuality it had been owned and occupied by the French director of the Sugar Mill. Three stone throws across the river lay the hapless village of My Thanh Dong, whose dirt trail along the riverbank faced incessant erosion from the wakes of river patrol boats. Northwest of district headquarters, the infamous "Parrot's Beak," a threatening finger jutting out of southeastern Cambodia, pierced ominously close to our operating area.

The villa was a mini-fortress, its northwest and southwest corners marked by fortified gun emplacements housing .50-caliber machine guns—a stark, powerful admonition that the villa was not a pleasure palace. An 81mm mortar pit sat at the northern end of the compound, and another .50-caliber machine gun was positioned facing the river on the second floor verandah. The villa compound contained a small housing and eating section constructed by Special Forces who had previously broken ground. A generator provided electricity, and large elevated holding tanks provided a supply of running water. Co Duc, Co My, and Co Hanh, three South Vietnamese locals, prepared the meals and performed general housekeeping chores.

Officially named Ap Hang Duong or Hang Duong hamlet, the compound was part of Hiep Hoa Village. By land you entered from the east, by an artery splitting off from Route 7A. A concrete wall, sporadically reinforced by sandbags, sheltered the northern, western, and southern perimeters, with concertina wire embedded on top of the west wall. An iron gate, its twin spurs secured by padlock and chain, also partitioned the west wall. Through that portal you gazed at a weathered wooden dock and beyond the river to no-man's-land.

A regional force company and one popular force platoon provided security; in case of attack, resident U.S. district personnel had specific assignments. A month before my arrival the Vietcong/NVA had launched an attack from across the river, pouring in B40 rounds and RPG grenades in addition to AK47 fire. Among those returning fire was young Sergeant O'Hare, who had manned the .50-caliber machine gun on the second-floor verandah, effectively pruning a large tree in the process.

About one hundred meters north of the villa lay the mysterious Sugar Mill. Owned by the French and operated by both French and Vietnamese labor, an eerie quiet prevailed within the mill, its walls holding silent the sounds of earlier combat. The mill's operations, save for scant rum production, were in abeyance. Exterior walls were perforated by bullet holes, and the high-ceilinged second floor, large-framed windows, in a perverted conversion, on occasion served as fortified machine gun emplacements. On the canal just south of the Sugar Mill, waves lapped gently at moored boats that used to ferry cane—boats whose throttles once generated a lusty rumble now floated in a watery graveyard.

Although the enemy lacked a formal navy, its surreptitious *armada* sailing under the fog of night functioned well. If a sampan was known to contain contraband, or if enemy movement was spotted west of the river, the Sugar Mill's second floor provided an effective firing platform. As an observation post, it was excellent. For an anti-personnel position, however, it was marginal since level, interlocking fields of fire were unattainable.

MAT III-56 AND DISTRICT PERSONNEL

"Lieutenant Thomas, I'm Lieutenant Smith, good to have you," he greeted his new second-in-command of the mobile advisory team.

"Good to meet you," I replied, anxiously scanning the area. First Lieutenant James C. Smith, Jr., made a poor effort to hide his amusement. I wore my soft OD jungle hat pulled down on my head as would a rodeo clown to keep the chopper's downdraft from blowing it away. When I looked up to a six-foot two-inch man with a kind, warm face, I felt an instant kinship for he possessed a friendly, easygoing manner. First Lieutenant Smith was a couple of years younger than I, which meant nothing, because he had six months—what seemed like a lifetime—in country. After OCS, Jim had completed the two-week jungle school in Panama and thought he was going to be a platoon leader.

Instead he had been reassigned to a MAT. Over the next six months we developed a bond that only soldiers can know.

Jim introduced me to the team. Officially a MAT included a captain as team leader, a first lieutenant as assistant team leader, a medic, and two senior NCOs. In reality, a team rarely operated at full strength.

Sergeant First Class (SFC) Louis R. Kerbow, heavy weapons advisor, and Staff Sergeant (SSG) Ronald D. Adams, light weapons specialist, were the noncommissioned officers and were serving their second tour. Both had trouble stringing words together without every other word being "shit," "fuck," or "goddamn." It just so happened that they knew the Army and how to manipulate it. They also mixed well with the Vietnamese.

Kerbow, a twenty-year veteran whose wife and children lived in the Midwest, was an E-7 who, in February 1970, would become an E-8 or master sergeant, a high rank for an NCO. Adams, red-haired and mustachioed, was from the West and had lived and worked in many of the places introduced to me by my father, places I loved—Bryce Canyon, Zion Canyon, Monument Valley, and Lake Powell. I learned a great deal from those two sergeants.

I can only imagine what must have been running through their minds when introduced to another rookie, as "Nice to meet you, Lieutenant" could be translated into "Well, fuck, I guess we have to train this green shit too. I wonder if he fucking knows anything worth a shit."

In contrast to MAT III-56's role, district advisory personnel operated out of the villa. District Senior Advisor (DSA) Captain Raymond A. Wing, who had majored in accounting at the University of Maine, held court. Captain Wing was an ROTC graduate, a career military man, and Special Forces qualified although not currently in such an assignment. I liked and respected this short, wiry captain who knew how to have fun (he was the proud owner of a pair of Budweiser shorts and matching shirt), but when he spoke in earnest, you had best pay attention. I felt confident in his presence, even when he swaggered about with a cane he brandished good-naturedly. Captain Wing's assignments ranged from serving twelve months on an A-Team in Kham Duc and the 25th Division in Dau Tieng to participating as a Revolutionary Development Cadre advisor and ultimately to serving as the S-5 (Civil Affairs) at Special Forces headquarters in Nha Trang. He knew a lot about the Vietnamese and their culture and displayed little patience with those who expended only a modicum of effort, such as his passive counterpart, the district chief, Dai-Uy Nghiem.

Another district favorite was Lieutenant David W. Ward. A University of Arkansas graduate, he served as the resident DIOCC (District Intelligence and Operations Coordinating Center) advisor, whose official function was to advise the South Vietnamese police and intelligence agencies on how to collect and share information to enable elimination of the Vietcong shadow government. Over time Lieutenant Ward and I argued good-naturedly about the merits of University of Arkansas football vis-à-vis those of the University of Texas. I respected Lieutenant Ward and valued his sense of humor, but in hindsight I believe everyone's performance would have been enhanced had we shared more information.

First Lieutenant Bob Trifiletti, U.S. Army Corps of Engineers, assigned to Duc Hue District as the Civic Affairs Officer, arrived a couple of months later. Due to the differences in the nature of our assignments, we did not spend much time together. His task was to work on civil projects for both the U.S. and South Vietnamese, including the laying of concrete and the construction, improvement, or repair of facilities such as schools.

Prior to my arrival Lieutenant Ward had accompanied Jim on several operations, and when joint operations with district were commissioned, the two of us occasionally linked up. Once, when mired thigh-deep in muck during an operation southeast of the Sugar Mill, Lieutenant Ward uttered his great war cry, "Lord, if I ever get out of this mess in one piece, I'm going to take a year off."

That was not the only war cry uttered by Lieutenant Ward. Another time the inimitable David Ward and his interpreter accompanied a joint Vietnamese and American CRIP (Combined Reconnaissance and Intelligence Platoon) on an amphibious operation west of the Vam Co Dong. Leaving the boats, the unit began patrolling westward toward Cambodia when they encountered an unusually large rice paddy dike. As they reached the top of the dike, they observed a squad of Vietcong emerging from a tree line on the opposing dike, roughly four hundred meters distant. The combined CRIP formed a skirmish line along the top of the dike and commenced firing. David judged that the enemy was out of effective range for small arms fire, so in true infantry fashion he raised one arm high and shouted, "Follow me!"

David then strode purposefully into the ankle-deep gumbo. Unfortunately only the American CRIP's medic, who happened to be unarmed, followed him. As this undermanned assault force of two proceeded, they heard an odd rasping, huffing, puffing sound. Abruptly halting their charge, they turned and saw on their right flank a heretofore-undetected herd of water buffalo. The largest, most truculent bull detached himself from the herd, and with David and the medic square in his sights, bore down on them like a freight train. The Vietcong became an afterthought. Lieutenant Ward and the medic made a hasty assessment of the situation and wisely decided that retreat was the order of the day. So retreat they did, faster than they had begun their aborted charge. David, while attempting a full gallop through the sucking mud, fired his M-16 over his shoulder at the raging beast.

The water buffalo, meanwhile, unable to decide which of his quarry presented the most suitable target, lost ground on his prey because he kept shifting his attack from one hapless soul to the other. Finally the American CRIP machine gunner leveled the water buffalo with a burst from his M-60. The water buffalo's indecisiveness cost him the battle, and then he lost his war. KIA.

For the most part, contributions from those behind the scenes at district, including work performed by valuable NCOs such as Sergeant First Class George R. Diggs, who served as district operations and intelligence advisor, and others whose names have slipped from memory, were appreciated by those of us in the field.

MISSION

MACV was established for the purpose of working more closely and coordinating with all South Vietnamese troops and civilians; therefore, each Vietnamese in his chain of command was to have an American counterpart who would report on his peer's effectiveness and convey unresolved deficiencies by kicking them up the chain. This required a lot of communication and cross-fertilization, and you can well imagine the Vietnamese were not always thrilled to have big American brothers looking over their shoulders.

When I arrived in country, there were approximately 350 Mobile Advisory Teams, with a goal of adding a hundred more during the year. Each district was supposed to have at least one MAT. Assuming there were 450 teams operating at full strength at the end of my tour, that meant 2,250 men. Not a large force, but this concept of teaching, support, and liaison was intended to permeate the South Vietnamese militia units.

A MAT was designed to operate at field level with South Vietnamese regional force and popular force units, generally working independently of other American units. The intelligence advisory effort served as the launching pad for many operations, but the data was often cold. The primary mission of a MAT was to advise and accompany regional and popular forces on military operations and advise and assist on tactics, logistics, civil actions, sanitation, and living conditions. MAT members were not designated to be primary combatants, although many wanted to be, and wound up doing so by necessity. We were to serve as the liaison, orchestrating artillery and air strikes when needed in periods of contact. Regional forces (RFs) and popular forces (PFs) were not part of the regular Army of the Republic of Vietnam, yet RFs and PFs made up approximately forty percent of South Vietnam's fighting forces. By volunteering to be a regional force or popular force soldier, a Vietnamese man could avoid being drafted into the ARVN.

Known as ruff-puffs, a regional force approximated company size (one hundred forty to one hundred sixty men) and a popular force, platoon size (twenty-two to forty men). In actuality, they operated at about half those numbers. (American units also were usually under strength.) In theory RFs and PFs operated in hamlets and villages contiguous to their homes, the idea being that proximity to family ensured diligence and conscientiousness. The contra theory: by integrating family members into the combat culture, the soldiers would become distracted and not be effective. Frequently RF and PF units were relocated.

As America began withdrawing ground troops, South Vietnam needed more fighting men, and ruff-puffs were called upon to assume a greater defensive role. The problem was that these units usually were not as well trained, not as well supplied with modern weaponry as the Americans and, without Big Brother, did not have coordinated air and artillery support available. Without advisors present on the ground, RFs and PFs often found themselves out on the proverbial limb. Our job was to help.

The sergeants had scrounged and traded for enough gear to outfit a team three times our size. In addition to the standard issue of M-16s, the NCOs had procured two .50-caliber machine guns (more of an anti-armor weapon than anti-personnel), two 81mm mortars, a 60mm mortar, and an M-79 grenade launcher. For a time we had an M-60 machine gun, a jewel of an anti-personnel weapon. For a party of four, transportation was provided by two Army jeeps, one three-quarter-ton truck and, for a short while, by a two-and-a-half-ton truck. One vehicle caught my attention.

"That jeep looks in excellent condition," I remarked to Jim. It looked immaculate.

"Uh, yeah, it's in pretty good shape," he replied cryptically.

"Does it take long to requisition equipment?"

"Depends on how you do it," he responded, again in a guarded manner.

"How long did it take to get this one?" I asked.

"About a day."

Turns out Jim had acquired the jeep in a clandestine exchange. His other jeep did not run as well as he would have liked—traversing rice paddy dikes tended to be a little rough on the suspension system—so during a jaunt into Saigon he *traded* the poorly performing jeep for one with better credentials.

SEEN, NOT HEARD

Initially I opened my mouth only to ask questions, gave no advice, and listened to the wisdom of Jim Smith and Sergeants Kerbow and Adams. I became more impressed with Jim for he had initiative and fortitude and was diligent in his approach. Though not a college graduate, Jim blended street smarts, experience, and initiative into the role of a MAT leader.

We practice-fired the 81mm mortar and witnessed across the river a dazzling display by "Spooky," a converted C-130 cargo plane outfitted with an awesome array of armaments. Among other weapons the plane carried at least two 7.62mm multibarreled machine guns (modified M-60s) configured to fire six thousand rounds a minute, ten times as fast as the regular M-60.

Jeep runs penetrating the operating quadrant's interior provided further insight into this anachronous realm. I became enthralled. Vietnamese children stood on the backs of water buffaloes, guiding them as they swam through canals. Fishnets, leveraged by long bamboo poles balanced on a fulcrum, rose from canals like plumes of smoke. Fragrances from freshly turned soil, water buffalo, chickens, dogs, dung, people, and canals coagulated into a thick, tart pungency. Monsoon rains washed the earth clean, leaving rich, saturated earth tones.

Remote farmhouses, as yet untouched by shelling, reflected the owners' unique artistry and expression of wealth or lack thereof. Like the Navahos in northeastern Arizona who inhabited clapboard shelters, some South Vietnamese lived under roofs of thatched straw and clay while others slept beneath faded red clay tile roofs that extended over open verandahs. A few homes sported awnings and intricate lace-like railings. Potted plants sprouted along multicolored exterior walls. It was difficult to comprehend the ongoing desecration of this land and its people.

Water buffalo pulled plows and carts. Rumor held that the Vietnamese valued water buffalo more than human life.[4] I did not believe it then and I do not believe it now. Encountering only stimulating conversation, local beer, oscillating fans, and the lovely, delicate faces of Vietnamese women, I could not believe there was a war going on.

That illusion was quickly shattered.

An American armored personnel carrier rumbled to an abrupt halt at the foot of the villa's grounds. Two American soldiers jumped out. Frightened, they carried a Vietnamese man, who had been shot with a .38-caliber pistol, allegedly by a South Vietnamese village policeman. The bullet had drilled a clean round hole in the center of the victim's chest. In their anxiety, thoughts of immobilizing the man were cast aside; they were about to witness their first fatality, as was I. The medics did everything they could, from administering oxygen to intravenous infusion of plasma. But it was too late; the damage was irreversible. Why the man was shot no one could say. What I remember are the looks on those two young soldiers' faces, a fusion of fear and concern. They did not want the man to die; they did the best they could. I had never been around death and was not particularly disturbed or uncomfortable, just surprised. I stood back and observed with a detached curiosity, like watching a movie unfold. The abstraction of death did not register.

～ ～

We never talked about death in our family—that it was part of life, the end of life. When I was in high school and my dad suffered his stroke, I remember him lying on the bed, but I do not remember feeling anything. When I relayed the news to my neighbor, Johnny, he asked plaintively, "Is he dead yet?"

After the war, when I uncovered the early strands of my father's life, I wondered how he felt about being born into a family whose world was encompassed by death. His mother Jennie died in July 1898, at the age of twenty-nine, so he never knew her nor she him. Three siblings—two sisters and one brother—died in infancy before Dad was born. Except for his father, he was the sole survivor. Unedited excerpts from old letters provide some insight:

～ ～

Undated, from my father's mother,

Dear Mother, Father, Sisters and Brothers. I will endever to answer your kind and welcome letter we received a few days ago. We are well. We have a baby boy. It is nearly a month old, its name is Lonnie. It has blue eyes, it is just as sweet as it can be. I washed today for the first time since he was born. Virve (?) stayed with me nearly two weeks. . . . We have planted some potatoes—we are having some nice weather now. I wish I could just slip in and see what your all a-doing just now. How I would love to see all of you. . . . Well Ma I don't know what John [husband] will do next year. I hope he won't stay in this place for we have seen so much trouble. . . . Well love to all

Jennie Thomas

February 15, 1898, from my father's mother,

John and the baby [Lonnie] is well. I am just able to crawl around a little my hip and leg is so bad I am nearly past going. Well I will send you the baby's picture. It looks just like him. Don't you think it is pretty and sweet. He has on short dresses now. He is so sweet. . . . I wish I could see you all but I can't so I just as well stand it the best I can. . . . Goodbye from your loving daughter/sister.

Jennie

Undated, from my father's mother,

Well dear mother it would do my heart good to see you but I know I cannot now but sometime if we live I hope to see you and if we do not live we can meet in another world where thair is no more trouble or sorrow. . . .

Jennie

Undated, from my father's father,

I can't find pleasure in any living thing. Every-thing is so still and lonesome. God alone knows what I have sufford since I lost my darling baby [one of Dad's sisters]. She was so sweet to me whenever she wanted to go anywhere she would say I want to go Papa and the last word she said was Papa how can I bear this bourden. I want you all to pray for me that I may be permitted to go where she has gone for I know she has gone to meet her brother and sister in heaven. Give my love to all. I will close.

> Your Bro.
> J.R. Thomas

May 31, 1898, from my father's father,

We are all up but Jennie is not well. She has got the sciatic rheumatism and she can't hardly go. I am not through chopping cotton. . . .

> J.R. Thomas
> Wagner, Texas

July 31, 1898, from my father's father,

This leave me well at this time but the baby is not well at present but he is better than he was last week. I am afraid he may have to be circumcised. . . . I do not know whether anyone has ever written to you the cause of Jennie's death are not. The cause of her death was Bright's Disease in acute form. Well I guess you can imagine how I feel I am so lonesome I can hardly live. I cannot be satisfied anywhere. I have felt as though I were lost all the while as I look around me at neighbors and friends the one I loved best I fail to see. It has not appeard to me even on that my Dear Companion was burried. It seems as though she is just out of sight. She said she could see our little babies with beautiful white robes on and I know she has gone to see them and as I can only be consoled by looking forward to the near future when I shall be permitted to follow her and if I am as well prepared as I think she was I will be satisfied. . . .

J.R. Thomas
Kellogg, Texas

J.R. Thomas was to remarry and live many more years, but neither he nor his new wife, a woman with only one leg, showed any interest or affection for Dad. I met my grandfather, John Richard Thomas, one time in the early fifties but retain no impressions of consequence. Did my father feel as his father had felt? Was he terrified at losing his family, choosing not to love them too much for fear they might go away? Dad lived with various aunts, uncles, and grandparents in a gamut of small towns or farms ranging from El Campo, Loraine, and Roscoe to Spur and Abilene. What I remember as a child from the few tortuous visits to one of his aunt's house was a sterile environment, a house that filled me with dread. Stiff, that is what it was. But that environment did not hamper my father's drive for, as already alluded to, he finished high school after his military service, then enrolled and worked his way through college.

In Vietnam my new dimension would open me up to a new realm of pain. Now that I had been introduced to the land and its people, it was time for escalating experiences to prepare me for what lay ahead. I had seen both beauty and death. I would see more, tasting profoundly the flavors of war. And I would need my father's drive to get through it.

3

THE DRILL

The barely audible sound, far off, is just like the
fluttering of a butterfly's wings . . . intimately close.
And it comes closer.

The staccato chopping of the blades slices the air
with powerful thrusts, creating irregular pockets
of waves . . . spreading, penetrating, in all
directions, with no direction.

The chopper arrives,
sending a tingling tremor
that permeates the whole of your being.

Your body flows into the cabin.
You are part of it now.
You sense it. You feel it.
The power has been transferred,
and you are magnificent.
You are powerful
in your jungle fatigues,
weapon at the ready,
bandoliers of rounds
slung around your chest.

The chopper is airborne, nose down,
skimming, searching, darting,
like a hawk before its kill.

You feel the chopper's speed.
And, as the gunner preps the landing zone,
tufts of earth are ripped loose
and thrown into the air
as if willed up by your eyes alone.
Lower. Then lower.
Quickly you are down,
off into the swirling dust, propelled
aside by the command of the blades
as they lift and carry away.

The sound is merely distant now, almost gone.
Slowly the power fades, and is lost.
Vulnerability recurs,
and your thoughts return
to the light fluttering of a butterfly.

"The Helicopter," a poem.

FIRST MISSION—EAGLE FLIGHT

Chopper blades rotated idly. The staged metal warriors waited patiently for their military passengers to board. Intelligence had reported a sighting of twenty Vietcong entering a hamlet nine to ten kilometers northeast of the Sugar Mill. Three regional force companies were to be airlifted and dropped as a blocking force. The choppers were to set down at a landing zone (LZ) and we would disperse from there.

The engines revved; escalated to a solid, steady resonance; and the warriors lifted sluggishly, hovering slightly before dipping their noses, gaining momentum, altitude, and grace. In flight, the birds exhibited a gallant symmetry. I trembled with excitement as my heartbeat mimicked the steady thumping of the rotors, and I wondered what might be encountered once we scattered from the LZ.

A hunter-killer Huey Cobra team reconnoitered the LZ. The lead gunship, nose down, skimmed just above treetop level in a brazen effort to surprise and startle the Vietcong, to force them into the open and draw fire. Bird number one was bait. The killer chopper, whose mission was to sweep clean anyone fool enough to show himself, hovered slightly above and behind the first bird. The frontal view of a cobra gunship presented both a slender silhouette and a frightening spectacle. Sharks' teeth often were painted on front of the fuselage. Armament configuration varied, but generally a combination of 7.62mm miniguns, grenade launchers, and 2.75-inch rocket pods were mounted. There was no return fire.

After landing, we moved out to our blocking-force position. Over the field radio came a transmission: "Discovered a small tunnel system. Blew in place two booby traps."

I heard rifle fire, readied my M-16, turned, and saw two Vietnamese soldiers shooting into the trees. "What are they doing?" I asked excitedly, wondering if they had spotted a sniper.

"Oh, they are just shooting at birds," replied the trung-uy (Vietnamese first lieutenant).

SECOND MISSION—NIGHT PATROL

Approximately three kilometers northeast of the Sugar Mill (seven kilometers by road) lay the hamlet of Rung-Tre, a scattered and sparsely populated enclave that had as its center of defense a well-fortified outpost manned by B Company, 2nd Battalion, 27th Infantry, 2nd Brigade, 25th Infantry Division. The perimeter of the outpost consisted of sandbag bunkers with roofs constructed of interlocking, perforated steel planks (PSP) overlaid with sandbags. The purpose of sandbags was to disperse the impact from direct hits, preventing the PSP from becoming a large fragmentation grenade.

To protect the perimeter, claymore mines—anchored in concrete to prevent sappers from turning them around—and trip flares were strategically placed within staked strands of barbed wire intertwined with spiraling concertina wire. Detonated by electrical contact, a claymore mine consisted of six to seven hundred steel projectiles propelled by plastic explosive in a sixty-degree fan-shaped pattern.

As I toured the inside perimeter, an infantry grunt took offense at my presence and said to another, "What the fuck is that lieutenant doing here?" The anger and bitterness appalled and concerned me, but the depth of his rage did not sink in for a long time. It did not matter then because the American unit soon pulled out and was replaced by 494 Regional Force Company under the command of Trung-Uy Nguyen Ngoc Hot, a forty-year-old soldier who had gone to military school and become an officer.

For my first night ambush I accompanied a squad of 494 Regional Force Company with Sergeant Kerbow along as my American mentor. We departed at dusk, heading west. Monsoon rains had flooded the rice paddies, turning the mud and buffalo dung into sucking quicksand as well as making the paddy dikes slicker than banana peels. The RF soldiers scampered as smoothly and quietly atop the crowned dikes as squirrels traversing a wet power line. Not me.

If there were any Vietcong in the area, they were probably laughing too hard to fire as this green lieutenant had yet to master the art of walking a slippery tightrope. I would slip off one side, then the other, resoundingly splashing progress reports to the enemy. Upon reaching the designated ambush site, I spent my first night lying in the mud. Other than the slurping sound of displacing mud whenever I moved, the most difficult challenge amounted to staying awake and keeping the muzzle of my M-16 out of the muck.

THIRD MISSION—RIVER PATROL BOATS (PBRS)

The Navy operated PBRs in inland and coastal waterways of Vietnam. Fast, maneuverable, and capable of reaching speeds of twenty-five knots, they constituted the sports-car genre of the riverine force. They were heavily armed, with a combination of .50-caliber machine guns, rapid-fire grenade launchers, perhaps a mortar, and other armament. In addition, sailors carried individual weapons. Among other objectives, their mission was to patrol the waterways, interdict suspicious traffic, conduct hit-and-run operations and on occasion ferry soldiers to an operating objective.

Timing is everything. I thought of my oldest brother. Richard, the one with the appointment to the Naval Academy, the one who graduated with honors from Rice University, the one who, after the third brother earned entry into his high school's National Honor Society, had looked me straight in the eye and said, "And you are going to be the next one."

"Oh, no, I'm not," I had replied silently and steadfastly, basing my response on a confluence of "cannot do" and "will not do," with no clear sense as to which was dominant. If I had to be perfect for my father's love, then I would neither succeed nor fail but excel in mediocrity.

Richard, a Lieutenant J.G. who just missed the Korean War, served in the Navy from June 1954 through June 1956 and performed his sea duty on the destroyer *Frank E. Evans* (DD754). Richard could have been commanding PBRs patrolling the Vam Co Dong. He could have been off-loading soldiers like me. He could have been in numerous firefights that PBRs encountered.

Nevertheless I looked forward with excitement to my first riverine operation, a joint effort of RFs, ARVN, and a U.S. unit. On this mission Jim would be my mentor, and it struck me as curious that he strapped on the PRC-25 field radio. Officers never carried radios, or so I thought. Whoever lugged the PRC-25 was an inviting target for a sniper.

"Jim, most advisors have a Vietnamese carry the radio. Why not us?" I asked.

A look of distress spread across Jim's face as he adjusted the load on his back. "When I was in Duc Hoa District, we had a contact. The regional force soldier carrying the radio got shot, but that didn't keep him from running off with the radio."

The implications were clear. Feeling vulnerable without the ability to call for artillery or gunship support, Jim had decided he would rather the team incur the burden of carrying the PRC-25.[5]

The weather was balmy, the sky hazy, as we completed our preparations and boarded the boats. Leaving trails of whitecaps, the powerful PBRs plunged six kilometers downriver into Duc Hoa District. We approached the drop-off point. The engines were throttled back, and the PBRs nosed into the east bank. Our unit disembarked.

As during my first mission the RFs again behaved in a slovenly manner. After scattering amidst the wild vegetation, we waited. Three hours later we still waited.

Jim and I asked several times, "What are we waiting for?"

To which we finally received a reply, "We are waiting for one of the Vietnamese commanders."

"Where is he?"

"He is at a nearby market and his soldiers won't go without him."

We could not command the Vietnamese troops to move. We could only recommend and apply pressure. The majority of Vietnamese troops and small unit commanders I worked with impressed me favorably. The soldiers needed strong leadership, and a bad apple tainted the entire unit. When there was a bad commander, you never knew if he was a poor leader or a Vietcong sympathizer.

Finally we swept a five-kilometer swath and found nothing. There is a term for this type of operation. It is called a cluster fuck.

Exposed to air, water, and land and seeing no action, I felt fortunate to experience these practice runs, which were to serve me well in the future. On one hand I felt talented and competent; on the other I was terrified of screwing up, letting crippling doubt set in, robbing me of my ability to perform.

Once on a small recreational lake in Tennessee, my mother, one of her sisters, and I, the kid, were in a small rowboat, the kind with the two oars secured in oarlocks. Mom let me row the boat, a task I was not prepared to undertake. If we moved at all, it was in a circle. Mom, becoming impatient and embarrassed, demanded the oars. I refused to relinquish them. "I can do it. I can do it," I said, feeling a strong need to succeed. Whop! I felt the sting as she slapped me, the blood rushing to my face. My aunt winced. I shed not a tear, but inside I was dying for I had failed. It was, by the way, the only time my mother ever struck me.

As the end of July drew near, I began spending more nights in the field. A clearer picture of the tangled operating environment—an oxymoron—was emerging. We also began spending time at An Dinh. This outpost lay approximately twenty-one kilometers northeast of Ba Thu, an enemy base-camp sanctuary on the Cambodian border, and fourteen kilometers east of the Parrot's Beak. Slightly off square, the outpost was less than half an acre in size, its perimeter defined by a bunker system wedged between stout bamboo and palm trees. The hedgerow afforded marginal protection from small arms fire and B40 rockets but offered little security from arching mortar shells.

4

Rumblings at An Dinh

The next day—
we found one in the wire,
clad only in blue shorts.

He was a guerrilla,
a sapper, a real pro,
only his life left him
a short while ago.

Live memories
of a dead mission
lay harmlessly about:
grenades, satchel charges . . .

A photograph—
of a smiling older man,
with an arm around his son,
much like my father had done.

"The Sappers – II," a poem.

Tuesday, 22 July 1969

My promotion to first lieutenant, while automatic, became effective. I felt prepared for what might lie ahead.

2000 Hours, Thursday, 24 July 1969

An Dinh received five rounds of 61mm mortar fire and the 158 Regional Force Company responded with its own. There were no casualties as the rounds fell harmlessly outside the perimeter, a typical Vietcong harassment and interdictory mission.

Friday, 25 July 1969

The ambush patrol unit of 158 Regional Force Company returned early and, failing to remove all of its own booby traps, lost one of its own to this collective oversight. He was dusted off.

1500 Hours, Sunday, 27 July 1969

While cleaning his weapon, a regional force soldier shot himself in the foot and had to be dusted off. By accident or intent? In the U.S. Army, we called it the million-dollar wound, as often this type of injury sent an American soldier stateside.

Night, Monday, 28 July 1969

An Dinh received several incoming mortar rounds as well as small arms fire from a force of unknown size. The Vietcong's and NVA's choice of hand-held weapon—the AK47 automatic assault rifle—delivered a distinctive signature, its "pop-pop-pop" easily differentiated from the M-16. Lieutenant Smith and Sergeant Kerbow accompanied a reaction force to pursue and engage the attackers while Sergeant Adams and I remained at the outpost, but not without an argument.

"I want to go," I exclaimed to Jim emphatically.

He replied just as emphatically, "No, Jack! Stay here. I need you to monitor the radio."

I wanted to experience contact and was chomping at the bit to undergo my christening. I felt like a little boy who had been told that he could not go out and play. A ridiculous feeling perhaps; nonetheless that is how I felt.

The reaction force pursued the attackers until they encountered a nearby graveyard. From the 3 August 1969 district senior advisor's report of events that followed:

> After departing at approximately 2115 hours and sweeping the initial area of contact, a platoon to the west spotted four VC and opened fire. Fire was returned from two directions. After grouping forces, gunships were called in [by Lieutenant Smith]. A weapon was picked up [a German pistol] and a blood trail spotted. The following day we were informed that two VC were killed and one VC seriously wounded in this action. As a result of this action and the actions of the 158 Regional Force Company, it was decided First Lieutenant Thom [the 158 RF Commander] be recommended for a valor award.[6]

29 AND 31 JULY 1969

We accompanied daytime sweeps and Lieutenant Smith used an M-79 grenade launcher to blow a booby trap in place. On the thirty-first, a need arose to evacuate a wounded Vietnamese from the outpost. A short trail connected the An Dinh bunker complex to Route 10, a laterite road running southeast to northwest, several kilometers east of and parallel to the Vam Co Dong. Calling in my first dustoff, I stood where the trail and the road intersected when, in the midst of my radio transmission, an American colonel and his aide stopped their jeep to ask, of all things, for directions. I was focused on sending the proper grid coordinates and ensuring that I had the bases covered to bring in the chopper, including having a colored smoke grenade to mark the location. I knew where I was, but I did not have my map with me; it was back in the outpost.

"Lieutenant, we need to see your map," ordered the colonel in a not-so-friendly tone.

I replied in a sheepish manner, "Uh, sir, I don't have it with me. It's in the outpost."

"What's this road we're on?"

"Well, sir, it goes up to An Ninh Village, then —"

"I want to know the number. What's the number of the road?"

By then I was so flustered I forgot the number of the road. The colonel chewed me out for not having a map on my person at all times, not a bad lesson. Later I realized that besides being lost, those idiots did not have a map either.

1930 Hours, Friday, 1 August 1969

The disruptive shelling continued. An Dinh received nine incoming 61mm mortar rounds which fell harmlessly outside the perimeter. There were no casualties. At 2000 hours an unarmed Hoi Chanh (defector) came to the outpost and turned himself in, probably defecting from the Vietcong squad that had just mortared the outpost. Hopeful of earning amnesty from the South Vietnamese government, the Hoi Chanh then led a small contingent to recover his AK. (See Chapter 8 for more information on Hoi Chanhs.)

Rumors: (1) The mortar tube the Vietcong was using might be a sawed-off version, resulting from the tube being damaged when a round went off prematurely. The senior South Vietnamese officer in the district good-naturedly chided us about not having captured the weapon. (2) An American unit operating in the area had uncovered a large cache of AK47 ammunition and shipped it to the United States where it underwent surgery. Sabotaged and shipped back for underground distribution to the Vietcong, the rounds were supposed to blow up upon impact from the firing pin.[7]

1142 Hours, Tuesday, 5 August 1969

I turned twenty-five years of age. Other than receiving cards from home, there was no celebration.

0400 Hours, Tuesday, 12 August 1969

At the An Dinh outpost, 158 Regional Force Company received thirty 82mm mortar rounds, five 107mm rockets, and an unknown number of B40 rockets and AK47 fire from an estimated reinforced squad of Vietcong, a classic military maneuver employed since this type of warfare began. Bombard and follow up with a ground probe. The first inclination of anyone on the receiving end of a mortar or artillery barrage is to scurry for cover. The most effective defense is to take the offensive, counterfiring as quickly and intensely as possible.

Whether the Vietcong knew American advisors were present is not known (none were), but there was no one to coordinate American artillery and air support. Under diversionary cover of the opening mortar salvos, Vietcong sappers, who were already in position, began their final approach, low-crawling under defensive wire positions. The strategy was to hit fast and hard. For the sappers, whose task was to breach the perimeter and fling hand grenades and satchel charges (bangalore torpedoes, i.e., bamboo tubes full of explosives) to disable and disorient interior defenses, it was often a suicide mission. A second line of guerrillas or NVA lined up to come in and mop up.

The fear of being overrun always lingered at the back of everyone's mind. But the regional force company acquitted itself well, countering with its own mortar, M-16 fusillades, and machine gun fire. Although .50-calibers could jam fairly easily, fortunately these did not as Sergeants Kerbow and Adams—who scrounged the unauthorized weapons—trained the RFs on their proper use and maintenance.

Early that morning we set out to survey the damage. The Vietcong had failed to breach the perimeter. The regional force company suffered several wounded and one KIA, a soldier who had been doing his job the best he could, by returning fire. A neat, round hole in the middle of his forehead marked the spot where the round had penetrated his skull and shattered his brain. An older soldier with gray hair, whose name quickly became purged from memory and who would never be known to Americans other than ourselves, would fight no more.

During my first visit to An Dinh I heard Kerbow ask, "Hey, Adams, which fuckin' side you want?"

"I'll take the one facing west."

"OK. I've got the south," Kerbow replied.

I did not know what the hell they were talking about until I walked the perimeter line. Two .50-caliber machine guns, the sound of which would send fear into the heart of a grizzly bear, dominated the western and southern perimeters. Sergeants Kerbow and Adams loved to man those weapons, getting high on the thump-thump-thump as six-inch shells shot out of the barrel at a muzzle velocity of two thousand nine hundred thirty feet per second.

This time as Smith, Adams, Kerbow, and I surveyed the outpost, we detected a somber but stoic attitude among the RFs. After all, these were soldiers, but they had lost one of their own, a good man. We covered the eastern and southern sides of the perimeter, made a right turn, and continued pacing the western line, reaching the .50-caliber machine gun position that faced west. Enemy fire had pulverized the bamboo window frame that sheathed this weapon. It was as if a threshing machine had been unleashed. I watched Adams, who, had we been present, would have manned that gun position. Imperceptibly, as the realization of what might have been sank in, his whole body trembled.

The enemy left one in the wire. By the time we arrived, the RFs had retrieved his body and searched for weapons and papers. Found on his person was some blood-spattered North Vietnamese paper money. Another keepsake, a photograph of an older man—the dead soldier's father, perhaps?—who was smiling and had his arm draped around this no-longer-living soldier, had been confiscated by the RFs.

As I began to grasp the meaning of death, the distinction between race, color, religion, and side began slipping away. I saw that the soldier's life had gone out of him; I was glad it was not I or a teammate, but I wished there were another way.

During my tour I never saw dead American soldiers. I saw wounded American soldiers, but no dead ones, as we simply were not around many Americans. The bodies I saw were all Vietnamese, both Vietcong/NVA and RFs/PFs, which made the war seem all the more foreign in respect to the experiences of my fellow American veterans who had not served as combat advisors. Yet, for me, it was quite personal.

When I departed Houston for Vietnam, my father lay flat on his back in the hospital and was unable to accompany me to the airport. As with many families in that era, expressions of touching and love were less than profuse; those that did occur were memorable, like tantalizing gifts of hope that made you want to hold on to life. I had performed poorly one semester in college. Mom and I were in my bedroom, and I was telling her how I felt—empty and lonesome. I had broken up with my girlfriend, had no goals, no purpose, and, in essence, ached deeply. Dad walked in. His first reaction, yelling, "What's going on here!" was typical. I held it in no longer and burst out crying. He came over, put his cheek against mine, placed his arm around me, and asked what was wrong. I told him, and he said, "Just do the best you can." I felt as if he had lifted a boulder off my shoulders. I can still feel the warmth of his cheek and the comfort of those tears. I still see the tattered black and white photograph of the two Vietnamese men.

While we had put in regular stays at An Dinh, we now received orders to spend even more time at this outpost. There were exceptions. From the 27 September 1969 Weekly Activities Report compiled by Captain Wing and addressed to the province senior advisor:

> MAT III-56 completed training of Popular Force
> Platoon 17, and accompanied one day and one night
> operation on 18 and 19 September with 158
> Regional Force Company. During the week, the team
> present for duty strength decreased from four
> personnel to one (Lt. Smith is on R & R, SSG Adams

is on Emergency Leave, SFC Kerbow is in the hospital). Team has had no medic for almost two months.

Little did we know, however, that the actions of July and early August were portents of events in November and December.

5

MURKY ENVIRONMENT

That is what the war was
that is what the war is
total confusion

go out on patrol
help vietnamese
kill vietnamese

three a.m.
stop for a pot of tea

"Oh, we killed two or three."

"You want a girl?"

"No, thanks, trung-uy."

"Confusion," a poem.

❧

In a sense, defending outposts and ourselves was the easy part. Understanding the environment was much more difficult because life's tentacles were a convoluted amalgam in South Vietnam, from economics to religion to politics to warfare. While this book is not intended as an in-depth exploration of economics, religious teachings, or political leanings, a brief summary may provide some insight into the chaos.

The economy was a mixed bag, a disharmonious composite of barter, cash, and black market trading. If you paid enough, you could obtain anything you wanted, from women to weapons, particularly in the back streets of Saigon. American dollars, while officially prohibited, played an integral role in the marketplace. Furthermore South Vietnam had the most powerful nation in the world telling them how to govern and live their lives, and, mirroring the discord of its parent, the village community of Hiep Hoa was not insulated from these influences. Regardless of the trickle-down effect, most farmers and villagers wanted to be left alone and allowed to plow their fields, but their fields were full of disruptive obstacles.

Regarding religion, there was no coherency. A Catholic is defined by Webster as "universal in extent; encompassing all; wide-ranging: . . . having broad sympathies; broad-minded; liberal . . . pertaining to the whole Christian body or church." The definition for Buddhism in Webster's is "life is full of suffering caused by desire and . . . the way to end this suffering is through Enlightenment that enables one to halt the endless sequence of births and deaths to which one is otherwise subject."

After the French were defeated and the Communists took power in North Vietnam, hordes of Catholics fled south. It seems logical, therefore, that Catholics would oppose Communism based simply on religious beliefs, and most did. However some, whether straddling the fence for survival purposes or genuinely opposed to the inept Saigon-based regimes, forged alliances with the Vietcong. Nor were the Buddhists inherently Communistic in their political support—to the contrary— but when Buddhist monks started to immolate themselves to protest persecution by the secret police force under Catholic President Ngo Dinh Diem and his brother Ngo Dinh Nhu, Buddhist followers did not exactly trample over each other in their rush to support President Diem. Driven more by lack of representation and recognition from various South Vietnamese governments, as opposed to adherence to a political principle or doctrine, the Buddhists in their frustration became vulnerable to the specious, manipulative practices of the Vietcong.

As already mentioned, the Cao Dai blended the teachings of Buddhism, Taoism, Confucianism, and Christianity. Again, while it may seem that this religious group would support a *democratic* government, the fact that, in the mid-fifties, forces loyal to then Prime Minister Diem routed their private armies did not exactly endear Diem to the multifaced Cao Dai.

All factions were present, and it would be inaccurate to say that everyone of any given religious persuasion supported a certain political program. As these incendiary incidents gained notoriety, however, it became obvious that America supported a South Vietnamese president who failed to practice true democratic principles. Diem attempted to squash all dissent.

The real issue was that no one strong and tolerant enough to assimilate and blend the disparate factions into a coalition government, with fair representation for all, stepped forward. The southerners in Vietnam did not want a Communist-backed regime to run the country. They wanted to govern themselves but could never put into play a leader who wanted to do anything other than eradicate all opposition. It is sad that no one emerged who could, or would, unite the South.

Strong leadership in the North further complicated the South's position. Their president, Ho Chi Minh, "He Who Enlightens," was a revered figure in much of South Vietnam. He was born Nguyen Sinh Cung in 1890 in Kim Lien village, Nam Dan District, Nghe An Province, in the central highlands of North Vietnam. Subsequently known as Nguyen Tat Thanh, in 1942 he adopted the name of Ho Chi Minh and became affectionately referred to as Uncle Ho. Upon his death on 2 September 1969, I naïvely hoped that the Vietcong and NVA would lose heart and abandon their prolonged aspirations to unify Vietnam. I was wrong.

Regardless of his political persuasion, Ho Chi Minh first and foremost was a nationalist; his goal was to free Vietnam of oppression. He wanted to unify Vietnam. This was remarkable considering Ho Chi Minh had left his country in 1911 as a cabin boy on a steamer and was not to return until 1941 when in the North he established in practice what he had been studying and preaching in principle: a guerrilla movement and a shadow government to fight the French and Japanese.

Thus, the North was the birthing ground of the Vietnam Doc

Lap Dong Minh (or Vietminh). Between 1911 and 1941 Ho Chi Minh had traveled worldwide, worked at the Carlton Hotel in London under a famous chef, studied in Russia while becoming a friend of Stalin, been imprisoned in China, and performed different tasks under varying aliases. However, he developed his "theology" for unifying Vietnam in Paris, where he also was a founding member of the French Communist party.

Ironically in 1945 Ngo Dinh Diem was offered the post of Minister of the Interior under Ho Chi Minh. Diem declined. Even more ironically Ho Chi Minh sought American support and later that year drafted a Vietnamese Declaration of Independence modeled in a vein curiously similar to that of the United States. An excerpt: "All men are created equal. They are endowed by their creator with certain inalienable rights." However, except on a microscale in which an American Office of Strategic Services (OSS) team trained and supplied arms to certain of Ho Chi Minh's new Vietminh, the United States refused him all other aid, choosing instead, if only by default, to support France. Twenty-plus years later, how interesting it would have been to know in the macrocosm the effectiveness of the OSS team's training guerrillas, who later would become our enemy.

Ho Chi Minh had invested considerable effort to negotiate a peaceful settlement for control and unification of Vietnam but failed. After the French were defeated in the 1954 epic, pivotal battle at Dien Bien Phu, Vietnam was bisected at the seventeenth parallel (DMZ) into two countries. Among the countries represented at the 1954 Geneva accords were the United States, Russia, China, and Great Britain. The United States did not sign, sending a foreboding, insinuative message to the people of North and South Vietnam. Uncle Ho got the North. From 1949 to 1955 the South continued under the reign of Bao Dai, an ancestral emperor and colonial puppet, whom the French placed in command as chief of state. He represented hypocrisy and the status quo. Ngo Dinh Diem, who in 1954 was named prime minister under Bao Dai, won the 1955 presidential *election* against his former boss.

Obviously Ho Chi Minh never gave up his lifetime goal of unifying Vietnam. In the South as well as in the North, that ideal was instilled in large numbers of Vietnamese. Many southerners who had risen up to fight French colonialism never changed their views; they merely shifted their emphasis to wage war against their perceived new aggressor, the United States. The roots of the guerrilla effort in South Vietnam were therefore firmly and deeply planted, and the unrest and discontent in the South provided fertile ground for manipulation.

In addition, a number of farmers in the South had been forcefully relocated from remote, rural ancestral homes to centralized, defensible positions among more populous centers. Generally relocation took place in geographical areas contiguous to original homesteads, but it was not home. I imagine the dispossessed were none too happy to become refugees in their own land, regardless of religious or political persuasion. Their lives were so intertwined with the past that it was difficult for dislocated villagers to sever connections and rally exclusively to one side or the other. Some of these folks had grown up and gone to school together or had worked together. Participants connected by bloodlines, or who once may have been friends or lovers, found themselves supporting diametrically opposed Vietnamese causes. Violently! What seemed to us to be rampant duplicity, a valid and justifiable observation in our view, was due to mixed loyalties.

I wonder how badly certain Vietnamese really wanted to fight their own kind. Political war, religious war, and civil war—on paper, clear lines of demarcation had been drawn, but before the ink could dry, water spilled all over the map. The lines blurred, lost definition, and faded into one another. Boundaries collapsed. Many Vietnamese did not trust each other and were not really sure which side of the fence their neighbor was on. Thus, they were not likely to be too vociferous in expressing their true beliefs because of the "I'm going to report you" mentality.

How much of this disruption could be attributed to both South Vietnam's and America's turbulent leadership changes in the 1960s is a matter of conjecture. The following table (not all-inclusive) depicts several abrupt changes of command in the two countries. It is no wonder both sides experienced considerable difficulty in achieving consistency and continuity.

VIETNAM	UNITED STATES
1955 to 1963—Ngo Dinh Diem served as Vietnam's first president.	January 21, 1961—John F. Kennedy took office as president.
November 2, 1963—President Diem and his brother, Ngo Dinh Nhu, assassinated; General Duong Van Minh (Big Minh) led military government after coup.	November 22, 1963—John F. Kennedy assassinated; Lyndon B. Johnson assumed office of president.
January 30, 1964—Nguyen Khanh, a Southern general, led a coup and overthrew Minh.	November 2, 1964—Lyndon B. Johnson defeated Barry Goldwater for presidency.
February-June, 1965—Khanh overthrown and Nguyen Cao Ky became prime minister, then vice-president under Thieu.	March 31, 1968—President Johnson announced he would not seek another term.
September 3, 1967—Nguyen Van Thieu elected president.	June 6, 1968—Robert Kennedy assassinated.
April 12, 1975—President Thieu resigned and was succeeded by Vice President Tran Van Huong.	November 5, 1968—Richard Nixon defeated Hubert Humphrey for presidency.
April 28, 1975—General Duong Van Minh appointed president.	November 7, 1972—President Nixon won reelection bid over Senator George McGovern.
April 30, 1975—South Vietnam surrendered to the North Vietnamese.	August 9, 1974—President Nixon resigned and Gerald Ford assumed office of president.

Data compiled from *Vietnam War Almanac* and *Historical Atlas of the Vietnam War* by Harry G. Summers, Jr.

Most Vietnamese of that period had never been without war. At one time or another France, Japan, China, and America had all tried to impose their will. I believe many Vietnamese were simply tired of fighting and wanted to align themselves with whoever could unify the country. One result was that the bread was buttered on both sides; the side presented at the moment was the one most likely to be favorably received. I cannot conceive of a more confusing and fearful way to live. In this shadowy, obfuscated environment, the people of South Vietnam subtly chose the side they would pour their allegiance into, regardless of outward appearances.

It was within this boiling cauldron of disparate beliefs, agendas, and motivations that we advisors were to help identify, isolate, and ferret out the enemy, a task similar to asking a cutting horse to cull out a specific cow when they all look alike. Nevertheless, if I was going to have to serve in this conflict, I felt fortunate to be assigned as an advisor in lieu of the traditional combat role as a platoon leader in an American unit.

Like most advisors, I had a fair degree of training and orientation regarding Vietnamese culture, religion, politics, and war. To live and work among Vietnamese engendered a viewpoint emanating more from the core of the conflict as opposed to a more detached, outside-looking-in perspective gleaned from experiences in American infantry units. But articulated advisory theory, looking good on paper and appearing sound in theory, was extremely difficult to execute. The combat advisors' destiny was to live and work with Vietnamese soldiers, some of whom were remarkably dedicated in their efforts to try to relegate to a level of insignificance the Vietcong and NVA. That they could not do so without significant American intervention over a prolonged period of time would soon become evident.

In reality, those of us at lower levels, whether U.S. troops, ARVN, ruff-puffs, or those Vietnamese endemically dedicated to the guerrilla effort, had little, if any, effect on military policy. We were pawns, sent out to do the bidding of our respective governments (yes, the Vietcong had a government too), all under the guise of doing what was deemed best for cause and country. And since I was assigned to one of the shaky spokes of this discordant hub, I made a commitment to carry the flag as best I could.

Just what was the nature of these Vietcong? They were different from North Vietnam's politicos and the North Vietnamese Army, who ultimately overran the South and took control of the country, which is not what the Vietcong and their political infrastructure desired.

The Vietcong were not a bunch of uneducated, undisciplined, ragtag peasants who ran around the country killing anything and everything they could. They were doctors, lawyers, engineers, mathematicians, teachers, housewives, laborers, village merchants, and farmers. Most assuredly, the Vietcong had the typical fringe elements of any organization, those who reveled in their thirst for violence, blood, cruelty, and sadism. Make no mistake, many were vicious, and they employed ruthless methods in assassinating South Vietnamese political cadre in hamlets, villages, and districts who supported the current South Vietnamese regime in power—as well as in fighting us.

That militaristic element had always been part of the Vietcong movement, the origin of which stretched back to the formation of the Vietminh in North Vietnam, who had been sent south to fight the French. Initially many southerners sympathetic to the Vietcong did not share their militaristic beliefs, instead first seeking and believing in political efforts for representation and acceptance in the governing of South Vietnam, using violence only as a last resort. All the doctors, lawyers, and teachers did not hail from rural areas; many were from large cities, such as Saigon. There had been a long history of clandestinely organized cells of youth movements and respected Vietnamese citizenry that either opposed existing governing policies and practices in the South, such as those employed by the repressive Diem, or, as long as they were left alone, desired to maintain the status quo. The escalation of repression, violence, and forceful removal programs against southerners alleged to be disloyal by successive, inept South Vietnamese leaders literally forced the elite of the resistance movement underground. But they were not necessarily Communists.

The Communist movement had intricately spun its deceitful web in the guts of the South, operating under typical front organizations, much like a Mafia group organizing legitimate businesses to launder dirty money. Only the Communists laundered ideas. One of the primary groups was the National Liberation Front (NLF), which had been formed in Hanoi in December 1960. The flag of the NLF was composed of two horizontal bands, the top half of the flag being red, the bottom half blue, each half representing its respective portion of Vietnam. A yellow star adorned the center, which represented the single purpose of uniting Vietnam. As Harry G. Summers, Jr., states in his book, *Vietnam War Almanac*, "The NLF was designed to disguise its Communist control and thus draw support from nonCommunist South Vietnamese disaffected with their government. The NLF stressed land reform, expulsion of foreigners, unfairness of South Vietnam's tax system, and other issues."

In the South the heart of the resistance movement did not have anywhere else to go; sick and bleeding, it needed a cure. In its desperate search for a savior, it found instead a group that promised what the people wanted to hear, but that, in the end, administered a fatal dose of poison. The Communists took over the country, and with that, washed away, at least temporarily, the hope for freedom. (In OCS I wrote my book report on J. Edgar Hoover's 1962 publication, *A Study of Communism*, in which he devotes half a page to North Vietnam and to Ho Chi Minh, who employed classic Communist principles. I doubt that even J. Edgar Hoover could have predicted that almost sixty thousand American lives would be lost in Vietnam.)

Other key southern resistance organizations were the Provisional Revolutionary Government (PRG), established in 1969 as the political arm of the Vietcong, and the Central Office South Vietnam (COSVN), created in North Vietnam to control the Vietcong in the South. Truong Nhu Tang is a former Vietcong who held the post of minister of justice in the revolutionary government. Educated by elite schools in both Saigon and Paris, Mr. Tang attained in Paris a master's degree in political science as well as a law degree. Among his overt jobs in Saigon was one as director-general of the Société Sucrière, the national sugar company that ran four sugar mills and related companies. I can only speculate that one of those sugar mills may have been on the Vam Co Dong River. (After one imprisonment Truong Nhu Tang returned to the Société as comptroller, poring through accounts and preparing and analyzing financial statements just as I would later pour over accounts in America.) In his book, *A Vietcong Memoir-An Inside Account of the Vietnam War and Its Aftermath*, he states, "COSVN was, and had always been, people rather than a place."

All three organizations (NLF, PRG, and COSVN) had southern

headquarters just inside the border of eastern Cambodia, between the Fish Hook and the Parrot's Beak, in geographic proximity to the Vam Co Dong River or one of its tributaries. (No doubt there had been ferried across the river large quantities of small arms ammunition and mortar shells destined for use in attacking the An Dinh outpost.) The Vietcong were also ingenuous in procuring weapons. In addition to supplies from Chinese or Soviet channels, they bought or traded for them from ARVN, who were supposed to be working with us. Weapons that had once been friendly were being fired at Americans.

Each of the three organizations was located several kilometers away from the others, with COSVN being in the northern sector and PRG headquarters in the southern sector. Tay Ninh Province, which was closest to the three headquarters, lay just north of Hau Nghia Province. The reasons for separate locations stemmed, in part, from a need for the organizations to fragment themselves so as not to present one target when the B-52s dropped their loads. It is also true that the three factions did not always cooperate. Another group—the Alliance of National, Democratic, and Peace Forces—was established to coordinate the ruling bodies. But as the guerrilla forces and Vietcong infrastructure continued to be decimated, North Vietnam, through the use of its political cadre and military leaders, took more control.

In the late sixties, as repressive pressure continued to mount against those known or suspected to be Vietcong supporters or sympathizers, the surreptitious southerners had no place else to go and began leaving the cities and contiguous countryside on bicycles, motorcycles, sampans, lambrettas, or on foot. Eastern Cambodia is where they congregated, healed, planned, and rebuilt strength. They moved control of an entire subnation to the jungle and underground. Unfortunately much of what they received from the North Vietnamese leaders was lip service. That a change in culture will transpire when new leadership takes over is a fact. There are no exceptions.

The life that guerrillas endured was one of deprivation and hardship, countered by an extreme motivation to unite their country and to be heard. Cause overrode physical constraints. Truong Nhu Tang describes a guerrilla's diet: "In addition to rice, each man's personal larder was rounded out by a small hunk of salt, a piece of monosodium glutamate, and perhaps a little dried fish or meat." Prior to annihilation and extermination of wild game, tigers, elephants, and monkeys were hunted. Again Tang gives a vivid description of guerrilla life:

> When neither sick nor fighting, the guerrillas spent their time building bunkers, raising vegetables, and training, constant training. It was a life of hiding and preparation: hiding from attacks, preparing to meet attacks, or training to carry out their own missions. If there were a half-day break in some movement, either away from or toward an engagement, they would dig trenches and bunkers. Food preparation, both in the headquarters complex and on the move, utilized what we called the "cuisine of General Hoang Cam" after a Vietcong general who had devised a system of smokeless cooking. We would build our fires in trenches or depressions, into the dirt sides of which we would dig a horizontal chimney. Almost all the fire's smoke would go into this chimney and be absorbed by the earth, very little of it emerging from the hole at the far end to mark our positions. Over thirty years and more of jungle warfare, the guerrillas had developed many tricks of this sort to shield them from their enemies—tricks that had by this time become second nature.

Tang states that what the guerrillas feared was malaria, snakebites, and then the American soldier in the jungle, in that order. The element they feared most of all, however, were the B-52 ground strikes. The U.S. had the correct coordinates for COSVN, NLF, and PRG and probably would have wiped out the southern leadership on sorties launched from Okinawa and Guam had it not been for advance warnings emanating from Russian trawlers patrolling the South China Sea. Similarly effective intelligence for sorties originating from Thailand was also in place. If time allowed, they would simply leave their bunkers and hide. But not always. Again in Truong Nhu Tang's words, "Equally often, however, we were not so fortunate and had time only to take cover as best we could. The first few times I experienced a B-52 attack it seemed, as I strained to press myself into the bunker floor, that I had been caught in the Apocalypse. The terror was complete. One lost control of bodily functions as the mind screamed incomprehensible orders to get out."

The bombing pressure was intense. The surreptitious southerners were on the move constantly and some broke down. Of course, we had no way of knowing what the Vietcong suffered, nor did we care. They were the enemy. In the field, we knew the air strikes and land incursions into Cambodia were going on, but we had no way to assess the impact, which makes it all the more remarkable that our enemy did not give up and surrender the cause.

6

Protect Thy Community

Hiep Hoa had a local barber;
we were not afraid.

We would let him cut our hair from time to time
and trim the inside of our ears with a straight razor;
we were not afraid.

He could cut only one at a time.
The other waited in a chair.

"The Barber," a poem.

~ ~

Even though the An Dinh outpost was our primary operating base, we continued advising other RF and PF units in the district. Also our rotation included spending time in the various villages and hamlets. Not only did we need to make our presence known, there was also much to learn.

A curfew was in effect, generally from 2000 hours to 0500 hours, depending on individual circumstances. Some villagers were allowed to fish at night. If there was to be movement during curfew, it had to be in single file and anchored by a flashlight or lantern. Who among these transformed into Vietcong at night we never knew. Somehow, amidst this quagmire, life went on. Children went to school, families attended church or pagoda, and farmers and villagers conducted transactions in the marketplace.

Hiep Hoa's primary school lacked amenities yet was functional. It had a rough tile floor, which must have felt cool to the barefooted children. The cutout windows were without glass and screens, but they could be secured with wooden shutters. The principal's office contained the barest of essentials—an open desk, three straight-backed wooden chairs, and in the rear, two wooden storage cabinets. When Jim and I met the principal, he had on a short-sleeved white shirt, slacks, shoes with no socks, and glasses. The teacher, standing five feet tall and wearing the traditional white *ao dai*, had thick, dark hair that lightly kissed her shoulders. Her smile brightened the room.

The teacher's desk and stool sat on an elevated wooden platform, and it was from there that she assigned lessons. Supplies were scarce. There was a propped-up easel but no blackboard. A few papers were tacked on one wall. The children, aged six to nine, sat on wooden benches at rows of wooden tables, four students to a table. Each child had a thin workbook. The girls wore the characteristic long black pajama pants and white cotton shirts while the boys wore shorts and white shirts. Cone-shaped straw hats lay at their feet. As the teacher faced the classroom, the girls sat on her right, the boys on her left. They were among the cutest children I have ever seen. Later in my tour I gave the principal and the teacher copies of pictures I had taken at the school. They seemed pleased.

This schoolhouse served another purpose—Jim and I utilized it to hold tactical classes for the ruff-puffs. Even though we understood that a few children might be effectively deployed as guerrillas, it seemed a disturbing oxymoron to teach soldiers methods of destruction in the same facility. Regardless, through our interpreter, we instructed ruff-puffs on tactics; the care, use, and maintenance of modern weapons; logistics; and sanitation. We wrote elementary lesson plans, made crude visual aids, and utilized the Army's simplistic but effective method of instruction: tell them what you are going to tell them, tell them, and then tell them what you told them.

While infantry tactics are broad and comprehensive, there are basic standards for small-unit tactics: mission; objective; expected length of operation in time and kilometers; starting time and place; type of terrain and vegetation; call signs; patrol leaders' competency at map and compass reading; grid coordinates; coordination of artillery and air support; use of color smoke grenades; location of friendlies in the area; sufficient water, sustenance, and ammunition; weapons maintenance; sequence of platoon movement; walking point and flank; position of officer(s), RTO, and medic in column; placement of automatic and heavy weapons; and noise discipline.

Other points: while on patrol, maintain sight distance of the men immediately in front and behind (but do not bunch up—one grenade will get you all); in contact, deploy on line; and, for riflemen, exercise firing control. At night: maintain light as well as noise discipline; utilize different routes and sites; do not settle in an ambush site too soon; and establish escape and evasion procedures.

Our sergeants taught the use, care, cleaning, and maintenance of machine guns and mortars. We taught the properties and employment of claymore mines, the use of protective barbed wire and trip flares, and how to take apart and reassemble an M-16 while blindfolded. If a magazine held twenty rounds, how many rounds should be loaded to facilitate a smooth feed for the first round? Some soldiers knew as much or more than we did, and on occasion assisted in the classes.

During the late summer and early fall Jim, Sergeant Thanh, and I often piled into the jeep and headed to an outpost to give on-site instruction. We critiqued ourselves after each class. The results of the day, whether they were an assessment of our teaching achievements or the outcome of an operation, were duly recorded in our operating log.

Once I taught riflery in a swamp. Entrusted to my charge was a platoon of Vietnamese who had only recently acquired M-16 rifles. Beyond the basics, few knew how to sight or "zero" a weapon, an essential element when taking aim. A safe locale was needed where there would be little risk of confrontation from the Vietcong and where friendlies would not be placed in the line of fire. Concerned about booby traps, I felt it less likely to encounter one in a swamp than in a hedgerow. I waded out thirty meters in waist-high water, pounded engineer stakes (metal posts) in the mud, and secured paper targets between the stakes. After conducting live fire, we disassembled the range.

Looking back, I would like to know what went on in the Vietnamese soldiers' minds when we taught. One sensation I recall is how vulnerable and scared some of them appeared. A few looked not much older than the schoolroom kids I photographed. Did these lessons help? I will never know.

By default, one unanticipated benefit of teaching was that it provided an opportunity to explore and embrace more deeply the culture, imbuing a tangible reality compared with textbook knowledge. Rural life unfolded in its most rustic sense. The villagers and farmers nurtured gardens and harvested rice fields. The marketplace, teeming with activity, functioned in the open or underneath canopies. Pigs were brought to market trussed up in wicker baskets. Women from nearby hamlets clustered, clamoring in high-pitched, excitable voices to barter chickens, pigs, fish, produce, and trinkets.

In contrast to the agitated market was the soothing effect of indigenous artwork. Suspended streamers with wild rushes of color flowed from anchors, as if trying to lift the villagers' spirits and dour expressions. Chimerical tapestries depicting harmony and tranquility rippled in the breeze. The Vietnamese commonly depicted gaiety in their artwork, perhaps portraying life as they would have liked it to be.

The French influence pervaded the south and many Vietnamese had French blood in them. Although the French had long since departed, I always sensed their presence and the impact of their culture—messages from fellow Caucasians nearly a generation removed that transcended time and physical contact. (Unfortunately the message of their futility in war failed to filter though the sieve.)

An alluring yet teasing occurrence was catching a glimpse of a more sophisticated and educated woman who moved with natural grace and elegance, her femininity accentuated by the sinuous rippling of her *ao dai* like the movement of a gentle breeze ruffling a lace curtain. The beautiful, delicate features of Vietnamese women served as a direct contrast to the harshness of their environment. I desired to be with such a woman, somewhere else.

Hiep Hoa Village supported an ornate Catholic church, situated adjacent to the river. Nearby a small Cao Dai temple, with its dominant eye, kept watch. The Vam Co Dong and its tributary canals—arteries of life—accommodated transportation, cooking, washing and bathing, waste disposal, and fishing. Usually the people fished with long, thin bamboo poles or nets. On some occasions soldiers pulled pins and chucked hand grenades in the water, then scooped up the fish knocked silly by concussion.

Tin-roofed structures, their rear stilts mired in the gloomy canals, became a cacophonous instrument when monsoon rains pelted the earth. The staccato rhythm, like the sound of an angry god unleashing his fury, sounded comparable to the firing of a 7.62mm minigun. The villagers used their conical hats as protection from the torrents of rain and to deflect the baking sun. It seemed the land and its people would just get tired, yet they persevered.

Common ground transportation consisted of bicycles, small cc motorcycles, and buffalo carts. Hitched to the rear might be a hand-constructed two-wheel trailer for ferrying people and produce. Often as many as two or three Vietnamese piled on a bicycle, and sometimes four or five swarmed aboard a motor scooter. Small rickety buses or lambrettas (three-wheeled motor-propelled vehicles) also serviced the area. The roads were rough, and more than once during the monsoon season we mired our jeep in the muck. Flats were common and new tires hard to come by. The sergeants did an excellent job of keeping the engines tuned, but to get flats fixed, we had to avail ourselves of a small repair shop in the village that could have come straight out of 1920s America.

Hiep Hoa Village appealed to me. In addition to the barber alluded to in the poem at the beginning of this chapter, Jim and I treasured another favorite in the village, a local carpenter who had been located by Sergeant Thanh, our interpreter. This kind Vietnamese man's principal commodity was coffins, and unfortunately supply was not likely to outstrip demand. We found him at his shop in the village. After we put forth our desires (which did not include a measured fitting for a coffin), he invited us into his modest home. There we sat, sipping tea, and discussing construction of small wooden boxes and tables. Successive visits allowed us to formulate simple designs and he willingly accommodated us. He crafted tables of hand-polished teak. Mine sits in my study today. The initial design called for RF and PF insignia to be tacked on to the table below Republic of Vietnam lettering. These were removed long ago, but the meaning behind both the RF and PF regalia is intriguing.

The ruff-puffs were not some thrown-together ragtag band of misfits and ideas. Deep thought went into the creation of the militia and their insignia. The regional force insignia consisted of a black coat of arms emblazoned on a field of yellow framed by a hexagon outlined in black. The yellow background signified race while the black denoted steel resolution. The crest symbolized bravery and fearlessness. Contained within the crest was a sword crossed with a mortar. The sword stood for fighting to win while the mortar depicted development of regional forces as fighting units. The crest rested on, and was lightly brushed by, unharvested stalks of rice, symbolic of prosperity.

The intricate, romantic popular force insignia used the circle to serve up its array of messages. The outer rim of the circle was composed of intertwined chains of rice stalks, associating PFs with the peasantry that inhabited rural areas. Grains of rice stood for abundance and prosperity. A yellow background again signified the Asian race. The focal point was a three-pronged star, with each spur split equally, one half being blue, the other white, and the colors being noncontiguous from one spur to the next. Between the three prongs of the star were three red arrows trying to pierce the star's core, with the tips of the arrows being blunted and absorbed by the core. These arrows signified the Vietcong's three frontal attacks being thwarted. The color blue symbolized the three phases of triangular warfare—integrated intelligence, psychological, and guerrilla actions. The color white depicted purity, wholesomeness, simplicity, and a high spirit of service.

Upon initial scrutiny, because South Vietnam lost the war, it seems to be a logical deduction that these units failed in their mission. But it is possible that, like other excellent ideas that have suffered a disreputable demise, the reasons for failure lie not with militia members themselves but with weak, ineffectual leadership, ill-defined goals and objectives, and lack of solid support and execution.

Fleeting excursions from field duty let filter into our subconscious a connectedness to these villagers—they were human and had a right to live their own lives. We became vested in the people, but that was only half of the duality. Hence the paradox—as sons of American mothers, we advisors were sent to fight a war in Vietnam to assist South Vietnamese in the desecration and killing of their own, just as some Vietnamese market mothers had sons who were Vietcong and dedicated to the desecration and killing of America's sons. The mutually destructive effort seemed something less than noble. It made it more difficult to separate the war from the people for the war was with and of the people, and the awareness of our human commonality created reluctance, *for me*, to want to go back into the field. Additionally I sensed a feeling of community, warmth, and sanctuary in the village. Even if it was illusory, to leave the refuge was to invite more risk. The internal conflict was as strong as, if not stronger than, the external one.[8]

7

WHAT THEY THOUGHT OF US

Every time I saw a mother,
did she see a son?

They sat differently.
Well, actually they squatted.

Vegetables, fruits, and rice
were bought and sold.

They looked at me.
I looked at them.

Did they see my mother?
Did I see their sons?

"Vietnamese Market Mothers," a poem.

In 1996 at the National Archives I found a 10 December 1969
unsigned draft report entitled, "Impressions of the People on
the American and ARVN Troops."

Unless it was an intentional fabrication by an American, the choppy

English indicates a Vietnamese wrote the report. Conducted at random among four villages in Hau Nghia Province, of which Hiep Hoa in Duc Hue District was one, the report summarized comments from forty-nine farmers, merchants, village officials, and drivers—whether Catholic, Cao Dai, or Buddhist—and came to the conclusion that

> Through the statement of the respondents, the team found that the people are disappointed with the American troops and ARVN troops due to the bad deeds of some troops. The people try to avoid contacting with them. . . . Although the American troops obtain the sympathy of the people, some bad actions of some individual American soldiers such as throwing empty cans or things at the people when they are moving, driving vehicles carelessly, arresting people illegally, shooting mortar carelessly killing people and animals, etcetera. Otherwise, American troops do not cause any direct inhumane actions as the ARVN troops. At present, ARVN troops are great anxiety for the people in rural areas when there is a operation. The people have a state of mind that ARVN troops are just interested in stealing property of the people.

The respondents treasured our delivery of medicines and foodstuffs but were fearful of misdirected mortar fire and angry at the destruction of property and at the solicitation of sex. The lack of a common language was a barrier, and one respondent said, "I thought the American troops are better than French troops but they are same."

While some respondents felt the majority of American degradations were unintentional, they were frustrated at the lack of discipline or punishment of Americans by Americans.

Early during my tour I did not help any. Initially aloof, a loner, I acted coldly to those I was supposed to help. An incident occurred at An Dinh, and while it may seem minor, it is one of my more unpleasant memories. Anxious about settling in at the outpost, I became irritated when a little boy kept clamoring for my attention.

I said to him, "*Di, di*" (go away).

The boy kept watching me. Like a cat that sensed you did not want his attention, the boy became more determined to win me over. And he was as cute as they come. Nevertheless I repeated the command. The boy remained in place. I looked up to see Sergeant Kerbow staring daggers at me. Even though I was emotionally uncomfortable in the proximity of young children, I had carried the doctrine of "familiarity breeds contempt" too far.

Kerbow knocked the arrogance out of this young lieutenant. "Lieutenant, it's obvious you don't like the Vietnamese people. They sense it. If you don't change your attitude, you're not going to make it."

I did not say a word. No need to. It took effort and courage for Kerbow to speak out. I believe that his admonishment, like the comments from my mother and Ron, helped keep me alive. I wish I had thanked Kerbow for his words.

8

Intel, Booby Traps, and the Square Lake

Booby traps
      obstacles
            to life

      a sure kill
            if unlucky

      disabling
            if unluckier still.

Ingeniously placed
      in the trees
            on the ground

      it makes you afraid
            to put your foot
                  down.

"Booby Traps," a poem.

Numerous intelligence agencies from both South Vietnam and the United States attempted to gather, sort, filter, and pass along to field operators useful interpretations of this political, religious, and war-infested quagmire. A joint effort, cryptically called the Phoenix Program, was designed to coordinate these intelligence-gathering efforts and neutralize the Vietcong's covert political infrastructure. This program also attempted to investigate and resolve inconsistent or contradictory reports. A passage from Harry G. Summers, Jr.'s book, *Historical Atlas of the Vietnam War*, states it best:

> But the shock of that attack [1968 Tet Offensive] prompted South Vietnamese president Thieu to issue a decree of 1 July [1968], establishing the Phung Hoang plan to coordinate government efforts to destroy the VCI [Vietcong infrastructure], defined as all non-military members of the Communist movement. Phung Hoang was a legendary Vietnamese bird that appeared in times of peace and prosperity. As the closest approximation for Americans was the phoenix, a legendary Egyptian bird that is reborn from its own ashes, the operation became known as the Phoenix Program.
>
> Enormously controversial in the United States as an "assassination program," largely as a result of a North Vietnamese propaganda campaign that made no mention of the fact that assassinations were part of their own policy, the program was nevertheless generally successful. Although assassinations were forbidden, some no doubt occurred, given the passions of those involved.

While indirectly affected, our MAT never directly participated in Phoenix. We were not specialists but generalists. Intelligence was not our forte. Nor did we participate in assassinations, and I was not aware of anyone who did. Those who participated in Phung Hoang operations were coordinated by the District Intelligence and Operations Coordination Center (DIOCC) or the parent organization at province level (PIOCC). The South Vietnamese we worked with were either a supply link for intelligence gathering or a reactionary force responding to *useful* intelligence information.

We had some contact with Revolutionary Development Cadre (RD Cadre), who, in theory, operated as liaison between the government of South Vietnam and the people in the hamlets and villages. Their mission statement seemed suspiciously close to that of a MAT. Whether or not it was a fair judgment, RD Cadre were not well thought of by the more competent RF and PF commanders with whom our team worked. In addition to the RFs, PFs, and RD Cadre, nine other organizations existed whose mission statements encompassed a security, intelligence, or potential combat role. This excluded regular ARVN and ranger units. (See the following chart.)

Unit	Purpose
Provisional Reconnaissance Unit-PRU	Target VC infrastructure
Peoples' Self-Defense Force-PSDF	Provide hamlet defense
Subsector Intel Squad	Deploy as reaction force against VCI and guerrillas
Sector Intelligence Recon Platoon	Conduct light reconnaissance; deploy as reaction force
Police Special Branch-PSB	Utilize agents, interrogators, and guides as directed
National Police Field Force-NPFF	Neutralize VCI; conduct surveillance
National Police	Control traffic, civilian, and criminal activity
Provincial Kit Carson Scouts (former VC)	Lead allied units to target objectives
Armed Propaganda Team	Persuade families of VC to rally to South Vietnam

See any coordination problems there? They worked about as well together as our Homeland Security, FBI, CIA, police, sheriff departments, and neighborhood watch programs. All had egos. Often what we saw in the field was, "This is mine, that's yours; no, it's not mine, it's his; or you take it." Doubt and uncertainty permeated field efforts, not only regarding which organization was responsible but also the direction in which the Vietnamese would turn when confronted with imminent action. And if they turned the other way, you could not necessarily say it was cowardice because they simply might have been Vietcong sympathizers.

Hoi Chanhs, Intelligence, and Disinformation

Each side tried various tactics to pilfer data or personnel from his enemy. Bribes, defectors, traitors, informers, double agents, assassinations, threats—you name it. By the time we got information in the field, it invariably had been filtered and delayed to such an extent that it was cold and ineffective. Captain Wing felt the intelligence effort at our level rendered impotent most follow-up efforts. At the outpost, reported intelligence of enemy activity occurred when the first mortar round hit.

One of the programs the South Vietnamese government employed, with U.S. assistance, was the Chieu Hoi or Open Arms Program, designed to encourage potential Hoi Chanhs to defect. Information was disseminated in a variety of ways, from word of mouth to dropping printed leaflets from aircraft.

GIAY THONG-HANH, read one such three-inch by six-inch leaflet. Essentially the document was a "passport." Set inside a border of yellowish orange, a large South Vietnamese flag—flanked left and right by six smaller flags denoting supporting allies—dominated the leaflet. Supporting nations were the United States, Australia, New Zealand, South Korea, Thailand, and the Philippines. The bottom portion of the document contained a message printed in three languages, to wit, "SAFE-CONDUCT PASS TO BE HONORED BY ALL VIETNAMESE GOVERNMENT AGENCIES AND ALLIED FORCES."

Simply put, a Hoi Chanh exchanged this coupon and his weapons for his life. He was granted amnesty—much like the amnesty subsequently granted by the United States government to Vietnam War-era draft dodgers—and was not treated as a prisoner of war. Hoi Chanhs received a receipt for their material possessions, a housing and monetary allowance, and a chance to contribute to the South Vietnamese government. Many loyal South Vietnamese, however, distrusted defectors.

The most effective use of a Hoi Chanh was to convert him into a Kit Carson scout. Assigned to American or South Vietnamese units, the scout led patrols into enemy sanctuaries or areas known to contain caches of weapons.

The Vietcong played the same game. One of our MAT's operations resulted in obtaining two pieces of Vietcong propaganda, the first of which was in poorly written English while the second waxed more eloquent. No one I knew took the messages seriously, but the enemy's efforts pointed out that stateside antiwar protesters had an overseas audience.

I. Unedited Excerpts

The Appeal of the South Vietnam Committee to U.S. Army men in South Vietnam oppose war

U.S. service men!

Johnson's administration have had to stop bombing and strafing in all over the Democratic Republic of Vietnam.

Clearly it is a suffering defeat in the policy of the escalations war of the hawk gangs in the white house and ((pentagon)), at the same time it is a sign of the U.S. capitalist's complete defeat in the South Vietnam aggressive war.

It is clearly the glorious victory in all side: South North who are struggling to defend and independence and freedom of our own country.

It is very great victory of the peace loving, justice people in the world and the United State who have rapeatly struggled and don't hesitate to demand an end to the immoral war waged by Johnson, Dean Rusk ringleaders in Vietnam.

And clear that's the first advangeous of the wise U.S. service—men an have conscience who are strongly refusing, don't go [?] battle to die in vain to get profit money for arm dealers and [? ? ?]

They are ((hawks)) ((Wall street)) who have many bills to take the war goods with their scheme . . .

They can not carry out their duck scheme. The Vietnamese people is very heroic and eulrgetic who are determined to check the bloody hands of aggression of the U.S. war mongers.

The millions of Americans and world people in the victorious position they are strongly struggling to demand the U.S. ring leaders must an end to the war and peace again in Vietnam.

U.S. service men!

You are directly suffered every danges and hardship in the fierce and hard war day by day certainly all of you don't want you being sent to the battle.

Your thinking and yearning certainly get a ship to take to your native port, lived in the sweet family.

With quick peace again in Vietnam and quick back America you must rise up to act:

—Determined don't go to the battle, reinforce, risist and search.

—Don't fight against the liberation Army when engaged battle you should lay down you arm you will be [?} treated.

—You! Unite with the Vietnamese, American and world people struggle to demand the U. S. governments.

—Ind to the war, peace again in Vietnam.

—Withdraw all U.S. and satellite troops back their country. The Vietnam affair settled by the Vietnamese themselves.

THE PEACE COMMITTEE OF SOUTH VIETNAM

II. A More Eloquent,
Unedited Piece of Propaganda

END THE VIETNAM WAR NOW!

The Vietnam Moratorium Day in protest against the Vietnam War took place seethingly throughout the States on Oct. 15, 1969. Millions of Americans of all social strata, all ages, wearing black arm-bands, among them many congressmen, state governors, retired generals, and numerous servicemen and war vetorans took part in teach-ins, meetings, demonstrations for an immediate end to the Vietnam war and the immediate and total repariation of U.S. troops from Vietnam. Church bells rang out continually in memory of U.S. troops who died an useless death in Vietnam. Addressing the meetings, senators, E. Kennedy, McGovern strongly donounced Nixon's policy of continuations of the war and trickle withdrawal of U.S. troops. They demand an immediate and total repatriation of U.S. troops. The foreign press and aide commented it was the biggest, strongest struggling movement of the American people so far. Peace-loving youths, students and people in many parts of the world also held meetings in suppert of the American people's just struggle for peace and justice.

AMERICAN SERVICEMEN IN SVN!

For the sake of genuine Americans' conscience, warmly respond to and participate in the anti-war movement of your fellow-countrymen, your parents, wives and children.

Perform realistic acts such as:

—Send letters to your families, to congressmen and to anti-war organizations in the States voicing your support to the American poople's anti-war movement.

—Hold meetings, sign petitions demandin the Nixon Government to put an immediate end to the war, bring home all U.S. troops, let the Vietnamese poople settle themselves their home affairs.

—Refuse to set out on operations, to sow destruction, commit crimes against the Vietnamese people. Leave your firearms aside refuse to move out and resolutely claim for your home return.

⌒〜⌒

The second message above, laced with improved grammar and spelling, clearly exuded more sophistication and education, an indication that cadre higher up the chain conspired on its construction. While I believe the NVA and their guerrilla henchmen, the Vietcong, had the drive, determination, and perseverance to continue the fray until they were either victorious or had been annihilated, stateside war opposition did not hinder their cause.

Realities of the physical nature of our assignment had a way of burning away disturbing academic and ethical issues relating to the conflict, keeping us grounded. In hindsight, one of my biggest regrets is that we did not make a greater effort to learn more of the language.

The problematic nature of communication between the Americans and the South Vietnamese is discussed in Stuart A. Herrington's book, *Silence Was a Weapon—The Vietnam War in the Villages*:

> Victims of the language barrier, most Americans were not fully aware of what was going on around them, and they depended heavily on interpreters to keep them in touch with events. This in itself was a crippling weakness since few interpreters could or would render faithfully what they heard. Most Vietnamese interpreters were caught squarely in the middle of the adversary relationship that often existed between the advisor and his Vietnamese opposite number. Failure to interpret accurately and completely was the rule rather than the exception. Many interpreters simply could not understand their American supervisor's English, but they would not dare to compromise their limitations. To do so was to risk reassignment of their cushy job back to the line units of their own Army. The most common result was an incomplete and often inaccurate job of

interpreting that was bound to lead to misunderstandings. And sometimes the interpreters' inaccuracies were deliberate. I have several vivid recollections of situations in which a Vietnamese officer was discussing something in Vietnamese with his staff when he turned to the interpreter and directed him not to share the discussion with the Americans. When a curious advisor asked what the discussion was about, the interpreter replied innocuously, "Oh, they just talk about how to get parts to fix jeep."

Understanding little Vietnamese, I quickly became lost in rapid-fire conversations, as most of them were. Also utilizing an interpreter raised the risk of lethargy. The lack of communication magnified the Asian mystique and hurt our effectiveness. How often our interpreters censored the underground grapevine I will never know. If I had to do it over again and were in command, I would demand that all advisors learn the language. Nevertheless I trusted Sergeant Thanh, who later paid a brutal price for his loyalty.

One language ringing clear belonged to Secretary of Defense Robert S. McNamara, who, in an attempt to prove by the numbers that America was winning the war, instituted a quantifiable measurement—the BODY COUNT. I believe that when this was put into play, a dehumanized American soldier began to emerge.

What the public did not know is that, in addition to the military aspects of the war, political and civic action efforts to win the hearts and minds of the people were actually carried out. Men like Sergeants Kerbow and Adams arranged for rural Vietnamese children to receive medical treatment for various ailments, such as severe eye and ear infections. American units conducted Medcaps, inoculating and treating villagers for common illnesses.

The simple BODY COUNT directive, however, changed the attitude of many American soldiers and the perception of the American public. America's occupation in Vietnam, never clearly defined, needed clarification and McNamara's sales chart provided it—kill and count, count and kill.

Commensurate with the issuance of the BODY COUNT directive was the development of the concept, "War of Attrition." With few exceptions, the most notable one being the retaking of Hue during the 1968 Tet offensive, villages and cities were not taken and held; battles were fought over territory that was soon relinquished. In the rice fields of Duc Hue District, as in much of South Vietnam, fronts pertained more to weather patterns than to classic warfare. So, to infuse substance to the engagement, killing numbers became the measure, as if the weight of enemy dead could tip the scales of victory in our favor. (How you obtained an accurate kill count of enemy troops who have been shelled by artillery or bombed from the air, and distinguished combatant KIAs from civilian KIAs, is beyond my comprehension.)

America consistently underestimated the resolve of the Vietcong and NVA. We believed we could inflict our will, methodology, and way of life on an alien culture. This attitude ignored their values and beliefs. We judged their worth by our standards and diminished the integrity of their being. You cannot dictate cultural change. Nevertheless I supported the advisory effort although intuitively I knew South Vietnam would fall without prolonged intervention from American combat and support troops. There were not enough strong South Vietnamese. From my 19 July 1969 letter home:

> I believe in the advisory effort. I believe that it will
> succeed if the U.S. government does not pull out
> too many too soon. I am firmly convinced the
> Communists have a total dedication to conquest.
> Even if a peace settlement is made, I believe that
> the Communists will try again. Their whole con-
> cept is based on one step backward and two steps
> forward. The one step backward may be to regroup
> and bring up their forces, or it may be to lull their
> enemy into a false sense of security, or both. The
> Communists have to be beaten, and beaten
> soundly. This means a military battle, a political
> battle, and a psychological battle, and they must be
> defeated in all three categories.

Booby Traps and the Square Lake

No amount of intelligence compensated for the angst of whether the militia would subvert our advisory efforts, or worse, take us out. No amount of intelligence mitigated the fear of tripping a booby trap. As the war progressed, the Vietcong and NVA replaced punji stakes with explosives, springing the trap either by command detonation—using a remote electrical charge—or employing a trip wire.

The Vietcong configured hand grenades in a variety of ways, often using carelessly discarded soda cans as repositories. Vietnamese children consistently beleaguered American patrol units by tagging along and selling Cokes. Entrepreneurial! Sell Cokes, pick up the empty cans, and turn them in. When someone breached a trip wire, the grenade would be extracted from the housing and a crippling explosion followed. An American grenade weighed a pound and a half and had a casualty radius of fifteen to twenty-five meters. It was no accident we advisors normally positioned ourselves in the middle of the column. The onus of detection fell on point and flank men, who, if they failed to discern the concealed booby trap, detonated the lethal contrivance with their body.

Summers, in his *Vietnam War Almanac*, writes: "Booby traps, some improvised and some imported from China and the USSR, accounted for some eleven percent of American deaths and seventeen percent of American wounds, as compared with three to four percent of American deaths and wounds in World War II and the Korean War." Those are significant numbers. It means that sixty-four hundred Americans met their deaths in that manner. There is no telling how many Vietnamese met their demise or were maimed as a result of encountering booby traps.

An unattended, hidden booby trap knows neither friend nor foe for it has no ability to distinguish between the two. One day, driving back to district headquarters at Hiep Hoa, Jim and I encountered the usual sights—children guiding water buffalo, women returning from market, and farmers working the rice paddies. The canals brimmed full and sampans glided over the murky surface. Villagers smiled and waved. A peaceful day, the temperature bearable, hostilities seemed remote. We turned into district.

"Someone's lying on the ground." I said to Jim as we pulled into the compound.

"Looks like a young girl," he said.

"What's she doing?"

"Christ! She's holding her leg. Her foot's gone."

A pretty, dark-haired Vietnamese girl, age seven, dressed in black pants and white top, stared at the sky as if in a contemplative trance, but in reality lay wild-eyed with fear and pain. Fully conscious, she clasped her hands tightly around her left ankle, trying to stem the river of blood. Warning signs, emblazoned with the Vietnamese words *Tu Dia* (deadly ground), were supposed to be placed in occupied areas, but they were not always effective. Or, maybe like most children, she did not listen to her parents that one time. She received care from the district medic, then medevaced out.

No booby-trapped terrain caused us greater concern than the Square Lake. Both American and South Vietnamese units suffered causalities there. Sparsely populated, located fifteen hundred meters west of An Dinh and forty-two hundred meters east of the snaking Vam Co Dong, the area remains an indecipherable, frustrating enigma, more for its personification of the enemy's quintessential will than for the terrain itself. Geographically close to strongholds of both the Vietcong and the NVA across the Cambodian border, it was used by the enemy elements as a temporary staging location for men and supplies.

A misnomer during the dry season, the Square Lake contained answers to many of our problems, but an intense concentration of booby traps, complemented by impenetrable undergrowth and hedgerows, encrypted and protected those answers. Intelligence indicated the area once entombed an underground hospital, and there still existed an extensive subterraneous labyrinth. This was a difficult way station to knock out. Even after the conclusion of the rainy season, with infantry and mechanized operations uncovering caches and tunnel complexes, we never unraveled the enigma that fueled the enemy's motivation.

The Vietcong's fighting strategy was like that of the American Indians: lure into ambush, hit and run, use cunning and deceit to offset America's vast firepower. Plot escape and evasion routes. Use the tunnels for temporary shelter and protection. We lived in their back yard, but we played at their discretion. Some South Vietnamese civilians comprehended the Square Lake and its secrets. But the Vietcong's roots splayed deep and wide, and the fear of retribution was an effective deterrent that silenced farmers.

A Buddhist monk lived nearby. More than once he materialized like a wisp from a dream. He never spoke. In the same way that our attorney-client, doctor-patient, journalist-source, and Catholic priest-confessor privileges are protected, the monk was shielded from the militia. Significantly our ruff-puffs denigrated neither religious shrine nor religious potentate, or none that I ever saw.

During one operation in which we encountered the monk, he was standing in front of his shelled-out pagoda. A gaping hole had been blasted through the front wall while the clay tile roof reflected structural damage. In the background several statuettes stood out among strewn debris. A stone religious icon—a cross between an angry dog and a feline—had been placed in front as if assigned to guard the pagoda. The monk was wearing rubber flip-flops, white pajama bottoms, and a burgundy thigh-length, collarless long-sleeved shirt rounded at the neck. His hair was closely cropped, and his hands were pressed together in prayer position. He appeared as impenetrable and implacable as the complex land itself, or so I thought at the time. Years later, using imaging software to examine the one photograph I have of him, I studied his expression. Although my earliest impression had been that his face reflected disdain, I am inclined, upon further inspection, to record a revised image of pleading and pain.

On occasion I still "see" the monk. His "presence" serves as a constant reminder of the terrible price paid for man's inhumanity to his fellow man.

Ironically, had I pursued my mother's wishes, I might have been in the same position as the monk . . . protected. "Have you ever thought of going into the ministry [as her father had done]?" she once asked during my senior year in high school. "You'd be a good one."

"No!" I replied, rejecting my mother's efforts to nurture a more positive flowering of my being. My mother's affirmation inadequately compensated for what my father withheld. Dad, whose own being was not affirmed by love, chose also not to affirm his sons. Had I listened to my mother's suggestion instead of choosing a rebellious path, I might never have seen war. But I would have missed an incredible journey.

9

LIFE IN THE AN DINH OUTPOST

Fun

    is not

        having diarrhea
        in a South Vietnamese outpost
        during a monsoon
            or
        having your friendly Vietnamese
        stand on your new commode seat.

    is

        taking a bath
        out of a well,
        a cigar, western novel,
        and Armed Forces Radio.

"Fun," a poem.

~~~

LIVING CONDITIONS

In early November MAT III-56 received orders to entrench itself firmly in the An Dinh outpost for gathered intelligence disclosed this area was to become a more popular nightspot. With that news we began constructing a command bunker, which took about a month for basic construction and another two weeks for refinement. As already alluded to, the logistics of funneling supplies to MATs, whether by design or poor planning, were shaky. Initially this did not bother me because it added to the swagger of operating outside the traditional chain of command of regular American units. As time passed, however, the lack of support became wearisome. For several weeks at An Dinh, our field command center continued to be the shell of an old Vietnamese house. From the 12 November 1969 Weekly Activities Report compiled by Captain Wing:

> Equipment [sandbags and PSP] for MAT bunker has
> not arrived; consequently, the team is forced to look
> elsewhere for its materials. This is taking a great deal
> of the team's time in trying to build a suitable place
> for its well-being.

Yes, our human resources could have been more productively employed, but as there was no one else to erect the bunker, the task belonged to us. We coveted empty wooden ammo boxes. When stuffed with filled sandbags, the boxes provided an element of structure and rigidity for a bunker, yet we could not get them. Where were the empty ammo boxes going? To the base camps for troops to sit on during the *Bob Hope Show*. This and similar incidents like it angered me—REMFs sitting on their asses when we had a more pressing need for the crates.

The house at An Dinh, a single-story structure placed in the middle of a hedgerow, had a high-pitched roof that hinted of a loft in days gone by. Composed of red clay tile, the roof's stalwartness offered a degree of safety from incoming mortar rounds which are launched in an arc. As the exterior walls had been destroyed, creosote-saturated rail timbers, stacked two feet high, provided a margin of defense from weapons such as B40 rockets, rifle grenades, and AK47s that discharged projectiles in a flat trajectory. Trees also afforded additional protection.

An adobe kiln, its baked clay crumbling from neglect, occupied one corner of the main room, the one we appropriated for our headquarters and where we stowed our gear. Our radios—PRC-25s, the communication workhorse for the infantry—were just as important as our weapons. So was the map board, upon which we plotted defensive targets and no-fire zones.

When first assigned to the outpost, I had remarked to Jim, "Makes it complicated, doesn't it, not being allowed to fire into certain areas."

Jim smiled sardonically. "You should have heard the briefing I received at province headquarters. 'Don't fire into Cambodia,' the major kept saying. Later, off the record, he addressed it differently. 'By the way, if you don't fire into Cambodia, you may not live.'"

The situation in Duc Hue District was similar. Since we were trying to pacify the area and win the hearts and minds of the people, the no-fire zones made sense—in a convoluted sort of way. You did not want to take the lives of those you were trying to save. The Vietcong knew this too; predictably they hustled into the settlements, pounded out a few rounds, and dissolved into the night. This was classic guerrilla warfare. If you returned fire, the enemy would capitalize on the propaganda value of American soldiers *intentionally killing civilians*.

There were civilians at the An Dinh outpost too. In many cases militia soldiers, who were also husbands and fathers, shared living quarters with their wives and children. Clotheslines and partitions adorned the venerable bamboo. Their bunkers were constructed of sandbags and support timber and had dirt floors which, during the rainy season, turned gummy. Of course, there was no electricity.

The Vietnamese used well water for everything—cooking, bathing, and drinking—even though the water was not potable. We either procured water from a purified source or sterilized the well water with iodine tablets, which gave it a rank taste.

"Hey, Jack. I've figured out a way to have running water," Jim said.

"Yeah! How's that?"

"After you haul up the bucket, you run around the perimeter with it."

The well became an amusement center, we being the entertainment. When we showered, some Vietnamese stood and watched, giggling. Perhaps they identified with a common human need. Subsequently we constructed an outdoor stall that afforded privacy and then fabricated a shower by suspending a canvas bag with holes punched in the bottom, providing the outpost wives with an easier way to wash their hair. The well and shower stall evolved from an amusement center to a community hub.

In an effort to ingratiate ourselves with the Vietnamese, we ate local dishes.

"How can you guys eat that stuff?" I asked my team members, whose digestive systems had apparently adapted to indigenous food.

"You'll get used to it, Lieutenant," the sergeants replied.

I liked the rice, Vietnam's staple, even though it was seasoned with green and yellow things pulled out of the ground, and tiny fishes whose bones crunched as we chewed them.

Then there was the seasoning. "Limburger cheese smells like perfume compared to *nuoc mam*," I complained.

"Don't worry, Lieutenant, you'll get used to that too."

"Yeah, yeah, yeah."

Nuoc mam, a primitively prepared sauce, could drill a hole through your stomach. To prepare it, the Vietnamese dug a hole in the ground, dumped in decaying fish, and laced it with other ingredients I never identified. When properly cured, the sauce was scooped up and used for seasoning. To the South Vietnamese it was a delicacy and a venerated tradition.

Poor nutrition sapped our bodies. Even so, we disdained C-rations. On occasion we were able to scrounge fresh food from American infantry units, treasuring these provisions like manna. One entrepreneurial scrounging technique Kerbow employed was to commission Vietnamese women to manufacture Vietcong flags and web gear, which he then sprinkled with chicken blood and traded as the real thing to unsuspecting novices in the 25th Infantry Division.

Late one afternoon I observed Sergeants Kerbow and Adams returning from Cu Chi, where the base camp of the 25th was located. "What the hell is that?" I asked, watching them unload a crate.

Smiling, Kerbow revealed his find. It was a case of milk, packed in ice, and in one sitting I drank half a gallon. It tasted wonderful. For most of the tour, there was no way to preserve perishables, so we had to consume any we had before they spoiled. Excess might be shared with our ruff-puffs, or destroyed, depending on the nature of the perishables. Normally RFs and PFs in the field did not like American food.

Sleep deprivation added to our discomfort. After slinging our narrow jungle hammocks between support beams, trying to get in the nylon-webbed hammock was like balancing on a G-string. We positioned ourselves with a modicum of comfort but invariably wound up in twisted knots. Turning was an exercise in futility because fatigue buttons invariably caught in the webbing, and you wound up buttoncuffed.

"Adams, how in hell can you sleep like that?" I asked incredulously, looking at the ends of his hammock tethered three feet apart. He slept in a contorted, horseshoe-shaped position.

"Lieutenant, it's an NCO secret," he said. "You have to earn your stripes."

Eventually we got cots out there.

Sanitation was pathetic. To say the militia employed ineffectual sanitation methods was a gross understatement.

"Jim, what's that noise?" I asked, listening to little twittering sounds during one of my first nights in the outpost.

"Oh, those are rats. Don't worry. You'll get used to it."

A favorite phrase, "You'll get used to it."

The rats reminded me of tiny Vietcong. They ran rampant, and there was no practical way to eradicate them. The troublesome creatures foraged nocturnally, the clattering of their feet within the bunker walls a persistent annoyance which exacerbated our fatigue. At a PF platoon outpost one night I found the rats' size and number so disturbing I spent the night sitting up, fruitlessly throwing my combat knife in an effort to pin one.

Other formidable issues confronted us.

Initially we shared a latrine with the Vietnamese. Accessible by a trail winding through defensive wire positions, the outdoor latrine, sequestered among trees and bushes, consisted of a large hole in the ground, with iron rails laid across it, much like a cattle guard. You perched on the iron rails and did your business. On occasion the latrine turned coed. A fertile breeding ground for maggots, the latrine was disgusting, even though we improved sanitation by burning the maggots.

"Man, I don't like going out there," I said to Jim.

"Yeah," Jim replied without sympathy, "but you don't have much choice. When you gotta shit, you gotta shit."

"Hey, Sarge, what would you do if you dropped your pistol down there?" I asked Kerbow.

With his guttural laugh he replied, "It's yours, Lieutenant. It's yours."

Having always valued my privacy while engaging in bodily functions, I was thrilled when our team constructed the consummate outhouse. Built from scrounged materials, it stood as a rustic work of art, even if not true and square. Not having enough material to make a secure door, we settled on a detached dividing wall for illusory anonymity.

The creative endeavor featured a slanted roof and steps up to the throne—a clandestinely procured commode seat—covering the drop zone. The Vietnamese also cherished this addition to outpost life and began frequenting the establishment. The only problem was that they assumed the more familiar, archaic European style of delivery, squatting on their feet instead of reclining on their buttocks, for what awaited us on the commode seat each morning were clearly defined sets of muddy footprints. We rectified the situation by fabricating a contrivance to lock the commode seat and guarded our keys. That the rustic, sturdy repository not only survived but also stood tall throughout mortar barrages attested to its sacredness.

Frequent bouts of diarrhea compounded my discomfort, the worst episode occurring during a miserable night of drizzle. I never wanted to use the outhouse after dark for literal fear of getting caught with my pants down. Feverish, I spent much of the night exposed to the drizzling rain, hunkered down just outside the bunker line, embracing the aforementioned archaic but effective release system.

We handled our illnesses with minimal loss of field time; besides, we had bigger problems. Imparting discipline among troops over whom we had no authority constituted a continual frustration for MAT III-56. One day as Jim and I returned to the An Dinh outpost after a short visit to district, we noticed a commotion going on inside the outpost.

"What's going on? Did somebody get shot?"

"I don't know. Let's check it out."

We parked the jeep and ran inside the outpost. Blood lay splattered on the ground. There had been a fight all right—a cockfight. To provide a diversion for his troops, Trung-Uy Loc of 221 Regional

Force Company allowed cockfighting inside the outpost. He admitted into the bunker complex villagers and farmers—any one of whom could have been an enemy infiltrator—with their designated fighting cocks. The owners prepared their cocks by talking to them and by biting them on their necks and drawing blood to further inflame the aggressive chickens. The militant cocks did not fight to the death; nevertheless I viewed the sporting contest with a mixture of intrigue and revulsion. Further, the MAT considered this practice a serious breach of security and discipline. The Vietnamese militia, however, viewed cockfighting as a natural extension of their lifestyle. Nevertheless when the new 221 Regional Force commander took over in late January, he prohibited chicken combat.

Life in the field was simplistic, priorities easy to set. Remote and isolated, we suffered little interference from higher-ups. We liked being left alone but nurtured cordial relations with nearby American support units. In the daytime we dressed in shorts and no shirts, a far cry from U.S. military specifications. At night we maintained radio watch, slipped into fatigues and combat boots, and slept with our M-16s at our sides.

DEFENSIVE POSTURE

"We've got classic fields of fire. The terrain is flat, open in all directions."

"Roger. But I'll be glad when the rice is harvested. It's too easy to hide."

An Dinh was a little nub smack-dab in the middle of an enemy infiltration route from Cambodia to Saigon. It was easy to target, as it stuck out like a sitting duck. The bright, richly saturated colors of the South Vietnamese flag—three red horizontal stripes symmetrically trisecting a blazing, yellowish orange background—served as a homing beacon for Vietcong mortars, yet the guerrillas never engaged us in the daytime.

Anchored close to the flagpole, an archaic wooden fire arrow, with tin cans placed along the prongs of the arrow, served as an alternative to the radio and strobe light. Absent modern communication devices, you lit the combustible oil or chunks of C4—an ignitable plastic explosive that needed a blasting cap to detonate—inside the canisters and pointed the arrow in the direction of enemy contact, hoping chopper pilots read it properly. We never had to use it.

The RF's 81mm mortar pit, the rounds supplied by scrounging sergeants, sat between the flagpole and the fire arrow. And it was the militia's mortar squad that plopped rounds into the tube.

Though not as formidable an outpost as Rung-Tre, An Dinh had protective wire latticing the exterior. Concertina wire was seldom available to ruff-puffs. Regional force soldiers, armed with M-16 rifles, grenade launchers, hand grenades, and older weapons such as the M2 carbine, filled in the gaps. Jim or I, of course, manned the radio and coordinated artillery and helicopter gunship support.

PSYCHE OF A MAT MEMBER AND TEAM DYNAMICS

Vacillation between belief and disbelief in the cause either fueled or sapped my commitment. Anticipation, trepidation, a desire for glory, fear of death—or, perhaps worse, being maimed—and the pseudo exhilaration from the combat high versus an impotent, forlorn yearning for home filled time. Conflicting emotions pooled, culminating in a heightened sense of awareness, an edge dulled by fatigue. Advisors, their teams seldom at full strength, scrambled to stay awake. Another hindrance: women in the outpost.

"Sergeant Kerbow, I don't want you messing with the women."

Total silence. I returned his glare with my own, "I mean it, Sarge."

Horror stories spread about advisors having their throats cut by Vietcong infiltrating a returning night patrol or, just as bad, meeting your demise at the hands of a "friendly" Vietnamese soldier with whom you were supposedly allied. Why give them a reason! In the outpost, the wives belonged to the militia.

What the women and children meant to their soldiers-husbands-fathers I can only speculate. Their mutual concern must have been immense, yet . . .

"How do the women keep smiling? It's as though they're unaware of their hardship," I remarked to Jim one day.

"I know," Jim said. "They work as hard as the men."

The outpost women helped us fill sandbags, dug trenches to bury excess explosives, and also performed classic matriarchal tasks. They could stabilize a basket of rice on their heads while balancing on one shoulder a bamboo pole straining from suspended buckets of water. They walked with a gentle, loping gait, the rhythm belying the weight of the loads they carried. When the older ones smiled, it looked as if they were bleeding from the mouth; instead, the blood-red substance came from the betel nut they constantly chewed.

No woman I knew participated in combat, but if called upon to do so, they would have complied. I am unable to fathom what these women must have felt when lying low, cradling a child, while close by the soldier-husband-father fired at probing sappers.

By the end of September province assigned another MAT to district, enabling us to narrow down our responsibility to three Regional Force companies and four Popular Force platoons. Generally reading body language, honoring my intuition, I felt the ruff-puffs sensed, accepted, and respected our role. Certainly we represented access to material and support otherwise unavailable. With that came a boost in morale for I choose to believe they perceived our sincerity, which in turn fueled their motivation to create for us a safety net. Challenge the purity of our motives if you will, but they wanted us alive which, in my view, was better than their wanting us dead.

Through October Sergeants Kerbow and Adams and Lieutenant Smith and I composed MAT III-56. We were short a medic. Overall I felt the team chemistry to be positive. Each member possessed a sense of humor, an essential element in warding off annoying trivialities that could have become divisive. Sergeant Kerbow's deep-throated smoker's laugh had a disarming charm that lightened the mood.

On operations Jim usually paired up with Sergeant Adams, and I with Sergeant Kerbow. Each pair had its nuances, but of the possible matches, these seemed best. You learned what the other could do. There was mutual interdependence, but it was not always smooth, even between Jim and me.

"Little Bear, this is Restful Fires Four Six Alpha. We just had a contact from the November/Whiskey [northwest] and I'd like you to take a look, over," Jim barked into the handset.

On the other radio in the meantime I fired off, "Little Bear, this is Restful Fires Four Six Bravo. We've just received incoming. Take a look west toward the river, over."

"Goddamn it, Jack. I just told them to go northwest."

"Then tell 'em again," I yelled back, as out of the corner of my eye I saw Sergeant Kerbow roll his eyes, wondering how this was going to turn out.

Later Jim admonished me, "Jack, we've got to stay in sync."

We had just experienced a typical shelling from the Vietcong. Unbeknownst to the other, both Jim and I took to separate PRC-25s, talking to the same chopper pilot. As team leader, Jim had the prerogative of having his order stand, which it did. I had embarrassed him, though unintentionally, by undermining his authority. And I had embarrassed myself by having done so. Fortunately no damage was done, and the situation was quickly clarified. The point was that there was constant pressure to know where you were, where the others were, and what each one was doing.

Shortly before Adams rotated to the States, Staff Sergeant George E. Brevaldo joined us. Brevaldo, who would be promoted to E-7 (sergeant first class) in February 1970, had a medic PMOS but seemed more interested in soldiering than in performing medical services. He knew the ropes and seemed to fit in relatively well with Kerbow and Adams. And I was glad we were at full strength, if only for a short while. Still, as the team had a new player, the chemistry changed, and the team had to find a new synergy. Brevaldo and I were to share several experiences over the next two months, and we worked fairly well as a team, in spite of personality differences.

SIMPLE PLEASURES

Little things became big things at An Dinh, brightening the day.

"Well, here it is. Wonder what goodies we got this time?"

"More stale cigars, stale pipe tobacco, stale candy bars, and paperback westerns," we mumbled in unison.

"Here, let me have that Milky Way. Man, that's stale. You could probably light the candy bar, eat the cigar."

"Not much difference."

"Who cares?"

We joyously tore into the sundry pack we received every month from U.S. logistical supply. No matter how stale our treasure pack, we ate, smoked, and read. We also received numerous batches of cookies and other sweets—baked by mothers, wives, and friends—all of which the team voraciously consumed.

"Jack, whatcha got in that package?" Jim asked.

"Nothing you'd like," I told him.

"Yeah, let me see. Your mom bakes some pretty good stuff."

"These are not good for you, Jim. You probably shouldn't eat any."

"Give me that box, Lieutenant."

Stickies—my favorite, as well as everybody else's, it seemed—was a pastry impregnated with healthy doses of cinnamon. We were lucky if they lasted a day.

Every soldier anxiously anticipated correspondence, and we were no exception. We responded with letters and tapes of our own. If someone received a letter of pain, it was tough, for there was no sanctuary—no one to confront, no one with whom to resolve the issue. Comrades provided some comfort, but in the end, each had to absorb it internally, sucking it up, tucking it away, and burying it so as not to dull his edge. I wonder how many men died as a result of "Dear John" letters.

One day I received from home a large brown envelope.

"Wonder what this is?" I mumbled to myself as I slit open the envelope. "Oh, a picture." And what a picture—one of the most poignant and memorable pieces of mail I have ever received.

My seven-year-old nephew Gary, the son of Harry, my second oldest brother, demonstrated no drawing skill. But it was his perception, rather than any proficiency in artistry, that was striking. A sheet of paper from a Big Chief writing tablet served as the canvas and depicted thereon was this: A bright sun shone from the upper right-hand corner, splaying over a simple landscape. Two inflated stick figures, both outfitted in green fatigues, stood on flat, green terrain embellished with a single tree. Identified by the caption "I'm Jack," I held what looked to be a blue cap-and-ball pistol—a most unique weapon. The other figure, his arms spread up and out, backed up against the lonesome tree. I assumed he was a Vietcong. And in an image that can only be conceived by a wonderfully innocent child, both parties had radiant smiles on their faces.

On occasion at An Dinh boredom threatened our edge. To break the monotony, we would pay a visit to An Ninh Village, which was nestled approximately two kilometers north on Route 10. Sitting in makeshift chairs alongside the road, we offered a tempting target for someone with a grenade passing by on a motor scooter. It was there, at a roadside vendor's stand, we ate off the local economy. Ba Mui Ba, a local brew known as Beer 33, numbed some discomforts. Blocks of ice, insulated by rice husks or sawdust, were brought in by truck or lambretta from larger cities, much like distribution to rural areas in the U.S. up to the 1950s. We cooled our beer with this ice, ignoring the possibility it could have been laced with slivers of glass.

There were other distractions. You could call home using the Military Affiliate Radio System (MARS) by placing a call that was picked up by a shortwave radio operator in the States, then relayed to a local phone destination. Fearful of getting homesick and losing focus, I never called. We browsed through camera equipment and stereo system catalogues, purchasing items and having them mailed directly home. Land lots in Florida or Taiwan? No problem, order sight unseen. Or arrange for stateside delivery of a Chevy Camaro or British Leyland MG or TR6. Petty distractions perhaps, but in a strong sense they offered hope for they gave us something to fantasize about—a fantasy accessible by a bridge of paper and dreams.

The South Vietnamese? Well, they had their own dreams. Americans were only temporarily displaced for if we survived our tour, we could leave the combat zone and return home. One day as Kerbow and I were milling about the outpost, I spied an old farmer in tattered clothes talking to some 221 Regional Force Company soldiers. "Who's the papa-san?" I wondered aloud to Kerbow.

"I don't know, Lieutenant. Never seen him before."

"Look, he's scaling that post up to the rafters."

"Got something in his hand. What in the hell's that?"

One of the dispossessed and relocated, he was paying a return visit to his former home. Fascinated, we watched him open a corroded tin box. He gingerly brushed aside decomposing paper that enveloped the contents of his treasure box, its existence apparently known to no other.

"Holy shit! Look at that stuff."

The peasant smiled broadly for his treasure had remained intact and unmolested. Proudly he displayed his collection of French and Chinese coins. I deciphered one French coin dated 1927. The Chinese coins had either square or round holes in the middle. I yearned to learn more of the history but felt grateful for this serendipitous encounter. We never saw him again.

When I think of that incident, it reminds me of my father's workshop, which housed a marvelous electric train platform, raised about three feet above the shop floor. You crawled on your knees under the platform to gain entry to the cutout control center. I longed to manipulate the Lionels on their runs of destiny. Over bridges and through tunnels the tracks ran. Whistles blew. A little man emerged from his hut. By the time I was old enough to drive, however, the engineers had retired and railroad operations terminated, the operation abandoned.

I played in that workshop, a connoisseur's repository for tools that any do-it-yourselfer would love—table saw, band saw, drill press, power grinder and sander, T squares, chisels, and every kind of hand tool you could imagine, including a wood-cutting set. Dad created there. He took meticulous care of his tools. In the shadow of his absence, I too created, using forbidden tools or machines but always cleaning up afterward to destroy evidence that might betray my intrusion. Like my father, I would rub my hand lovingly over a smoothly sanded board—and much also like the farmer who stroked his coins.

10

FIELD NOTES

I do not advocate war.
I do not advocate peace.
I do not advocate anarchy.

I do advocate
>*the right of an individual*
>*to pursue just interests*
>*with no interference*
>*from any source.*

Sometimes—
>*for that,*
>*you must fight.*

"The Advocate," a poem.

PATTERNS

When our patrols made contact with farmers and their families, I consistently came away with the impression that they just wanted to be left alone. They worked. They swept their floors daily. Furniture was sparse but coveted, armoires a prized possession. Stashed away might be one or two sets of extra clothing, a photograph or two. Beds were raised a foot off the floor, the mattresses constructed of wooden slats. Pillows were nonexistent. Doors and windows were open to the wiles of nature.

"Let me farm; let me live my life."

This message was intended not only for our ears, but also for those of the Vietcong and the NVA. But it was not that simple. A farmer might work his rice fields or tend his meager cluster of livestock by day, eat a rice-based dinner supplemented by homegrown vegetables and *nuoc mam*, then go to his night job, which entailed laying a land mine, planting a booby trap, or dropping a few rounds down a mortar tube.

The militia questioned farmers and their families about their activities, unusual movement in the area, and whether they had contact with the enemy. Trouble was, they might have been the enemy. You just did not know. Even the South Vietnamese commanders had to rely on their gut feeling regarding the veracity of what they had been told. A farmer might know what we needed to know, be sympathetic to our cause, but not inform us out of fear. He did not want to lose what he had, so he danced. Of those farmers we encountered, the majority treated us courteously, as we did them. Some offered fresh cucumbers and, on rare occasion, thumb-sized bananas from dwarf banana trees. I saw that they ate first.

Humor was a common denominator. "Trung-Uy, look," one of the regional force soldiers said.

Under a tall bamboo hedgerow, two pigs engaged in propagating their species. The regional force soldiers pointed, giggled, and laughed, just like American soldiers did.

VILLAGE PATROL VIGNETTE

Living in the midst of an elusive, invisible enemy, faced with objectives as clearly defined as a stirred-up river bottom, and aware of America's waffling support, MAT III-56 patrolled. When working with ruff-puffs, many advisors wore the light brown beret that was part of the popular forces uniform. This was not standard garb for the U.S. Army, but who was to know.

In a rare escalation of participation by American advisors, our current three-man team merged with three district members, became a force of six, and joined a Popular Force platoon to see that all was well in the pacified village of Hiep Hoa. At 2000 hours on a clear night we began our sweep, the aura as peaceful as that of a small community tucked away in the rolling hills of Texas. Treading ghostlike through the village, we heard low, intimate murmuring. Soft rays of light emanated from within the homes, the faint illumination provided by candles and oil lamps silhouetting shadowy figures as they quietly settled their day. Perhaps they talked, told a story to their children, played a game, or made love. Thinking of all those things exacerbated my feeling of loneliness.

As we approached Hiep Hoa's marketplace, the heart, pulse, and soul of community life, unexpected voices floated our way, as did the steady hum of a generator. Rounding a corner and coming closer, we ascertained the cause and resolved our conjecture. A sizable group of villagers had gathered, eyes riveted upon what lay before them—a television.

HELIBORNE

Reconnaissance. The pilot revved the OH-13's engine. The blades escalated in rhythmic cadence, lifting the small craft into the sky. Like a wiry, shifty running back, the bird maneuvered nimbly. Thrusting forward and upward in a great display of freedom, the agile craft flitted and darted to views of broader perspective. I was interested as much in the thrill of flight as I was in reconnaissance. When the bird dipped its nose and skimmed the treetops, I felt my stomach knot just as in a roller-coaster ride. The terrain appeared deceptively tranquil as if the intervening cushion of space systematically dissolved conflict. As we hovered over a swamp, the pilot used his blades to blow back the flora, endeavoring to expose hiding places used by the elusive Vietcong. I kept my weapon on safe.

Eagle Flight. Flying under saturating cloud cover in a symmetrical, staggered formation, the olive drab choppers complemented the green gradations of inundated rice paddies and lush bamboo. A detached, illusory feeling of power and invulnerability permeated my being as if I were absorbing the chopper's power. Abruptly the door gunners shattered the whimsical feeling when they cut loose with their M-60 machine guns, prepping the landing zone. Puffs of smoke dissipated into the atmosphere, and as the rounds struck our earth, chunks of sod were ripped loose and tossed into the air. At touchdown we bounded from the choppers and dispersed into a defensive position until the birds were airborne again. It was a cold LZ.

Sergeant Kerbow and I, carrying standard fare—.45-caliber pistols, knives, M-16s, bandoliers of seven magazines with eighteen rounds each, smoke and hand grenades, canteens, and PRC-25 radio—continued our mission, accompanying this regional force company airlifted beyond the boundaries of Duc Hue District.

We began a five-kilometer sweep through an unpopulated area ripe for the Vietcong. The point and flank encountered no booby traps, and the patrol discovered nothing of consequence. If not for the rain, it would have seemed like an afternoon stroll. Either we swam or we waded across canals, then mucked into the swamps. I relaxed and continued what I had done from the air, taking photographs. The most significant event of the patrol occurred after Kerbow had waded through chest-deep water, holding his weapons aloft to keep them dry. Reaching the other bank, he placed his .45-caliber into a holster full of H_2O— this from a man who had been an Army officer in 1953 (he had been downsized in a rift). Kerbow laughed at himself, which was one of the characteristics that endeared him to the South Vietnamese people.

Whenever I went up in a chopper, I thought of brother Harry, the one who wanted the military. I was nine years old when Harry got married. I remember my father bellowing to no one in particular, "He couldn't have hurt me worse if he'd stabbed me in the back." Harry had fathered two children by the time he finished his sophomore year at Rice.

After graduation he used his ROTC commission as a springboard to a regular Army commission, becoming both a ranger and a chopper pilot. To me he was the maverick of the four brothers for he cut a different swath. In 1966, at the beginning of my fourth year of college, where I focused first on pursuing girls, second on planning next summer's trip to Europe with my friend Bob, and third on studying, brother Harry flew helicopters on an abbreviated tour in Vietnam, which was cut short because of his wife's illness. A similar incident had occurred during his tour in Korea. Holding the rank of major, but with hurdles too difficult to overcome, he resigned his commission and left the Army he loved. While holding a nagging fear for his safety while he was in Vietnam, I never thought I would follow him there.

GROUND PATROLS AND TRUNG-UY HOT

On a waning, sultry afternoon in early September Trung-Uy Hot waited patiently as Sergeant Kerbow and I arrived for a night's stay after a grinding, meandering jeep ride through mud and bamboo. A smokeless pipe dangling from one corner of his mouth, he greeted us with his customary swagger.

Our purpose: to accompany an early morning operation with Hot's 494 Regional Force Company. Before going into his command bunker to plan and coordinate for the evening, we practiced the fast draw. Yes, the notorious Western movie had made its way into South Vietnam, and I hailed from Texas. Kerbow joined the fray, to the delight and amusement of the regional force soldiers. Next Trung-Uy Hot demonstrated his fencing skill. Then we retired to the relative seclusion and safety of the bunkers.

After inheriting the Rung-Tre outpost from the American infantry company, Hot had fortified it more formidably with RPG screen, similar to cyclone fencing. No women and children were present. Kerbow paired up with RF enlisted men and took care of himself for the evening. Hot posted guards and sent out a night recon squad, which culminated in a protective ambush position.

By far the most competent and dedicated RF officer we worked with, Trung-Uy Hot taught me more than I taught him. There was no pretense with Hot. In a rare display of trust and companionship to an American, he released his feelings in drawn-out English.

"I've been fightin' for seventeen years. I am tired. I am weary. I want to be with my family in Saigon."

Imagine, growing weary after "only" seventeen years of fighting. Still Nguyen Ngoc Hot collected his professionalism and persisted in his calling.

The inside of Hot's command bunker was Spartan but cozy. Trapped by the thick humidity, dust particles hung in suspension, reflecting light from a small battery-powered bulb. We used the light to illuminate the map, and under its dim glow reviewed the targeted sweep area, assigned primary artillery coordinates, and fixed our blocking-force position. Another regional force company was assigned to search out and drive suspected Vietcong into the blocking force. That unit would not have any advisors attached.

I got anxious before any mission, not so much from fear of possible contact, but from fear of not being properly prepared. If a thorough working knowledge of the M-16 and PRC-25 instilled a specious feeling of physical security, then complete understanding of map and lensatic compass reading instilled a similar feeling of emotional security.

Topographical maps (those with contour lines depicting degree of elevation—the closer together the lines, the steeper the terrain) for our operating area were useless; the land was as flat as a pancake. The map of choice was a pictomap, which was an enhanced aerial photograph. You learned to orient yourself by visually matching trails, trail intersections, hedgerows, and hamlets from the ground to the map, then translating the image to a numerical grid coordinate. All maps utilized grid coordinates, reading right and up from prenumbered grid squares to obtain the correct grid. If inaccurate, death by friendly fire could ensue.

Repeatedly I reviewed the objective, then memorized the radio frequency and call signs and ensured that my M-16, ammunition, and canteen were in readiness. Seldom wearing my flak jacket or steel pot, I carried the rifle with the sling over my right shoulder, barrel protruding from beneath my armpit and canted to the right, my hand clasping the trigger guard. The safety was on, but within easy reach of my thumb. It became a source of continuing frustration and lack of mission fulfillment that I never employed the weapon. I felt cheated, never having sufficient provocation to discharge and justify my fear. This was a paradox: not wanting to kill versus wondering how it would feel to kill someone directly. It was as if by consummating the latter, an inbred rite of passage would be satisfied. Mostly, though, I think the need for self-preservation ruled supreme.

After the mental walk-through, we relaxed and spoke of other things. A chung-uy, or aspirant, a youngster who had been to officers' school but was not yet a full-fledged lieutenant, joined us. There was no equivalent rung on the American chain of command. A chung-uy ranked lower than a second lieutenant (a thieu-uy), and an aspirant earned his bars in the field. The youngster spoke fair English, and the three of us discussed world events, political leaders, our families, and hopes and dreams.

We looked at advertisements in American magazines, which depicted cars and stereos. The two militiamen could not believe the multitude of material goods available to Americans; they had difficulty fathoming the existence, much less the possession, of these products. Hot asked why I was not married and I did not have a good answer. I remember feeling a warm tingling in my soul and a silent flood of emotion engulfing me. We connected.

Next morning the DSA canceled the operation. The 604 Regional Force Company that was to have served as a sweep team had encountered an obstacle. Tangential to Route 10—which ran northwest from Duc Hoa, through the villages of Bao Trai, Tan My, and An Ninh, and then continued farther into Trang Bang District—were several unkempt, rugged, rural roads and cart paths that penetrated deeper into the land of the unfathomable Vietnamese.

One of these offshoots had been mined once a week for the past three weeks, never on the same day. The road, frequented by military traffic and cautious civilians, was rough and difficult. Vietnamese civilians knew the dangers and either bypassed it or waited for the road to be cleared. Apparently afraid either of missing or being late for the kickoff, the regional force company forged ahead of the minesweepers. Their truck hit a forty-pound land mine, killing two regional force soldiers and wounding six. Three additional mines were found in the immediate area.

Brother Steve might have had to clear mines. The third brother, one of two I thought had won our father's admiration and respect, had committed an unpardonable sin. As stated earlier, he had been a football star in junior high and high school. At five feet eight inches tall and weighing one hundred sixty pounds, Steve was smaller than I was, but he was a fiery running back who led Bellaire High School to its first championship season. He received a partial football scholarship to Rice, but his lack of size hampered him, as did previous leg injuries that slowed his agility and speed, so he quit college football. In his last football season at Bellaire he missed the first few games due to a leg injury. When he returned to active duty, Bellaire did not lose another game until the playoffs. Playing against Port Arthur, Steve was carrying the ball and charging toward the goal line. Inches away from scoring a touchdown, he took a hard hit that forced him to cough up the football. The fumble cost Bellaire the game, and this error became a wound that deeply haunted Steve thereafter for Dad never let him forget it.

"We would've won if Stevie hadn't fumbled the ball," became a familiar phrase in our family.

The fumble became a sin-in-perpetuity, overriding the fact that Steve had been the spark plug that got the team as far as it went. For now Steve too was less than perfect; he added to our father's pain. Steve, the one whom brother Harry goaded into becoming an officer by saying, "You'd make a good private," was commissioned in the U.S. Army Corps of Engineers. From March 1963 through March 1965 Steve spent his enlistment in Germany, practicing combat demolition.

I believe my brothers would have liked Trung-Uy Hot. In addition to being warm and playful, he was bright and a sound tactician. Hot was also a stern disciplinarian. He would put an insubordinate soldier in a tiger cage—a wire cell of a size such that one could neither sit down nor stretch out—as punishment. The lack of mobility combined with loss of face generally sufficed as an effective deterrent. Trung-Uy Hot was also known to take his rifle butt and whop an inattentive soldier on the side of his head.

Only once did I witness him getting tough with a peasant. Inside hamlet homes and isolated farmhouses, it was common to have small, adobe-style bunkers the residents could duck into for safety, like a storm cellar. At one farmhouse Hot interrogated a woman suspected of harboring a son belonging to the Vietcong. We found no weapons but did find incriminating articles of clothing. Hot did not like the woman's answers and struck her broadside with the butt of his M-16. The blow was not severe, but she cried, more from emotional fear than physical pain.

Trung-Uy Hot also worked hard to keep up the morale of his troops. Though he pushed them, he supported them. Once Jim and I were giving a class on the claymore mine to Hot's 494 Regional Force Company. After five minutes of our explaining the mine's characteristics, Hot took over the instruction, then noticed that his troops could not stay awake, their heads bobbing like corks on water. They had been on ambush patrol the night before, and, once settled down, they were done for. Hot did not admonish his soldiers, accepting with equanimity that his Vietnamese militiamen needed rest. He could have reacted with embarrassment when his soldiers fell asleep in front of two American officers, thereby committing the Asian sin of losing face. Instead he turned to us with a pleading look and said, "They are so tired. They need rest."

We respected his request and rescheduled the class. I felt that his openness was a sign of brotherhood.

In one instance Hot became miffed with us. We were trudging across swollen rice paddies. Jim was in front with him, and I was near the rear of the column. A couple of regional force soldiers gasped and pointed to the muddy waters. There, a viper swam arrogantly in his domain. I took aim, and with one shot recorded my only confirmed daytime kill. The Vietnamese were impressed, and Lieutenant Smith used the event to impress upon the soldiers the importance of aligning front and rear sights. Not to be outdone, Jim found his own snake whose life he mercilessly took. Hot looked at us and said, "Lieutenant Smith and Lieutenant Thomas play."

On another patrol I carried the PRC-25 radio as we slopped through muck and buffalo dung in the rice paddies and shallow canals. When we reached a deep canal, I found myself up to my chest in water and held my M-16 aloft to keep it dry. I got stuck and, with both feet mired in mud, could not move. My chagrin was in stark contrast to the amusement of the regional force soldiers, especially when it took three of them to pull me loose.

During one visitation to the Rung-Tre outpost several 494 Regional Force Company soldiers—barefooted, pants legs rolled up, and wearing sheepish smiles on their faces—were plodding about in a circle, mixing mud and straw with their feet. Their mission was to create adobe for use in constructing a larger oven. The problem with warm, fuzzy encounters was that it dulled your senses and sapped your resolve, making you vulnerable to drifting away. That was dangerous for potential hazards continued to manifest themselves, whether through the enemy's contrivances or not.

In another incident, as Jim was getting out of the jeep, his M-79 grenade launcher discharged, plunging the round into the ground right at our feet. Fortunately inherent in the design of this weapon was a built-in safety factor. The bore of an M-79 contained rifling grooves that caused the projectile to spin when it emerged from the barrel, and the projectile's spinning released weights in the fuse mechanism which armed the round after thirty meters. The M-79 had an estimated range of one hundred fifty to three hundred fifty meters, and upon detonation, its killing radius was five to twenty-five meters. Jim picked up the miscreant round and heaved it.

Another patrol resulted in our finding a booby trap without anyone tripping it. Buried in the ground, with just the head protruding and no trip wire attached, the wicked, pressure-detonated contrivance was pointed out by each soldier as he gingerly tiptoed around it. I felt relieved no one ignored the "wet paint" sign.

THEFT

Sergeant Thanh and I spent one night at a regional force company outpost where the personnel were unfamiliar to me. East of Tan My Village, bordering a swamp, there lay an old French fort with intricate underground fortifications. In my persistent naïveté I took a stroll around the perimeter at dusk, leaving my .45-caliber pistol in its holster in a bunker with Thanh, who fell asleep. Five minutes later I returned to an empty holster. It is the only time I remember getting angry with Thanh. I yanked him out of his slumber and badgered him to find the pistol. I will never forget his response, "Maybe they need more than you." I mulled over that one; still do.

Our southerners were poor. They viewed Americans as having unlimited resources and an infinite reservoir of re-supply. For some, theft was an acceptable means of acquisition, innate to their value system. On our part, the fear existed that plundered weapons might be traded on the black market, ultimately winding up in the hands of the enemy. This type of behavior exacerbated feelings of frustration, building upon those already derived from fighting an elusive enemy in a foggy environment. Theft occurred frequently enough to sharpen feelings of mistrust, and at times it was difficult not to harbor an acrimonious attitude toward those you were supposed to serve.

As in any culture, only a minority stole, but those who practiced the profession did so with impunity. If they wanted something, they went after it. They also siphoned gas from our vehicles. Generally this divisive activity transpired at larger compounds or villages with less security, where there was an eclectic mix of Vietnamese groups.

You could say I was careless, even negligent. Since there were no repercussions, you could also say I slipped through the net of accountability, through either charisma or luck.

11

NIGHT MANEUVERS

A hellfire erupts in the blackness—
slowly whirling, drifting
to the earth.

The slow descent—
the brightness
mesmerizes.

Enrapture.
     Horror.
         Guilt.

A helicopter—
     five men
         snuffed out.

"Whirling Fire," a poem.

~ ~

In contrast to day sweeps, night patrols were exercises in futility of a different sort. But the opportunities for inadvertent mistakes were amplified, the margin for error narrower. We taught the ruff-puffs not only to take different routes to ambush positions but also to select different sites, a difficult proposition to implement. Seldom was anyone surprised for it was safe to speculate the enemy knew where we were and chose to avoid our location. Still, the fact our presence was known might have helped curtail potential activity because we had massive firepower only a voice-speak away.

Imagination could easily run amok. Lying on my stomach in a wet, muddy rice paddy conjured up images of crawling centipedes and slithering snakes. When it rained at night, I got cold. Alternatively when it was hot and steamy, the stifling heat and humidity fogged my glasses. I needed tiny windshield washers and defoggers.

Typically our night patrols started at dusk, just when physical movement was more shadowy and difficult to detect, with jungle fatigues conveniently blending in with the dark green foliage. We patrolled beyond the designated ambush site, as in a recon, and when it was completely dark, surreptitiously doubled back, taking up our position.[9]

After the mining incident in which two RFs were killed and six wounded, we tried to induce that unit commander to pull an ambush position on site, only to be met with entrenched resistance. A few nights later an unusually large number of advisors clustered at the outpost. Included were Captain Wing, Lieutenant Smith and myself, and three enlisted men—two E-7s and the other an E-8. Scheduled to have joined us was a platoon from a nearby American infantry company, but the company commander backed out at the last moment. Allegedly his company was to move across the river the next day, and he wanted to rest his men. I think he did not want any part of the militia.

Nevertheless we spent the night at that outpost and pulled our own ambush. Using a midsized starlight scope, we surveyed the approach to the mined sections of the road. The visual effect was surreal, something like monocolor dreams. Taking turns peering through the scope throughout the night, none of us spotted enemy movement. It was an uneventful night.

During one night patrol on the outskirts of Hiep Hoa Village, Sergeant Adams and I, along with a popular force squad, hunkered down on one side of a narrow canal. Hours later, still prone, we tried to stay focused and alert. Moon and stars provided ambient lighting, softly illuminating our limited field of view, which consisted of the other side of the canal where it melded into a line of primitive structures. A light breeze agitated the trees, creating haunting shadows that danced spasmodically in tangled confusion. Across the canal a solitary figure in black flitted among the shadows. The sergeant and I raised our weapons. The Vietnamese commander moved quickly, deftly flicked my muzzle aside, and whispered, "No!"

The Vietcong probably still laugh about another occurrence. A regional force squad was in place, having stealthily slipped behind a rice paddy dike. Quiet reigned supreme until one of the Vietnamese soldiers jumped up, flailed his arms, and registered his complaint in low muffled screams.

"Thanh, what the hell is he doing?"

"He say something crawl on him."

The frequency of such occurrences categorized these events as common phenomena. Roger Voss, a fellow lieutenant who served on MAT III-76 in Duc Hoa District shortly after Jim Smith's reassignment to Duc Hue and who completed his tour in Hau Nghia Province's headquarters at Bao Trai as RF/PF S-3 (operations and training), related the following stories at our OCS Company's twenty-five-year reunion.

It was dusk—a time when noise and light discipline became paramount—and a segment of his RF unit assembled and prepared to move out. Only one member was not ready for he had to move his motor scooter, which was relatively light and effortless to push. Before anyone could stop him, the proud soldier-owner cranked up the bike, revved the whining engine, disengaged the clutch, slipped into first gear, and raucously moved the scooter from one side of a house to the other.

A second story revolved around one of Roger's assigned outposts. His troops were securing the outpost for the night, closing wire gates and intentionally obstructing access to the adjacent dirt road. But one unfortunate villager with his water buffalo and trailing cart were about to miss curfew.

All of a sudden, above the quiet was heard the Asian equivalent of "Hyah, hyah, hyah," amid sharp retorts of a cracking whip.

Roger inquired delicately, "What the shit's going on?"

His counterpart responded, "We told him if he did not get his cart off the road, we were going to shoot him."

Roger's third report: he was advising an ambush patrol unit and his counterpart was a lower-ranking regional force soldier who spoke little, if any, English. There was no interpreter.

"Where are you going?" Roger asked incredulously as the Vietnamese began to pick up and move position.

No answer.

"Where are you going?" Roger asked again.

Still receiving no response, Roger wrestled the squad leader to the ground and sat on him until he could extract some semblance of intelligent information. Turned out there was an ARVN unit nearby and Roger's action probably prevented an inadvertent contact.

I feel certain that if I canvassed comments from the comparatively small number who served as MAT members, I could fill a large volume with incredible anecdotes. There would be common threads such as botched ambushes and mistaken objectives. What is remarkable, perhaps bordering on the miraculous, is that there were not more incidental friendly casualties.[10]

One of the more oxymoronic ambush patrols I accompanied centered on its point of origin. The rendezvous was at a Cao Dai temple (not the one in Lieutenant Smith's past). Dusk was falling. Villagers milled about in shadowy eeriness, seemingly floating in suspension. Young couples held hands. I felt weakened by the specious calm, felt my vitality drained—using a place of worship for instigation of a patrol. The commencement of ambush patrols always held something of a dreamlike quality. Colors, voices, movement—everything took on muted tones. Fireflies flitted in random flight patterns. Even water buffalo seemed to move with a lumbering grace. It was a mellow, seductive time, the time of day when the villages and hamlets grew sleepy, when the poignant scents from incense, cooking fires, *nuoc mam*, decayed vegetation, mud, dung, and body odor melded together. The perfume was not unpleasant, but sharp, like curling smoke that leaves a residue upon all it permeates. The aroma heightened a feeling of intimacy. As darkness closed in, however, and we began our movement, the tranquility fled.

"This doesn't make sense, meeting at a place of worship, planning a patrol," I said to Kerbow.

"Yeah, LT. But what the fuck are you gonna do?"

"I'd rather stay here . . . but we're going on patrol."

You never wanted to make the Vietnamese lose face, particularly in front of their comrades. During the dark days of November I accompanied another ludicrous night patrol, one that could have culminated in sexual gratification had I so desired because what was offered was not an opportunity to kill or maim, but a temptation illustrative of the irony of all conflicts—the chance to create life rather than take it. In the early morning hours, after a fruitless ambush position, we were working our way toward the An Dinh outpost when we stopped at a remote "friendly" farmhouse for night tea. A thatched roof covered the small home. Several soldiers sat on the swept dirt floor while I was given a simple wooden chair. A thin candle faintly illumined the interior, casting an eerie glow. Between sips of tepid tea, we whispered softly in the diffused light.

A young soldier approached me and flipped open his wallet to a picture of a young Vietnamese girl in all her naked glory. "Trung-Uy, would you like this girl?" the soldier delicately asked in competent English.

Replying as respectfully as possible to the young soldier, I said, "No, thank you," somewhat fearful my rejection might be construed as an ugly slight.

So I elaborated and said I had a girlfriend back home—I did not—and wanted to be true to her. First of all, you could not expect to receive favors gratis; something was always expected in return. Secondly, my professionalism would have been compromised. But last and most important, I visualized myself banging away while Vietnamese soldiers lingered about, affording any of them a prime opportunity to cut my throat. Of course, venereal disease was a concern, and rumors circulated about the possibility of a woman concealing a razor blade in her mouth or vagina. Myth or not, I refused to bargain under those conditions. That was something I could control.

On yet another infamous black night at An Dinh we started taking incoming. I was in the open. Sprinting to the shell of the Vietnamese house (we had yet to complete our bunker) so I could get on the radio, I clotheslined myself on a wire. I was wearing my steel helmet, and as I tumbled to the ground, the helmet and my glasses flew off into the darkness. Panicking because I could not see for what seemed like an eternity but was probably less than a minute, I crawled around on my hands and knees, kneading the ground with my fingers, trying to retrieve my glasses. As the rounds were impacting and exploding—they hit outside the bunker line—I was groping and hopping around like a spider on a hot plate while a few militiamen, in relative security and safety, stood back laughing. Finally a soldier picked up my glasses and handed them to me. I was infuriated and indignant for I had been going to the radio to call for support. As already mentioned, at times it was hard to want to help these folks.

Often nights begun serenely soon turned treacherous. On one occasion, as twilight evanesced to black, our team enjoyed treasured moments of peace and relaxation. We wound down, discussed the progress of the bunker, and shared food and drink, experiencing the cherished camaraderie that exists among men confined by physically intimate conditions and bound together by a common enemy and the will to survive. An American infantry company from the 25th Infantry Division had an operating element in the area, so we were content merely to monitor the radio and happenings in the night sky. While we knew there were things scurrying in the dark, the evening unfolded calmly. A little later, while wandering inside the outpost, I happened to be gazing at the stars when suddenly a gyrating ball of fire erupted. In an aesthetic moment I thought to myself, "Oh, how beautiful."

As this flaming ball spiraled slowly to earth against a charcoal canvas, a mixture of horror and guilt annihilated my short-lived "high." For what I initially thought was pretty proved to be a hellfire engulfing an American helicopter as it plummeted earthward, carrying with it soon-to-be-extinguished American lives. There was no certainty regarding the cause of the explosion. It could have been hit by ground fire. As the chopper was not far away, however, that deduction did not ring true for I heard no immediate sound. It could have been hit by friendly artillery—a high explosive round or a flare gone awry—or something might have exploded within the helicopter itself. The American ground commander asked for permission to move from his night position to search for the crash site. Permission denied! Nothing could be done, and the Vietcong likely would have been sitting there waiting. The next day Lieutenant Smith was ordered to accompany a ruffpuff patrol to search the area, with recovery of bodies the objective, but the patrol failed to find the site.

These nocturnal encounters delivered a strong message. The Vietcong gave us the days, but they took the nights.

Tormenting monsoon rains made the nights worse. The rain penetrated our being and was perhaps God's way of shedding tears. Smith and I, along with Sergeant O'Hare, were at the outpost. I do not remember if any other team members were present. A muffled explosion ruptured the wet blackness. We went out to its source and found a grisly scene. A regional force soldier had cradled a grenade, pulled the pin, wrapped his body around the grenade, and taken his own life. When Jim reached the man and turned him over, a last gasp of air gushed from the dead soldier's lungs. Sergeant O'Hare remembers the gaping hole in the man's chest cavity. The reasons for his suicide remain a mystery. The act could have been precipitated by any number of factors, but we wondered. Could he not take it anymore? Had he engaged in a duplicitous act for which he felt an irreparable sense of shame? Had he lost his woman?

Death had struck again—close, yet far away. The finality and the horror of death confounded me. So did the fear of it. For two nights in mid-February I witnessed an event that may or may not have been related to the suicide. Nevertheless neither the training at the MATA school nor at Di An had prepared me for such a spectacle. The genesis of the story was a regional force soldier who allegedly had died without a soul. The medium who infused this poltergeist into the being of a living regional force soldier was called the "Sand Spirit," whose specter visited his human expurgator at midnight. The living regional force soldier was clearly in utter anguish as he tried to purge himself of this unwelcome visitor by attempting to contact the missing soul of the dead soldier through the "Sand Spirit." Sitting cross-legged on the ground, rising, laughing hysterically, wailing, talking in a high-pitched excitable voice, then sitting down again, the living regional force soldier attempted to reach the lost spirit existing perhaps in a state of prolonged, or possibly eternal, purgatory. On occasion he stretched his arms to the heavens, as if trying to physically grasp and make corporeal this apparition, while at other times he savagely beat himself in the face and chest with both his hands.

His comrades in arms stood helplessly about, mesmerized. No one knew what to do.

"Trung-Uy Thomas, what do we do?" asked the new commander of 221 Regional Force Company, evidence that this was an exceptional occurrence, even for the South Vietnamese.

In my most authoritative tone I replied, "Trung-Uy, I have absolutely no idea!" That one was out of my league. We merely stood back and observed, trusting that the regional force soldier would successfully purge the spirit or beat it into submission. What we were witnessing was an attempt at exorcism.

12

DISTRICT VIGNETTES

The Vam Co Dong had a tide
like an ocean—
it ebbed and flowed.

It reminded me
of being on a fence,
afraid to cross to either side.

"The River," a poem.

～

THE VILLA

Paradox defined both the people and the land. Nature, in its benign state, with its inherently beautiful sunrises and sunsets, its infinite, resplendent array of colors, shapes, patterns, and changes, instilled soothing impressions. I never reconciled the marked contrast between the softness of nature and the destructiveness of war. Yet nature is not always soft, and perhaps like the violent, destructive tornadoes, floods, and earthquakes it unleashes, man feels the need to emulate nature's malignant moments.

Often we needed a respite. Intermittent days and nights at the district villa provided relief from the darker side of our mission.

We showered, watched movies, drank and played cards, and, best of all, consumed more palatable food. The villa was like a base camp, a haven from which I did not want to detach myself emotionally. It felt safer. The villa never got hit during my tour, exaggerating perhaps a false sense of security.

The second floor of the villa housed one great room and a few smaller ones for offices and sleeping. The great room had a bar, high ceilings, and tall, wide doors. It breathed freely, seemed grand. Dogs, cats, and chickens roamed at will. Dogs barked, cats chased rats, and roosters crowed. The compound reminded me of the old *Ma and Pa Kettle* comedies.

Snowball, a dog with snow-white hair accented by a black splotch encircling his right eye, was the favorite. Lieutenant Trifiletti taught him how to swim by throwing him in the river and letting him fend for himself. In spite of this externally induced self-sufficiency, I am afraid that Snowball ultimately wound up on someone's dinner table.

Another dog, Lit'l Shit, wounded while traipsing through a minefield in Duc Hoa, avoided execution by certain militia because Jim rescued him. A cat made his presence known by frequently depositing his coup on our district doorstep, but we declined to partake of its offerings. If only because there were more Americans present, the villa was more than a quasi-resort; it was a home away from home.

Captain Wing ordered a bow and arrow set from Sears that we employed to launch volleys of arrows at makeshift targets. A basketball goal and volleyball net branded the compound American, but Vietnamese participated, transcending cultural differences.

Certain activities might have seemed foreign to our South Vietnamese . . . and to our enemy. Sergeant First Class Clifford Simmons, a former three-year POW in Korea who was as tough as nails, had commandeered a Boston Whaler, a flat-bottomed boat constructed like a bass fishing boat. In its other life, the boat had been used by Army engineers.

Churning swaths through the squalid Vam Co Dong, one advisor piloted the boat while another rode shotgun with his M-16, his eyes flitting between the western bank and the precious cargo towed behind the boat. Imagine the enemy's intelligence report: a villager scurries from the blistering market, hops on his battered bicycle that has multiple tire patches, and pedals feverishly to his relay point, where he says to the next messenger . . .

"Tell Duong American advisors will not be present today."

"How do you know?"

"They are *waterskiing*."

We began by riding a two-foot-wide board, then escalated to a set of water skis Captain Wing obtained. Absurd? Perhaps. But diversions like waterskiing—akin to planting rice seedlings and anticipating maturation into glorious fields whose pre-harvest flowering shapes a waving sea of green—planted seeds of hope for the future. It also demonstrated our unbridled youthful machismo.

The Vam Co Dong, a curious river with a tide, served as an apt metaphor for the ebb and flow between comfort and violence. From the villa's second-floor verandah, you overlooked the isolated My Thanh Dong hamlet nestled in a coconut grove across the waterway. Beyond the hamlet lay untended fertile hedgerows and swampland speckled with dormant rice and sugarcane fields. I witnessed beautiful sunsets that silhouetted both the heavily armed PBRs sprinting north and the protective barbed wire that pierced through the seductive illusion of tranquility. Sanguine skies filled with gradational rings of magenta enveloped the enticing bamboo hedgerows and burned into the drab river, transforming it into deep purple and muted green.

Yet, here as everywhere, the most meaningful touch came from a human hand. One day as Jim sat at the edge of his bunk, he was locked deep in sadness, betrayed by a tear falling down his cheek. Co Hanh, the least outwardly attractive of the three women who worked at district, happened by. She walked over to Jim, stroked his head, and gave him a loving kiss on the forehead.

THE RTO

District radio control was sequestered in a ground-floor, closet-sized alcove. One wall held a large pictomap that depicted the coordinates of all district advisory personnel. When in district, even if not permanently assigned, every person pulled his share of radio watch.

Typically each district had a permanently assigned radio operator (RTO). For much of the time ours was a jocular, roly-poly young man named Miles M. Hayward. Affable, in command of a quick wit,

Specialist 4 Hayward happened to be taking an intermediate accounting correspondence course. On occasion I assisted Hayward in his studies, which reminded me of my college career. After completing three years at Southwestern University and then two years at the University of Texas in Austin, I wound up with a BBA and decent B average. Even though not officially enrolled in graduate school, I completed one extra semester of study, achieving an A on a post-graduate course in accounting theory and problems, the only A in accounting I ever made. I sat for the CPA exam in May 1967 and found out three months later I had passed three of four parts, having flunked only auditing.

I carried my stupid auditing textbook all through my military tenure, even letting it gather mortar fragments at the An Dinh outpost. I never opened the book. I should have thrown it in with the *nuoc mam* pit where, I am sure, the text would have dissolved in the fiery sauce.

Hayward answered a late-night radio call.

"What's the deal, Hayward?"

"Sir, a regional force company reports three wounded Vietnamese civilians near their outpost," he replied.

"What happened? Which outpost?"

"I don't know, sir. I'll try to find out, but the details are fragmented. He [the interpreter] says that one or more are seriously wounded and in dire need of aid. He's afraid if we wait until morning they may not make it."

I briefed Captain Wing, who elected to bring in a medevac escorted by Huey Cobras. Sergeant Thanh and I would accompany the mission. Kneeling at the chopper pad, illuminated by the whirling dervish's spotlight, I brought in the medevac, a UH-1 Huey armed with a 7.62mm minigun. Since neither the NVA nor the Vietcong abided by the Geneva Convention, the Red Cross symbol on a chopper functioned more as a target than as an emblem of immunity.

We jumped on board. Thanh's job was to interpret communications from our Vietnamese counterpart on the ground while mine was to act as liaison between Thanh and the pilot as well as to coordinate grids. Soon after liftoff we received a radio transmission.

"What's going on?" I asked the pilot.

"An American unit is in contact. We've been diverted."

The birds flicked off on a new azimuth.

"Where we go?" Thanh asked.

I shrugged my shoulders but felt a wicked excitement about the diversion—exchanging mercy for destruction. The choppers sliced through the night air for fifteen minutes until reaching the alleged contact site. I had no idea where we were. The door gunner turned his head, looked at us, and put his hands over his ears, the signal for us to cover ours.

He cut loose. The deafening sound rattled my chest. The rapid firing action overwhelmed me. Like thousands of luminescent angry bees, only deadlier, the rounds struck their target, devastating any living thing in their path. After the ordnance was expended, we were released to complete our original mission. Without further mishap, we picked up the wounded civilians.

INSPECTION

Sergeants Kerbow and Adams successfully procured another .50-caliber machine gun. I surmised the sergeants thought each of us should have his own. In their benevolence they deposited said weapon at Jim's and my doorstep. Impeccable timing enabled Jim and me to rendezvous at the weapon site exactly when Captain Wing and Lieutenant Ward arrived with a full colonel from the Office of the Inspector General—the only time the Army's internal assassination squad assaulted the area. Well, the .50-caliber looked as if it had spent the better part of its life immersed in a swollen, muddy rice paddy for it was covered with sufficient slime and mud to render it inoperable.

The colonel, immaculately dressed in starched fatigues and highly polished boots, asked, "What's that weapon doing there?"

And I, like an idiot, responded before either Jim or Captain Wing could stuff a bandanna in my mouth. Lieutenant Ward silently mouthed, "No, Jack. No!"

"Uh, sir it's not ours."

He blew a gasket. "What do you mean it's not ours. That's United States government property and . . . LOCK YOUR HEELS WHEN I'M TALKING TO YOU! Get that weapon cleaned up." It was the worst ass-chewing I ever had in the Army. The tone was ugly and hateful.

Sergeant Kerbow asked later, "Lieutenant, what do you want us to do?"

"Get rid of it," I said. For all I know, that machine gun rests at the bottom of the river.

The incident disturbed me. Opening my mouth was dumb, but my feelings were real. I felt maligned. The colonel's callous disregard for those of us in the field, his insensitivity, his lack of awareness, and his detachment from reality affected me like poison. How we lived, what we did, and what we were trying to do under extreme risk seemed to be of no consequence. Worse, I felt intimidated and had responded like a child as I had done when I felt unjustly admonished and criticized by my father.

It was similar to when Dad ordered my brother Steve or me to fetch tools, a dreaded task. Dad gave a meticulous, precise description of the tool and its location. When both Steve and I were present, the one not called upon to perform breathed a huge sigh of relief, thankful the other had drawn the black bean, since invariably we retrieved the wrong tool. We would race to locate the tool, fervently hoping we would make the right choice. Dad doled out his contempt in direct proportion to the number of times we erred, compounded by the time it took.

Often he welcomed my failures with, "Jack, you make me tired."

It was not so much the quasi-executions we endured, the denigration of our character and the humiliation and shame at failing, but the tone in which he spoke. For life was not to be savored or enjoyed; rather it was to be lived with reluctance and resentment for the misfortune of having been put on earth. Years later Steve said, "If I had known how to pray then, I would have prayed for divine guidance."

I interpreted the colonel's message similarly. I felt executed. I was just as afraid of being emotionally blown apart as I was of being physically blown apart. Often internal demons overshadowed external ones.

Mr. Nghia

Mr. Nghia, a South Vietnamese civilian, was the DIOCC interpreter who worked in Duc Hue District but resided in Saigon. His uncle, a full colonel in the South Vietnamese Army, served as judge advocate general, a position of influence and responsibility. Well-connected, Mr. Nghia got things done others could not, and he also held himself above the fray. In wartime South Vietnam, he was one of those in a class above the rest.

Brimming with wealth and education like many of the elite, Mr. Nghia stood apart from the pack. He possessed an insouciant air. Dressed more like a westerner than like a traditional Vietnamese, he emanated the aura of connection, power, and self-assurance often innate to a person of fortunate birth. As the saying goes, "He chose his parents well." He was proficient and articulate in English and appeared to be what we called a good guy, but none of us could be completely sure. It was difficult to tell how dirty he got his hands. I envied his mobility and apparent freedom but asked myself, "Why am I, a twenty-five-year-old American infantry lieutenant, put in the untenable position of fighting this person's war?"

SERGEANT O'HARE

Buck Sergeant (E-5) Richard O'Hare, a gregarious, outgoing young man, dropped out of college and ended up in the military. Scheduled to enter OCS, he decided not to attend. A seasoned veteran at the ripe age of twenty, he had already spent one tour near Hue with the 82nd Airborne as part of a troop contingent airlifted to Vietnam in response to the 1968 Tet offensive.

O'Hare was in charge of hamlet security; his task was to rank the quality of RF/PF fortifications, but he also accompanied several operations while working out of district. After he left his Duc Hue role, he spent some time working with the Vietnamese Airborne but said he got bored. O'Hare possessed an engaging, infectious sense of humor that lightened the load, no matter how burdensome it seemed, and he was affably mischievous. I suspected O'Hare or Kerbow of labeling Jim and me Batman and Robin. We embraced, even embellished, that concept, to the point of stenciling MATMOBILE in bright yellow block letters on our jeep.

We did not see a lot of O'Hare, our time limited to the few morale-boosting nights he stayed with our team at various outposts or when our MAT visited the villa. This brown-haired, blue-eyed sergeant with a perpetual smile also left an indelible impression on a few others. In a single hair-raising action, O'Hare distinguished himself.

In O'Hare's words: "On the morning of 23 July 1969 Lieutenant Baldwin and I left the District headquarters bound for Cu Chi for the main purpose of scrounging food and other supplies for the team and our counterparts, the Vietnamese regional and popular forces. We were driving a jeep towing a trailer in anticipation of our success on the mission. The route led from our team headquarters at the Sugar Mill on the Vam Co Dong along the only road out to Tan My. We then went to Bao Trai, the province capital along Route 10 and then on to the base camp at Cu Chi.

"While in Cu Chi, we scrounged a trailer-load of food, both refrigerated and canned, as well as several bound packs of sandbags, a badly needed item for both us and our Vietnamese regional and popular force comrades. Silly as it must seem, inexpensive items such as sandbags were difficult to obtain at that time and any opportunity to obtain them was seized on.

"Hau Nghia Province, especially its western reach, was *Indian Country* and the rule was that we were always to travel in two-man teams. Upon our arrival in Bao Trai Province Headquarters, we stopped in to check for mail, etcetera. Lieutenant Baldwin was informed that some sort of paperwork was in need of completion and that he would have to spend the night. Since we had perishable goods, I said that I would head on to district headquarters, a daylight drive of about thirty minutes and fifteen clicks [kilometers]. My only wise move of the day was to exchange my .45-caliber pistol for Lieutenant Baldwin's M-16 and claymore pouch holding ten M-16 magazines.

"Away I went, enjoying a nice ride through an area between two PF outposts that we had always thought to be relatively secure. About three kilometers from Bao Trai, along Route 10, in an open area surrounded by rice paddies, where the road was elevated, I came upon a group of Vietnamese with weapons surrounding a Honda motorcycle. There was one body on the ground and on my right, a person running away from the others.

"I stopped my trailer-equipped jeep about fifty feet away and jumped out to size up the situation. Within seconds, gunfire started and the running man reached a rice paddy dike behind me. It was evident that he was a South Vietnamese soldier. When I asked in my broken Vietnamese if he had a weapon, he answered that he didn't. Then I realized that I was in deep shit. Here I was alone with a bunch of VC and no support. At first I was angry that he had dropped his weapon for the VC to take, but I quickly realized that he and his comrade, even though they wore uniforms, were unarmed and simply riding a motorcycle, like so many RF and PF soldiers did.

"I started to fire at the group, which was by this time running away and firing back at me sporadically. I took on the closest VC to me, dropped him, and when he didn't fire back, I started on the rest. They were about one hundred to one hundred fifty meters away and running. I believe I hit another one because he stumbled and it seemed like another of his group helped him along.

"At about this time they returned fire with accuracy. I don't know if it came from the group I was engaged with or others, but a bullet hit the jeep and I felt a thud on my left shoulder. I suspect it was from another VC who had been left for security in a wood line about thirty degrees to my left. Frankly at that time I was seriously concerned. I was getting a little tight on ammo, had no radio or protection other than the jeep since it was open all around me, and knew I was vulnerable to capture if wounded. There was no way that I could run or drive off because the trailer made turning around impossible and to drive straight would mean going toward the VC. I later found out that the bullet had gone through the radiator and battery and embedded itself in the fender, making a dent that hit my arm, didn't cause a scratch, but felt pretty solid when it hit. Thank God for lead in the battery!

"I let out a full magazine in the direction where I suspected the fire was coming from and all firing ceased. After a few moments I left the cover of the jeep to check on the VC who was closest to me and had not fired in some time. Approaching cautiously, I confirmed that he was dead; an M-16 rifle lay by his side.

"Then a small number of local popular forces soldiers showed up and helped me carry the dead VC to the jeep and we put him in the trailer. I insisted that he be placed in the trailer on top of the sandbags and would not let anyone search him. We loaded the dead PF in the back seat of the jeep after I stripped him of his watch, ring, and wallet. I did not want anyone to loot his body and later I turned over his personal articles to his commander to give to his family. That was a reaction to our suspicion that the Vietnamese were dishonest but, in reality, I think they were honest and especially reverential to their dead. The soldier, whose life I probably saved, left with the PFs and I did not see him again. All I remember of him is that fearful but thankful face as he hid behind the rice paddy dike.

"As we were loading the bodies on the jeep, several APCs of the 25th Infantry Division came upon the scene and I used their radio to call to Duc Hue to tell them of the situation. The 25th troops wanted to pursue, but it would have been futile due to the time elapsed and the rice paddy dikes that they would have to cross.

"I drove the jeep back to the TOC [Tactical Operations Center] in the Province HQ compound in Bao Trai with the two bodies and turned them over to the Vietnamese. I then went into the small bar in the HQ and thanked Lieutenant Baldwin for lending me his rifle. He was pretty startled by the event. I had a beer and headed back to Duc Hue since I had the load of perishables. When I got about a kilometer or so out of Bao Trai, several of our team members came out to escort me back to Duc Hue.

"After the action Co Duc, our cook, asked me about what happened. She was happy that I had shot a Vietcong as her husband had been killed earlier in the war. I also remember that later we had to throw out the sandbags (old cloth type) as the blood stank so bad that they were unusable.

"What was significant about the action was that the VC or NVA launched it in broad daylight on a major highway and within close proximity to two outposts. There was also little cover for them to hide in. At this time the 25th Mechanized troops were patrolling the roads and we thought things were secure so perhaps they were showing that they really controlled the area. The Bronze Star for Valor that I received had a bunch of inaccuracies but the above account is as I remember it."

Had O'Hare received American corroboration, he probably would have been the recipient of a Silver Star. At district that night he was, as we say, pumped up, the adrenaline still flowing. The remnants of MAT III-56 happened to be in town, and we joined in the district celebration, vicariously sharing his experience while slowly defusing the charged atmosphere with several rounds of beer. Deservedly O'Hare was the center of attention and was popular with the local friendlies for word spread. He had saved a life.

13

JEEP PERILS

Colors—
I have seen black, I have seen white
and worked with brown and yellow too
seems most of each are quite all right
seems some of each you should eschew.

Ideas—
The ideas of man, since time began,
all have a regal plan for his ascent
but the historian inevitably records
man's descent.

Whys—
The ideas seem good, most quite fair,
ineptly man seeks perfection
repeating mistakes unaware
slighting perhaps God's direction.

Future—
The stage is set, the players are in place
there is not much new of man to discuss
whether or not we end up in disgrace
depends on the people who are us.

"Man," a poem.

JEEP RUNS

At the An Dinh outpost one morning when Jim, Kerbow, Adams, and I were going to a meeting in district, someone had placed bamboo branches and palm fronds across the road. Adams tried to clear the area by popping a few rounds from the M-79 grenade launcher. The bamboo remained in place, unscathed. Jim walked up and took a look.

"What are you going to do?" I asked, incredulous.

Jim replied in his easygoing manner. "I'm going to remove this stuff so you guys can get off your ass."

He grabbed the branches and threw them out of the way. No booby trap. This was a gutsy move. Still, was the Vietcong sending a warning? Or had a few regional force soldiers set the barrier as a joke? We never found out.

Returning to district from Rung-Tre one afternoon, Jim and I encountered a group of South Vietnamese militiamen walking along Route 7A. They begged for a ride so we let them pile onto the jeep. Now we numbered sixteen. With bobbing heads and flailing arms and legs obscuring all but the vehicle's tires, our assemblage resembled a Hydra.

Jeep runs were not neighborhood trips to the corner grocery. They were necessary to accomplish our mission, regardless of where we laid our heads. During the rainy season we often got stuck, even in four-wheel drive. Sometimes the mud sneaked up on you, as it did once when I was behind the wheel. I hit a bump, plopped down in a mud hole, and sprayed mud all over a Vietnamese woman standing by the road. This was not a good way to win her heart and mind.

Another time Jim admonished me to slow down. "Jack, we're not in a race, for Christ's sake." As I turned to acknowledge his comment, I inadvertently steered into a well-disguised road hazard with sufficient force to launch one First Lieutenant James C. Smith off the back seat, depositing him on his tail beside the road.

Patience was never my strongest virtue. On one occasion my interpreter and I were driving to district. Turning right on a heavily traveled but narrow road, I encountered a South Vietnamese tank just sitting there, idling. I waited a few seconds, but soon tired of listening to the rumbling diesel engines and pressed the jeep's accelerator, intending to skirt the tank while avoiding a canal on the right. I missed the canal but not the tank, skidding into its left forward track, destroying the jeep's windshield.

Unfortunately horror was never far away.

Like most mornings, this one dawned hot and stuffy. After the roads were cleared, Jim and I left An Dinh and rumbled southeast down Route 10 toward Route 7A for a rendezvous at the villa. Jim drove while I cradled my M-16.

"What's that in the intersection?" asked Jim, downshifting from third to second.

"I don't know. Pull up closer."

When we arrived, my stomach knotted up. Three bodies lay in the road.

"Jesus Christ! They must have taken a direct hit from a white phosphorus round."

The charred bodies were burned beyond recognition—a deep, dark frightening black, like midnight in a coal mine. I tried to imagine what they must have felt when hit. How much pain? How quickly did they die? We surmised they were Vietcong, but even so I could not escape in relief or pleasure. The blackened bodies made their terribly painful death seem more vile and evil. I chose not to photograph the sickening scene because to have done so would have been invasive. Today when I think of that pyre, I remember gawking at their nothingness and not comprehending the immensity of their death.

THE GIRL ON THE BICYCLE

In the confusing climate of war, where ambivalent feelings ruled, anything could happen when you got behind the wheel. Saigon was no exception, as graphically illustrated by a jeep run that ended tragically. Journeys into the southern capital required justification. Often, transporting a stateside-bound comrade to Tan Son Nhut or picking up a comrade returning from R & R sufficed. Scrounging for supplies unavailable through regular channels was another valid reason.

Hotels were something else. One particular hotel was a twelve-floor refuge hosting lonesome soldiers, journalists, and civilians looking for intrigue or sex. A restaurant, bar, and poolroom occupied the top floor. GIs and girls converged in throngs, the activity as frenetic as on a stock exchange trading floor.

"Release your magazines!" the hotel manager said as Adams and I approached the front desk.

Going first, I inserted the barrel of my M-16 into a three-inch-wide tube contained within a larger cylinder about three feet long, then pulled the trigger. Clear! Adams followed suit. We handed our weapons to a Vietnamese clerk behind the counter and received receipts in return. I felt vulnerable, surrendering my weapon in the midst of war.

After securing a room, Adams and I took to the streets. The day teemed and steamed. The confluence of jeeps, two-and-a-half-ton trucks, bicycles, motorcycles, buses, lambrettas, Renaults, Peugeots, and vintage American vehicles congealed in the streets of Saigon. Exhaust fumes hung heavy. Impatience reached the boiling point. The prickly heat suctioned fatigues to your body and pasted the sweltering mass to the hot canvas seats. Sergeant Adams drove while I, in the passenger's seat, languished in a near-hypnotic state, a heat-induced stupor.

We were stuck behind a deuce-and-a-half. Underneath the frame in front of the truck, through half-open eyelids, I saw bicycle tires. A cyclist was riding in the wrong lane, heading toward us from the opposite direction, and was looping around to our left in front of the truck. The sergeant gunned the accelerator, propelling the jeep around the left side of the truck, which put us on a direct collision path with the bicycle and its teenaged girl rider. "Sergeant, watch out!" I wanted to scream, but, like a man suffering from a stroke and unable to formulate his speech, the words never burst forth from my mouth, instead simply swam inside my brain. We struck the bike, blasting its rider to the pavement. The girl's mouth opened in horror just before impact. The sergeant never saw her until it was too late.

My silence on the streets of Saigon fit a destructive pattern. When I was thirteen and bicycling on the wrong side of the street toward junior high school one morning, I noticed at the next intersection a car driver about to turn right. He was going to plow into me so I jumped off the bike. The car smacked it, and gasps of alarm sounded from bystanders. Concerned, the driver stopped, got out, and asked if I was okay. He then took from his trunk a crowbar and used it to straighten the left pedal. Unscathed, I went on to school, expecting to be called to the principal's office and punished. I was not, of course, but never told my parents. Self-preservation prevailed.

During my twelfth year my mom, my sister-in-law, and I were seated at the kitchen table. I watched my two young nieces, their little hands groping for a cookie jar, a jar easily within my grasp. I knew what was going to happen and watched the event unfold, making no effort to intervene. The older niece fondled the jar and dislodged it from its perch, whereupon it crashed to the floor and shattered. Mom exclaimed, "Jack, you could have stopped it."

I could have. Instead I sat motionless and speechless, frozen in a cocoon composed partly of indifference but mostly of fear—fear of taking action. The cookie jar could be repaired. The girl? She was immobile and unconscious when we departed the scene. The Vietnamese police said, "No sweat," and carried her away. The extent of her injuries became buried in anonymity in the bowels of Saigon. Yes, it had been an accident. Preventable?

One Saturday in March 1999 I dreamed again about Sergeant Adams. We found each other, two apparitions floating through time and space, at a church in Houston. Adams, sporting a neatly trimmed beard, looked much the same as he did in 1969. The dream—wavering between extraordinary clarity and frustrating obscurity as dreams are wont to do—transcended our differences. We sat in a pew. I leaned over to an older man sitting beside us and told him how many years it had been since Adams and I laid eyes on each other. It was as if two long-lost brothers had come together, and what needed to be said flew between us in seconds.

> *"Look, I need to be straight with you," I told him as I put my hand on his shoulder. "I have tried to find you, to talk with you."*
>
> *Sergeant Adams patted his side, looked me in the eye, and said, "I've got pancreatic cancer." He reached into his pocket and appeared to be pulling out a calling*

card. "I've been living in Colorado, but most everything I own is in a van."

For a brief moment, we are transported and I see the weathered, wood-frame structure in which he had been living. "I've written a memoir," I told him. "In it, I've changed your name because of the unfortunate occurrence that year."

He looked at me, his face radiating both acceptance and grace, and said, "That's okay. Those things happen."

His image dissolved beneath a bridge over water, amidst unintelligible voices connected with unrecognizable faces. I could grasp neither him nor the surroundings any longer, yet in a twist of perspective not previously considered, the thought occurred that Sergeant Adams might have looked to me that day to prevent that awful accident and held me responsible. Is it possible that he was giving me what I had never acknowledged I needed—his forgiveness?

In Vietnam the consequences of inaction could be as severe as those from taking the wrong action.

14

AN DINH HEATS UP

They streak down from the heavens
and up from the ground.

The lights, red and green,
provide a dazzling array of color,
filtered into visual perception
by the blackness of a night sky.

The slashing speed
is awesome, enthralling.
A time photograph of stars
comes to life in fluid motion.

But beauty is merely a facade;
the sparkling lights are a deadly burst
of steel projectiles from which
nothing can escape.

"Night Sky," a poem.

❧

A report from the province senior advisor, dated 1 November 1969, stated in part:

Information gained from POWs, Hoi Chanhs, captured enemy documents and agents point to an enemy "high point" of current so-called Fall/Winter campaign. At present no starting date can be established, however dates in mid-November are frequently mentioned. Current intelligence shows that, if this increase in enemy activity does occur, it will be in form of Emulation High Point designated to bolster morale of enemy troops. The captured enemy documents suggest strongly that the morale of some enemy units . . . is low with a high rate of desertion. It is believed that during the coming week, enemy-initiated activity will remain at current low level. The Enemy Main Force Units will remain in their sanctuary with small recon elements operating in the Province. The Local Force and guerrillas will work on the preparation of projected Emulation Phase. The activity will with all probability increase with approach of mid-November.

This document was found during my research in early 1997 at the National Archives located in College Park, Maryland.

15

DESTROY AN DINH

We all have those places—
some more poignant than others,
ones that tell it all.

The places where
we lost part of ourselves,
found part of ourselves.

An Dinh is Jack's place—
where it all happened,
where it all did not happen.

He can see it from anywhere
indelibly planted
irrevocably stamped
               in his mind.

Detached—
Jack watches himself
               watch Jack.

"Jack's Place," a poem.

merican infantry units, deployed by helicopters, sporadically conducted operations west of the river. This was before the U.S. high command "authorized" units to hit known enemy sanctuaries in Cambodia. As already indicated, the innocuous An Dinh outpost stood at the heart of an infiltration route to Saigon, so the Vietcong wanted to obliterate our sanctuary. The Vietcong's and NVA's ability to escape detection perplexed and frustrated us. Radar, infrared sensors, and air recons all combed for the elusive Vietcong, but they were constantly on the move. The VC not only continued to infiltrate the area, they also accelerated the process, regardless of the cost to themselves.

0130 Hours, Sunday, 9 November 1969

The first round slammed hard on the clay tile roof of our confiscated Vietnamese home—we had yet to complete our command bunker—raining shrapnel and fragments of clay tile on the ground below. Sergeant Brevaldo reached the radio first, but I yanked the handset away. In the blink of an eye I knew I had hurt his pride. No doubt he would have performed well, but as the only officer at the outpost that night, I resolved to take charge.

A second round hit the roof. Sergeant Brevaldo screamed, and before I could hit the "push to talk" button on the handset, my legs quivered as though someone had just twanged two taut rubber bands, the first and only time I experienced uncontrollable fear.

"Are you hurt?" I yelled at Brevaldo.

"I'm okay. A piece of tile hit me in the head."

His scream scared me more than the incoming rounds. Intuitively we sensed this was not a harassing, sporadic attack. They had us zeroed in.

"Restful Fires, this is Restful Fires Four Six. Over."

"Restful Fires Four Six, this is Restful Fires. Over."

"This is Four Six. Be advised we are receiving incoming. Over."

"Roger, Four Six."

Incoming rounds pounded the outpost with heightened intensity. The 221 Regional Force Company commander immediately ordered his mortar crew into the pit to return fire at suspected positions.

I recovered my composure and my legs stopped shaking. Brevaldo ran the bunker line to coordinate with the militiamen.

Artillery support seemed to take forever but actually had been on call for less than a minute. I could have called for artillery from the fire direction center by using six-digit grid coordinates or by using the outpost coordinates as the reference point, then giving an azimuth and distance in meters for high explosive impact. Both procedures were cumbersome and time consuming. The more expedient method, the one most logical to employ, incorporated the use of predetermined defensive targets for quick retaliatory response. Even if the rounds were off target, it bought time.

"Blue Lightning, this is Restful Fires Four Six. We need HE [high explosive] rounds now. Over."

"Restful Fires Four Six, this is Blue Lightning. What grids? Over."

"Blue Lightning, this is Four Six. Fire Delta Tangos [defensive targets] two and three. Over."

When the first rounds whistled overhead, I felt like the cavalry had arrived. There had not been enough time definitively to assess the direction and distance from which the incoming rounds were launched, but Jim and I had preplotted known hot spots that we then shared with the fire direction center and district, a common tactic used by units in static defensive positions.

Brevaldo charged back. "Adjust arty right and drop," he said.

On line, he had heard the thumping from enemy mortars. I radioed Blue Lightning. "Delta Tango three—right one fifty, drop one hundred [meters]. Over."

A brief lull fell. I knew we had seized the enemy's attention. More important, the quick response enhanced the morale of the regional forces. They hunkered down, not knowing what lay ahead. Would they hold?

I relayed other Delta Tangos. Once begun, it became easy to "walk" the artillery.

Still the onslaught continued. The distinctive, clipped retorts from AKs filled the night as concealed enemy riflemen poured out covering fire in support of sappers. Incoming mortar rounds and B40 rocket shells pummeled the outpost. From a distance a Communist .51-caliber machine gun raked our position. Our regional forces countered with an interlocking fusillade of M-16 and machine gun fire. Sappers breached the perimeter wire, but our RFs repulsed them from crossing the bunker line.

Too much ordnance was being dumped on us for this to be exclusively a Vietcong operation. They had brought along their friends, an undetermined NVA force. For the first time since I had been in country, the possible reality of being overrun slapped me in the face.

I lost track of time. I had already called for helicopter gunships, but until they got on station, artillery support hammered the distant hedgerows and rice paddies. Things settled into a tempo and I felt confident. Brevaldo and I knew what we were doing. Our training was paying off.

Amidst the muzzle flares and smoky haze, the sharp smell of cordite filled the air. Part of me wanted to turn the radio over to Brevaldo, pick up my M-16, and cut loose, but the flare ship, Little Bear, arrived on station so I returned to the business at hand. To diffuse the harsh, unforgiving blackness and give our riflemen definitive targets to shoot at, I called for illumination.

"Little Bear, this is Restful Fires Four Six. Light us up. Over."

"Restful Fires Four Six, this is Little Bear. Flares are on the way. Over."

During the brief periods of illumination from friendly flares I felt a deceiving gentle radiance as if the artificial light would render the enemy's efforts impotent. But the illusion quickly passed for just as the flares fell to earth, so did my artificial high. Then another flare popped and again my spirits rose. It was like being on an emotional roller coaster.

Then the gunships arrived.

"Restful Fires Four Six, this is Diamond Head Three One. Over. Fires Four Six, Diamond Head Three One. Over."

"Roger. Diamond Head Three One, this is Fires Four Six. Welcome aboard. What's your situation? Over."

I gave the situation report. The fire direction center curtailed the artillery fire as the Huey Cobras—the sharks, the hunter-killers—arrived on station. After confirming our position, I briefed the lead pilot as to the ground attack and mortar barrage situation and then directed them by azimuth and distance to suspected enemy positions.

With the Cobras on station, we felt invincible, and I believe most pilots exhibited that kind of bravado.

The flare ship continued to circle high above the contact area, dropping flares and trying to spot enemy positions and ground movement. By now we had a better fix as the regional force soldiers examined incoming shell craters indicating from which direction mortar rounds were being fired. Brevaldo continued to bring in data, and his assistance was invaluable. The gunships oriented themselves and took charge of their destiny. They reported receiving .51-caliber machine gun fire but were not hit.

I listened as the lead pilot transmitted, "Fires Four Six, I see a couple in the open. I'm gonna go down and grease 'em, then come back on station. Over."

The chopper pilots' radio transmissions, their voices made staccato by the rhythmic fanning of those elongated blades, sounded as if they were speaking with mouths full of gravel. The first team expended its ordnance; a second Cobra team would soon replace them. During the interim I had artillery fill the vacuum. But the incoming mortar, rifle, and B40 fire continued. Before the contact was finished, a third Cobra team would come to our aid.

The 221 Regional Force Company numbered about eighty men and persevered with return fire. They had plenty of ammunition. Before the third Cobra gunship team expended its load, a higher authority in the chain of command called for additional support—an old, converted C130, affectionately known as "Spooky." I could have requested, not ordered, the aircraft. We were grateful for the assistance.

Now in radio contact with Spooky and using our electronic strobe to mark our position, we ensured that the pilot had a proper identification of our location. No one wanted to make the mistake of being on the receiving end of such a lethal volley. Using the outpost as a pivot point, the pilot circled to his left, then cut loose to the west and south a torrent of destruction that could only instill abject fear in the hearts of any NVA in the open. It was the coup de grâce. At approximately 0430 hours contact broke, replaced by a stunned silence. They had withdrawn.

Brevaldo approached, and we clapped each other on the shoulder. "Good job," I said.

"Thanks."

When you are under attack, defense and survival assume the lead role, relegating morals and ethics to the rear, at least temporarily. You return fire with everything at your disposal to rid yourself of an unwanted intrusion. It gets real basic. They are trying to kill you and you are trying to kill them. Reflection comes later.

The assessment: we received approximately eighty-five rounds of mortar fire, both 61mm and 82mm, .51-caliber machine gun fire, and indeterminable numbers of small arms and rocket fire. The Spot Report (a handwritten log maintained of all incidents called in by radio) estimated the enemy force to be company-sized and composed of both Vietcong and NVA. The report also indicated one more confirmed enemy KIA than I remembered. Other than the blow to Brevaldo's head, neither of us received a wound. To Brevaldo's credit, he did not ask for a Purple Heart.

As a testament to the effectiveness of well-fortified sandbag bunkers and how difficult it was, without overwhelming numbers, to root out those so entrenched, the regional forces suffered only one KIA and one WIA, the result of a sapper having turned a claymore mine around so that it was fired on the outpost. We had one NVA POW, a sapper who got through the wire unscathed but who inflicted no damage within the outpost. We found one NVA KIA in the wire. At first light the RF commander ordered a perimeter sweep, and a chorus of shouts went up for the sweep uncovered another sapper who was alive and hiding in the bushes. He had been wounded, but not seriously. I joined the ruckus and saw grenades lying all around him. I think he was relieved it was over, and glad to be alive.

It seemed strange to me, but I felt absolutely no animosity toward the POWs. They were just doing their job although I questioned whether their motives were completely altruistic. The RFs treated them humanely. As one POW was being fed, I walked by and spoke to him in fragmented Vietnamese. "You eat rice, huh?" He looked at me as if I were from another planet, and at that time all I can say is that I felt compassion. He seemed young, a kid. How many others were killed, wounded, and dragged away we would never know. And the number decimated by the artillery barrage, helicopter gunships, and Spooky also remains unknown, but we know they had confirmed kills. Without the artillery and air support, the result would have been different.

To this day, only in my wildest dreams can I imagine doing what the sappers did. Either drugged or ferociously dedicated and heroic— or possibly both—the sappers would have begun their suicidal low crawl through the tanglefoot wire hours before the first incoming rounds hit. Their mission encompassed breaching the perimeter and creating havoc within the outpost by throwing grenades and satchel charges, thereby allowing support troops to pour in behind them and mop up. Sappers often carried grenades and satchel charges tied to their bodies and flung the whole package at their adversary.

When the 221 Regional Force Company commander searched the NVA KIA, he found tucked in the soldier's shorts a drawing of the outpost that clearly depicted routes of ground attack from both the southwest and northwest. The attack from the west proved logical. The Square Lake area, with its tunnels, thick undergrowth, and proximity to the river, sheltered many Vietcong. The drawing also contained a diagram of the position of the house. That he had an accurate drawing of the outpost was no surprise for the information could have been obtained from any number of sources, including nearby farmers who, while harvesting their rice, probably counted strands of protective wire, pinpointed gun emplacements, and marked the exact position of the house.

We found on the NVA body papers identifying him as a platoon leader, the lead sapper. His body was not mangled, but his life had left him. When I gazed down on him in death's repose, a bewildering array of conflicting emotions engulfed me—emotions battering each other from extreme ends of the scale—from a sadistic feeling of superiority to gratefulness to remorse.

Subsequent intelligence filtered down from both the South Vietnamese and 25th Infantry Division said this: the attackers had come out of Ba Thu, on the eastern boundary of Cambodia, and had been briefed on the military strength of the An Dinh outpost, which reportedly contained approximately twenty regional force soldiers, possessed no machine guns, and had no artillery or air support. No mention was made of American advisors. Talk about lies by omission. Rumor had it that they had been told to attack the outpost or die in place.

The impact of the enlightening dawn felt surprisingly cleansing as if the sunlight washed away all the evil perpetrated the night before. Visitors arrived—Colonel Weissinger, the province senior advisor; Captain Wing, the district senior advisor; and their Vietnamese counterparts. All were gracious with their commendation of our performance under fire.

Captain Wing, who never said a lot, complimented me in his baritone voice, "You really had your shit together."

"Thank you, sir."

That and other comments, including those from Colonel Weissinger (with whom I had a subsequent falling-out), made me feel good. Brevaldo, Sergeant Khanh (my interpreter), and I were awarded the Bronze Star for Valor, as was the 221 Regional Force Company commander. Also we were told we would receive the South Vietnamese equivalent, which we never saw. Perhaps the informal South Vietnamese rating system was more meaningful anyway as they rated their American brethren on a scale of one to ten, ten being the down side. While I was standing on the road, several RFs encircled me, smiled, and said, "Number One."

Jim, who had been at a PF platoon outpost the night before, had by now returned from that location. He shook my hand—he had monitored the battle via the other radio—and congratulated me on my performance. But he also had a puzzled look on his face.

"What's up?" I asked.

"The colonel chewed my ass for not being here."

We both just looked at each other and shook our heads. [11]

Not only were Colonel Weissinger's comments stupid, they also countermanded our mission, which was to split up and cover more units. We strongly felt that only those of us in the field really knew what was going on.

Rumors began circulating about civilian casualties.

Unfortunately the battle was not clean. Battle is not clean. Shrapnel has a way of spilling over boundary lines. It is impossible to restrict such voluminous, destructive bursts of fire to a confined area. Rounds go astray, falling outside the thin curtain separating free-fire zones from no-fire zones. When a mortar or artillery shell strikes, the shrapnel splays not horizontally, but at an angle, out and up. And it does not remain airborne; it has to come down. The majority of rounds fired from airplane-mounted miniguns hit the target area, but it is inevitable that some will ricochet or stray. An M-60 machine gun, which uses a 7.62 mm shell, has an effective range of eleven hundred meters.

Shortly, a small group of villagers approached from south to north along Route 10 and stopped at our location. Consisting of mama-sans and papa-sans and raggedly clothed children, the group seemed to be an extended family. Jim witnessed what occurred. A broken-toothed peasant woman in tattered clothes broke through the cluster, looked directly into my eyes, and began to gesture. I could not read her face or her emotion. She did not appear particularly angry or anguished, but perhaps I denied what I saw. I did not know if she was accusing me or simply making a statement. She looked at me and pointed to a small box lying on the ground. Inside the box lay a Vietnamese baby who appeared to be asleep. He was asleep, all right—the sleep of death.

My first thought was, "Oh, my God, I'm responsible for killing the baby."

In reality, I had no idea what had caused the baby's death. Could a disease have been the reason? Had he been killed by small arms fire from either the NVA or the regional forces? By a wayward mortar shell? Or had he been killed by my directing artillery or gunship fire in an area where civilians might have been exposed?

What had transpired earlier in the contact had gone something like this:

> "Restful Fires Four Six, this is *Spooky*. There's a house
> to the sierra whiskey about three hundred meters
> from your outpost. Do you want me to fire? Over."

Being aware of this house—one that was occupied from time to time—I hesitated before making my decision. Then I spoke into the handset. "*Spooky*, this is Fires Four Six. Fire. Over."

It is important to note that the pilot did not ask for permission to fire but whether I wanted him to do so. There is a difference. I had the option to say no; however, since one direction of attack had come from the southwest, I elected to go for it. As a result, I claimed responsibility.

Was my decision the cause? If so, why only the baby? If there were other civilian casualties, where were they? Why would the infant have been exposed and no others? The questions will never be answered. Upon reflection, I do not recall seeing any visible signs of external wounds, but the baby may have been wrapped in a blanket. I just do not remember. Regardless, the infant was dead, never having a chance at life. That is a tragedy. Also my earlier illusion of perceived glory for having done something *significant* was now tainted by this death.

The incident became my epiphany of war.

Was this the kind of shame felt by my father who, as a child, had rummaged through trashcans for shoes? Or was his a different shame? For bequeathed to my father was a legacy of hard work and no joy. Even more important, he inherited the pain of guilt after the death of his mother and three siblings—the heinous crime being that he was the sole surviving child—and the accompanying shame for his emotional deprivation and penury. Perhaps guilt and shame were the traits my father and I had most in common.

When I think of death by intent, I think back to a day in my sixth year when I tagged along with some older neighbor boys as they hunted blue jays in our spacious backyard. Unlike them, I did not have a BB gun. I remember watching with a detached curiosity and fascination as one of them drew a bead and fired. The shot pierced the lungs of a defenseless bird, causing it to tumble to the ground. As I watched the jay gasping its last breath, I asked, "Why did you kill it?"

"Because blue jays are noisy and messy birds. They cause a lot of trouble," was the boy's self-justifying response.

My father did not like blue jays either. On many early summer mornings, he could be found throwing rocks to drive raucous blue jays from a tree in the front yard, so the neighbor boy's response fit.

What had the blue jay done to the boy? What had I done to my father?

Kill or destroy what we do not like, do not understand, or cannot control. There's a senselessness about it . . . on all sides.

16

FOLLOW-UP ACTIONS

They had a fanatical dedication—
a motivation through fear?
I will never know for sure.

Patient. Cunning.
They would lie in wait
for hours.

And then begin the crawl—
the four-hour crawl
to cover thirty meters.

Deftly snipping wires,
tying off trip flares,
turning around claymore mines.

Not a sound—
They made no sound!

Until they entered
the compound.

"The Sappers–I," a poem.

In the face of clearly overwhelming firepower, the Vietcong and NVA relentlessly kept after us. Not only did they have to escape detection, they also had to carry their heavy mortars and ammunition with them. An American 60mm mortar weighs just over forty-five pounds, an 81mm mortar one hundred thirty-two pounds, and a .50-caliber machine gun one hundred twenty-six pounds, before ammunition. The Vietcong's and NVA's equivalent weapons could be assumed to be of comparable weight.

Was it fear, drugs, or an absolute faith and belief in their cause? Or a combination thereof? The Vietcong and NVA had suffered a tremendous number of casualties since the U.S. became involved. While the 1968 Tet Offensive did open the world's eyes to the fact that the NVA and the Vietcong could launch coordinated major attacks across the country, it really decimated their ranks. North Vietnam, however, kept sending troops and supplies down the Ho Chi Minh trail, the guerrillas kept training, the wounded and maimed continued to be treated in underground hospitals, and so they persevered. The guerrillas left to fight were augmented by NVA regulars who increasingly took over the leadership role.

EVENING, THURSDAY, 13 NOVEMBER 1969

Nothing went right. This should have been a Friday the thirteenth. At 2055 hours they hit us again—a typical skirmish that involved an exchange of mortar fire and retaliatory artillery. There were no casualties. It was as if our enemy was saying to us, "I don't care how much firepower you have at your disposal. This is our country. We intend to unite it and will not give up before we do."

At 2145 hours a regional force soldier shot himself in the hand while on guard duty—a million-dollar wound. We called a dustoff.

As if there was not enough tension existing between the ruffpuffs and ourselves resulting from normal efforts at co-existence, other incidents occurred that had nothing to do with trying to superimpose one culture over another but were the consequences of human error. The worst, and potentially most volatile, incident occurred during an ambush patrol's return to the An Dinh outpost. This botched patrol illustrated the dangers of inept Vietnamese leadership and poor tactics, coupled with the actions of an overanxious American sergeant. A 13 November 1969 Spot Report stated, "At 2020 hours, ambush patrol returning to outpost left two men behind. The two men tried to catch up. They approached the right flank and were shot by own unit. Two RFs WIA."

That was a partially true report, but it was not the whole truth. In this highly active period, nerves were already on edge. Lieutenant Smith and Sergeant Adams were accompanying a platoon of 221 Regional Force Company on a patrol that culminated in setting up a temporary ambush position. Kerbow and I remained at the outpost. It was common for returning night patrols to maneuver under cover of darkness; this one was no exception. But two regional force soldiers got separated from the column, breaking physical contact and line of sight with the rest of the unit. No one was aware of it. Adams detected movement coming in from the right flank. There were not supposed to be any friendlies there. He pulled the pin on a white phosphorus grenade (a highly destructive incendiary device) and lobbed it in the direction of the perceived threatening flanking movement. Then Adams opened up with his M-16. He killed one regional force soldier and seriously wounded another.

Was Adams wrong? Trigger-happy? Judge as you may, he feared his life and the lives of those he was supposed to protect were in danger. The black night reduced vision to just a few meters, and the Vietnamese unit failed to use call signs. Adams acted; he did what he thought he was supposed to do. It was a mistake, a tragic one. Death by friendly fire.

When the patrol returned to the outpost, there was considerable consternation and clamor. Some of the RFs were overwrought. Kerbow and I were afraid that a classic Vietcong tactic was being employed— that of tacking on to the end of a patrol and infiltrating undetected into the outpost, where they would unleash a flurry of grenades. But that was not the case. What happened was that a regional force soldier took his M-16, and in a most threatening manner, jammed the muzzle into Sergeant Kerbow's gut. Fortunately no round was fired, but it was some time before we defused the situation. Kerbow was understandably upset, and no one got any sleep that night. I can only speculate how Sergeant Adams felt about the incident. Who knows what stresses might have been accumulating in his soul! Weapons are unforgiving, somewhat different from an intercepted pass or a missed ground ball.

Jim confided that he initially thought his patrol had been fired on first, and that's what he told the Vietnamese commander. But that observation was quickly erased once Jim recognized the familiar sound of American weapons; he knew those being fired upon were not Vietcong. There was no AK47 fire. That was a strange and uncomfortable patrol for Jim for at one stage he found himself on point. Upon reflection, Jim wondered if the patrol had accidentally interrupted an intended run on An Dinh that night since, as already mentioned, we were hit shortly thereafter. Nevertheless the event only heightened our apprehension and feeling of intrigue about the behavior of this unit.

Two regional force companies occupied this outpost during my tour—158 Regional Force Company, with Lieutenant Thom as the outstanding commander, and 221 Regional Force Company, which stumbled onto the playing field in late October. Considering that the 158 Regional Force Company was on loan from Tay Ninh, the province just north of us, the notion that these units operated in familial areas was somewhat dispelled. The first 221 Regional Force Company commander was not as effective or as aggressive as the second company commander and, to my relief, the first was relieved of command in January, after most of our action subsided.

To say that getting a Vietnamese commander relieved of duty was a clumsy, cumbersome task is an understatement. We had no authority to do so directly and had to work through our chain of command in order to get our superior officers to convince their counterparts that a particular unit leader should be removed. Jim wrote an emphatic entry in our log. "The 221 RF Company is extremely weak on night ambushes and patrols . . . if 221 RF Company fails to improve, it should be replaced due to the fact that An Dinh is a critical area." One thing rang clear—the enemy was testing the mettle of this unit. Still, giving the first company commander his due, he functioned competently when the An Dinh outpost came under attack.

Interestingly enough, the heightened enemy activity had the miraculous, positive effect of funneling to us sufficient quantities of supplies for completion of the bunker. On 20 November we took turns using a twenty-pound sledge to embed engineer posts in the ground to frame the sides, packed ammo boxes stuffed with sandbags between the posts for the walls, and drove eight-inch spikes into timbers to support the PSP for the roof. In a sense, the physical labor was rewarding as it took our minds off worrisome issues out of our control, such as when we would be hit. We completed the task by the twenty-fourth, having set one layer of sandbags over the PSP.

So by late November we had fairly decent living quarters, including a butane-powered refrigerator in the separate screened-in kitchen area. The rectangular main room would accommodate five, with enough headroom to stand. We lined the interior with bamboo matting, which created a more homelike atmosphere. We had some crude handmade furniture for storage. Since night light discipline was of paramount importance, we fabricated tiny light fixtures by inverting small plastic cups, punching a hole in the bottom center, running a minuscule flashlight bulb through the hole, then powering it with a small battery. Using these quaint but effective fixtures, we read cherished letters from home, wrote letters of our own, and even read an occasional escape novel.

Inside the bunker we stored all hand-carried weapons, bandoliers of ammunition, canteens, poncho liners, and an extra set of jungle fatigues. We made it as livable as we could. Essentially meals were a continuation of what we had been consuming. If we ever had anything resembling breakfast, I do not remember it. A jar of peanut butter was worth its weight in gold.

Thanksgiving was coming, and with that, a brief lull. But it did not last long.

17

THANKSGIVING RESPITE

The futility of man's choices
continues to present itself.

He builds, neglects, abandons, and destroys.

Nature
crawls back
reclaims its natural wildness
wondering
why man ever even bothered.

"Futility," a poem.

❧

THURSDAY, 27 NOVEMBER 1969

The weather in late November provided a taunting interlude by cooling off somewhat, adding a fleeting pinch of crispness, and stimulating wistful yearnings to be elsewhere. Stateside, my mom and dad were building a vacation home on a hilltop overlooking Lake LBJ in the rolling Texas Hill Country (as a way of diverting their attention from the war). My oldest brother, Richard—by age thirty-five he had made partner at the large public accounting firm of Arthur Andersen—celebrated Thanksgiving Day with his wife and two daughters at their Houston home. The next brother, Harry—two years removed from the military and working for IBM—lived with his wife and four children in Austin, where they consumed their Thanksgiving meal. The last brother, Steve, who had also worked at Arthur Andersen, had left the firm to join Browning Ferris Industries, the large trash-hauling company. He and his wife were living in Atlanta for several months while he worked on an acquisition. So, the Thomas sons were spending turkey day in Houston, Austin, Atlanta . . . and Duc Hue.

Yet there was solace in South Vietnam. Sergeant Brevaldo, who previously had been assigned to a medevac unit based in Cu Chi, had stealthily procured a turkey from a 25th Infantry Division mess hall there. This same Brevaldo had earlier engineered for Jim the opportunity to go up in a chopper where, for an all-too-brief period, Jim took over the controls and flew the bird. As to the other bird, Brevaldo infiltrated the mess hall from the rear while Batman Jim kept the jeep's engine idling. It was not long before Brevaldo charged out the door yelling, "Let's go, let's go!"

As a result, a wonderful Thanksgiving Day dinner prepared by Co Duc, Co My, and Co Hanh awaited us at the Sugar Mill villa. We stuffed ourselves and washed the meal down with champagne of forgotten vintage. The district advisors were present, and we needled each other, arguing which was the best college football team. Also I had a debt to pay. Upon promotion to first lieutenant (July last), I had to pass NCO muster by undergoing an initiation ceremony, albeit a belated one, concocted by Kerbow and Adams. And a concoction it was—a ten-ounce glass full of straight liquor blended from anything they could get their hands on, diluted by one ice cube. I got that baby down, then proceeded to drink beer as a chaser. Playing poker afterward, my motor skills systematically deteriorated, eventually culminating in the inability to hold my cards. The evening ended with my staggering to quarters and subsequently becoming violently ill. But I passed the test.

Thanksgiving in Vietnam was a true celebration. It was basic. We celebrated being alive. We celebrated being with each other. How easy it is to lose sight of what is important! In his later years, with his health declining and his eyesight failing, my father became more moody and despondent, still angry at the cards he had been dealt. After a Sunday meal, he would not say a word but enacted his shake-a-plate routine in which he shook his empty plate in the air, the signal for Mom to retrieve this potential airborne saucer. No one said a word; we just sat there. And no, Dad never threw a plate.

EARLY MORNING HOURS, MONDAY, 1 DECEMBER 1969

Relatively speaking, it was a light hit. This time it was Sergeant Kerbow and I who manned the outpost. Earlier in the day I had set up a small battery-operated tape recorder to capture any action. I had intended to switch the recorder on when the first incoming rounds hit, but I forgot about it for the first fifteen minutes. We received approximately twenty rounds of incoming mortar fire, along with AK47 small arms fire.

The RFs countered by firing their 81mm mortar and M-16s while Kerbow blasted away on his beloved .50-caliber machine gun. I had come to relish the awesome thumping of that 126-pound weapon, its six-inch shells launched at a maximum rate of one hundred rounds per minute, up to a range of eighteen hundred meters. I called in artillery support from the 25th. First up from their four-deuce mortar squad were illumination rounds, which also functioned as marking rounds in the night sky. Then I gave fire adjustments based on the position of the illumination. I considered the need for gunships but elected not to bring them in. Two regional force soldiers were wounded, one seriously.

The flare ship Little Bear 23 arrived on station and we coordinated to bring in a medical evacuation helicopter. As always, chopper pilots needed to know all of the circumstances surrounding the contact. The dustoff pilot was responsible for deciding if and when to come in, or whether to wait for gunship support.

"Restful Fires Four Six, this is Dustoff One Six Three. Understand you've had contact. What's the status? Over."

"One Six Three, this is Four Six. Affirmative. Contact broke approximately two zero ago. Your best approach would be to come in to our location from the November to the Sierra. Suggest you come in with your lights out. Over."

The pilot was still hesitant and wanted me to describe nature of contact and direction of attack. I told him we had received approximately twenty rounds of incoming mortar as well as AK47 small arms fire from the southwest. Our chopper pad was fifty meters west of the road, close to the outpost, and marked with yellow paint. Plus we would activate the strobe light. No good. The pilot wanted gunship support.

There was nothing we could do but wait and worry about the more seriously wounded soldier. In the meantime Sergeant Kerbow worked to get the regional force soldiers to move the wounded to the chopper pad and secure the LZ with a fifteen-man security team. Kerbow and I communicated by yelling to each other since Jim had the other radio at another outpost. The Cobras came on station, and the dustoff pilot readied his approach.

Kerbow did a good job guiding in the chopper with just his strobe and no radio. When he returned to the bunker, I told him so.

"I didn't think he was ever going to land the fucking bird," the sergeant said.

"Think our soldier will make it?"

"Yeah! He'll make it," Kerbow said.

It felt good to know that with chopper aid, the seriously wounded regional force soldier's life would probably be saved. Just as hearing the first artillery rounds whistling overhead had reminded me of the old U.S. Cavalry bugle call, hearing far-off chopper blades approaching, whether from a dustoff or gunships, was like receiving aid on angels' wings.

Once the action had subsided, Vietnamese soldiers gathered round and together we laughed nervously in a simultaneous effort to purge our fears and express relief that no more damage had been inflicted. Kerbow, as only Kerbow could do in his laconic but eloquent manner, said, "I caught one in the wire, hit him, saw him crawling away, and hit him again, blasting him another fuckin' twenty feet. Un coca, trung-uy?"

EARLY MORNING HOURS, TUESDAY, 2 DECEMBER 1969

It was Jim's turn; my role when he was there was to assist. He took charge in his comfortable, authoritative manner as we received approximately twenty rounds of mortar fire, accompanied by AK47s. Included in the incoming were a few rounds of high explosive that neither Jim nor I could identify as to weapon of origin. They were louder than any we had heard before.

During the engagement, an incoming round hit close to the mortar pit where Jim had been standing. He came running into the bunker, laughing as if he had just heard McNamara had been drafted, and said, "Jack, when that round hit, it lifted my steel pot off my head and it landed on top of the mortar tube."

We were getting used to this.

0230 Hours, Sunday, 7 December 1969

While another Sunday morning in Vietnam, stateside it was Saturday, 6 December. The Southwest Conference still basked in its glory as Arkansas and Texas vied for the conference football championship. Texas was undefeated, but Arkansas had a strong team. Lieutenant Ward and I had previously placed a wager on the outcome of the game. Armed Forces Radio broadcast the game live, which I picked up on a solid, compact portable radio. Reclining on my bunk, I dissolved into a time of not-too-long-ago naïve innocence when priorities were focused on having a date and the outcome of the game.

In Texas there is nothing like a crisp autumn day for football amidst an electrically charged atmosphere from a cheering crowd. Texas fell behind in the first quarter, and it was then the Vietcong rudely interrupted my reverie by lobbing in a few rounds. It was the usual stuff. A couple of hours later the enemy broke contact. There were no casualties. I remembered the game was on and went to the radio just in time to hear Texas score the winning touchdown in the waning moments. It seemed absurd, listening to a football game in the midst of war.

Tuesday, 9 December 1969

We received three rounds of B40 rocket fire and one 107mm rocket. There were no friendly casualties. District Senior Advisor Captain Wing was visiting the outpost and spending the night in our command bunker. We were asleep, except for the radio watch, and the concussion from the first round dislodged Jim from his slumber and catapulted him onto the dirt floor. He must have been dreaming because in the fog of initial consciousness he exclaimed, "They've breached the perimeter. They're in the outpost. They're in the outpost."

No sappers had breached the perimeter; nevertheless we responded with the customary retaliatory fire. Later, in his throaty horselaugh, Captain Wing inquired, "Who said they were in the outpost anyway?"

FRIDAY, 12 DECEMBER 1969

We received mortar fire. No friendly casualties.

From 9 November through 12 December the Vietcong/NVA hit us seven times. In addition to Captain Wing's support, Colonel Moore, battalion commander of the 2nd Battalion (Mechanized), 22nd Infantry, 25th Infantry Division, visited us after every significant contact.[12] We received more moral and tangible support from him than we did from MACV beyond district level. Colonel Moore had the horses, and he is a man I will always remember. He had no direct authority or control over us but always came to our aid. He gave us whatever he could, from excess food and supplies to rounds for the 81mm mortar. To have him nearby was a comfort. We had confidence his fire-support teams would back us up in times of contact, and they did. Colonel Moore was the epitome of a good leader for he was out in the field with his troops, making himself vulnerable in order to assess the ground situation better. He led by example.

A feeling of anticipation permeated the atmosphere after the last assault. That the monsoon season had lifted was a boost in morale since we would not be exposed to so much muck. The beginning of the rice harvest was another encouraging event. Sappers would lose some of their protective cover. The completion of our bunker was perceived favorably because it added to our comfort and security level. The command bunker at An Dinh had become home.

With Christmas drawing near, we decorated the inside with a three-foot artificial Christmas tree that my folks mailed to us. Jim and I carved out some time to play a football board game, and we pilfered some extra PRC-25 radio batteries that we used sparingly to power a small black-and-white Sony TV. In addition to the proverbial supply of cookies, one of my cousins sent a package of small rubber bouncing balls that I gave to the children in the outpost. The simple gifts delighted the children for they had so little. The period of calm was gladly received but was tainted by the fact the chemistry of MAT III-56 was about to change.

Monday, 22 December, found First Lieutenant James C. Smith traveling to Saigon on the first leg of his journey home. We had become good friends and I was going to miss him. I felt an emptiness due to his imminent departure for we had no secrets and supported each other, one picking the other up when he was down. We had shared our fears and dreams, our common interests of photography and stereos, and the common male bond of a love for sports. But perhaps most significant was our mutual acceptance. There is no stronger bond than the one sealed by mutual interdependence for survival, where you believe and trust in your fellow man. Of such circumstances, friendships are made. A poor excuse to have war, but it is there nonetheless.

Jim was a good officer, and our friendship did not interfere with respect for command and leadership. The highest compliment I could pay a man is that I trusted him enough to share a foxhole with him. Conversely, if he could say the same of me, I would consider this the supreme accolade. If I could have chosen one person with whom to serve, I could not have come up with a better choice. Moreover I was envious because Jim had endured the hard year in primitive circumstances laced with unforgiving conditions. He had put in his time and was to be rewarded by returning home in time for Christmas.

Sergeant Brevaldo would leave the team at the end of January, and Sergeant Adams had already departed on a special thirty-day leave since he had re-upped for a different assignment. Kerbow stayed with us off and on for another couple of months. Captain Wing, who not only visited us by jeep but also flew out on medevac choppers in support of our efforts, would soon complete his assignment and be replaced by Major Glenwood L. Cooper. Colonel Moore's assignment was over. The team numbered three—Brevaldo, Kerbow, and myself—and would remain undermanned for some time. While all of us came from dissimilar backgrounds and we did not always see eye to eye, we functioned well as a team. The chemistry would never be the same. I would miss them all.

As for the An Dinh outpost—a bunker system and a shell of a

house on one-third of an acre wrapped within a bamboo hedgerow—just what did we defend? Moreover, what was the purpose of the attacks? Were the Vietcong/NVA trying to take out the outpost? When you consider the concentration of dates surrounding the attacks, primarily late July to early August and November to early December, it suggests a possibility the attacks were diversionary, perhaps to clear a corridor to transport men and material ever closer to Saigon or simply to allow collection agents to gather rice and taxes.

Regardless, you cannot just bundle conflicting emotions, extinguish those deemed undesirable, and bring to the surface only those which make you look the best. The antithesis is also true: there is no need to suppress the positive and present only that which portrays the most negative. At that point, given the prevailing circumstances and what we knew, we did our jobs. It was far from perfect, the most damaging event being the Adams incident. Lieutenant Smith and I, Sergeants Brevaldo, Kerbow, and Adams, and the 221 Regional Force Company commander and his soldiers, along with the aid of American artillery and air support, saved RF soldiers' lives, probably kept the outpost from being overrun, particularly during the morning of 9 November, and sent a strong message to the enemy.

Five and one-half months left to serve . . . .

18

SQUARE LAKE FINALE

Let them
steal his camera
steal his gun
steal not my son
Amen!

"A Father's Prayer," a poem.

◆~◆

Tuesday, 30 December 1969, turned out to be a narrowly averted bad day at "black rock." The day started out innocuously enough, as Sergeant Brevaldo and I, along with a platoon led by Aspirant Lam from 604 Regional Force Company, accompanied an element from the 2nd Battalion (Mechanized), 22nd Infantry, 3rd Brigade, 25th Infantry Division in a daytime sweep, search, and destroy mission in the Square Lake area. Again Sergeant Thanh was my interpreter. Our role was to patrol to the objective and set up a blocking force. It was one of the few times I participated in a combined operation with a traditional American unit.

The dawn broke clear. As the morning sky rolled into a rhapsodic blue, cotton-puff clouds suddenly materialized as if launched at random from 105mm howitzers. The end of the monsoon season boded well for the Americans and not so well for the NVA and Vietcong for as the land dried up, tanks and armored personnel carriers (APCs) were released to plow through the fields, disrupting scattered farmers working the harvest. A Combat Tracker Team (composed of dogs, handler, and tracker) tasked to sniff out tunnels and caches reinforced American infantry. The once tranquil sky became blotched with teams of Huey Cobra gunships amid rising swirls of brightly hued smoke from grenade-marking rounds. Artillery waited in the wings. The confluence of offensive firepower followed the strategy taught at Infantry OCS in Fort Benning, Georgia. These were classic American tactics, even if inappropriate for an unconventional guerrilla conflict.

As the tracked vehicles got on line, the powerful rumbling of diesel-powered tanks and APCs positioning for a pincer movement made the ground tremble. The menacing Cobras unleashed their potent rockets at suspected targets. In a rare display of authority over a militia unit, Brevaldo and I were leading the regional force platoon to position. For a while! Brevaldo and I took turns carrying the PRC-25 as the weather was hot and we were moving at a fast clip. NVA were in the area and, believe it or not, we surprised them as some were caught in the open.

Our platoon sighted one and gave chase. The regional force soldiers were as excited as we were for seldom had the enemy been flushed out in the daytime. The RFs forgot their tactics—604 was the same unit that had struck the land mine—abandoned discipline, got off line, and barnstormed forward in a state of disarray, the faster soldiers leaving the dilatory behind. We looked like a scatter graph. For over a hundred meters I sprinted as best I could with a twenty-three-pound radio on my back while shouting at the aspirant to get his troops on line. The effort was of no avail. We were too late for the blue-shorts-clad soldier eluded us by disappearing down a camouflaged spider hole. I was frustrated. It was the closest I had come to an enemy soldier in the open, but he faded away before I—armed with only a .45-caliber pistol—or anyone else could fire a shot.

We regrouped and patrolled to our designated position, a blocking force on the western edge of the pincer maneuver. The platoon lined up behind a rice paddy dike, and I radioed our coordinates to the American forward observer. He acknowledged us and had supporting artillery launch a smoke round, which I used to define our position in relation thereto. The shell was perfectly launched, the smoke popping almost directly overhead. This I confirmed to the forward observer, but no sooner had the words been transmitted through the handset than a high explosive round hit close, no more than fifty meters to my left.

I actually saw the shell burst, saw the raging shrapnel fan outward and upward, and heard the shrapnel whizzing overhead. There was no time to move, no time to react. I was mesmerized. No one was hurt, but I burst on the radio, "Adjust fire! Adjust fire! We are right under that goddamn artillery." The forward observer anxiously responded, "Okay, okay." He adjusted fire and walked the point of impact into the tree line, where I had placed one squad of the RF platoon. They came charging out like a pack of wild hyenas, giving the nervous laugh of fear. Sergeant Thanh came to me wild-eyed and asked, "Why they fire so close?"

The American unit continued to pinch in from three sides. Brevaldo now had the radio and was handling the liaison. I briefly left the unit and joined a group of American officers as their soldiers attempted to penetrate the hedgerows. Like bulls on a rampage, the APCs and tanks tried to crash through the undergrowth, but the thick vegetation impaired movement. There was no finesse; a dog-team leader or commander of a long-range reconnaissance unit would tell you that all tracked vehicles did was destroy the trail. Nevertheless an American lieutenant followed some of his men into the thicket when immediately we heard a muffled explosion. Someone had tripped a booby trap, a familiar sound, and soldiers dove for cover. Wounded, the lieutenant was carried out to the open, and a medic was quickly at his side, checking the severity of the wounds before administering first aid. I handed the medic my knife so he could cut the field dressing to size. Before the operation terminated, ten U.S. soldiers were dusted off, but no friendly KIAs.

I walked over to a group of American officers, and we congregated alongside a tank, which provided a shield between a hedgerow and ourselves. As we were discussing the operation, I felt a solid bruising blow to my upper left arm as if someone had balled up his fist and slugged me. I looked at my arm and noticed that a jagged piece of hot shrapnel about an inch thick and the size of my palm had landed flat and stuck on my fatigue shirt as if glued there by someone. We all looked at each other, then dropped to the ground.

"Do you want a Purple Heart?" the captain asked, somewhat in jest.

"No, thanks, I'm not hurt. All I'll have is a bruise." I had already seen several Americans dusted off, some of whom were ambulatory. It was the closest I came to getting wounded, and it was from our own artillery.

No NVA were flushed into our blocking force as they had chosen to stay ensconced in their tunnels, but there were several confirmed enemy KIAs that day. The pounding continued and then we began to move. Brevaldo handed me the radio. It was then I entered a mode where I came close to doing what was nearly done to me.

There was contact in a tree line and an American M-60 machine gun squad was ripping the hedgerow. Some distance behind the gun placement, a husky black sergeant lofted grenades over and well beyond the machine gun position. I decided to help him in his endeavor and pulled the pin on one, launching it in the same direction, only I forgot I had the cumbersome PRC-25 on my back, which bound my arm and restricted the toss. I watched in abject horror as the grenade landed only a few meters in front of the machine gun squad.

"Jesus Christ! Please roll! Please roll!" I screamed to my soul. And oh-so-fortunately, like an end-over-end punt, the grenade rolled far enough away before exploding. The machine gun squad crouched as low as they could to avoid the shrapnel whizzing over their heads. The gunner turned around and yelled, "Sergeant, who threw that goddamned grenade? Shrapnel was flying all around us."

When the sergeant looked at me, he knew he did not have to say anything for I ducked my head in shame. This was a narrowly averted catastrophe, one I attributed to luck, fate, or perhaps an infrequent intervention from God. But if so, why protect me and the machine gunners but not others? It is a difficult question to answer. Since I believe God seldom intervenes, I credited the outcome to luck.

But "what if" scenarios still dance in my head! What if my

throw had been a little shorter? What if the grenade had not rolled out of harm's way? I could see the gunners and machine gun being riddled by shrapnel. The mistake of forgetting that I had a twenty-three-pound radio on my back while throwing a hand grenade, which resulted in friendly casualties, itself an oxymoron, would not have been acceptable or forgivable. Had I taken American lives, I believe I might have snapped, screaming my head off and charging into the hedgerows. But it did not happen and I have to thank someone, so I thank God, if only for the luck. I cannot imagine the anguish endured by those who knew they were inadvertently but directly responsible for deaths by friendly fire.

I have often wondered what the regional forces that I was with thought of that incident, or if they were even aware of it, for shortly thereafter I experienced the most positive and obvious instance of their taking care of me. After the grenade incident, I took over point of the regional force column, if only for a brief time, because I felt the only way I could atone for my near-fatal mistake was to draw fire. Extremely embarrassed, I wanted to leave the scene as quickly as possible to distance myself from the mistake and block it out. If fired upon, better still, for if not erased myself, then I would return fire and inflict enemy casualties, thereby redeeming my virtue. I do not think, however, I would have done much damage with the .45-caliber pistol. The chance for redemption did not occur; I was not fired upon. What did happen was that a couple of regional force soldiers quickly walked abreast, one on either side, and each firmly grabbed one of my elbows and relegated me to the center of the column. I was still their umbilical cord for coordination of air and artillery support, and they were not ready for that link to be severed. Another possibility . . . the RFs action was an act of love.

Three days later impact awards were handed out. A Colonel Parker and a second lieutenant each received the Silver Star while one captain was awarded the Bronze Star for Valor. I received an Army Commendation Medal with "V" device. It ranks a rung below the Bronze Star and was more a token or courtesy, probably because I left myself exposed during the contact. My performance at the Square Lake that day had been questionable, and even though my ego needed the medal, I should have refused to accept it.[13]

Today, when I reflect on the incident, it reminds me of close calls in relation to the fragility of life.

19

THE DRY SEASON

O Captain!
You made your bold presence known to all,
you did not think you could possibly fall,
but a cocky man can wind up alone,
too often he reaps the seeds he has sown.

My Captain!
You did not listen you must now agree,
vanity dictated its own decree,
and now you are floating distant and free,
it is a shame you did not hear or see.

"O Captain! My Captain!" a poem.

~~~

JANUARY 1970

The month of January passed disturbingly quiet. In a last-minute comeback, Texas defeated Notre Dame in the Cotton Bowl, which was far more exciting than what transpired at An Dinh. Officially the team numbered three, and I was the team leader, but in reality it was not functioning for Brevaldo spent a week in the hospital for treatment of a spider bite and Kerbow spent a week with MAT III-

69, a team I subsequently took charge of for a few days. MAT III-69's assignment was at the old French fort east of Tan My Village, where earlier I had *donated* my .45-caliber pistol.

Being hit by the Vietcong/NVA had become addictive. The combat high. I was coming down and did not like it. To vent my frustration, I wrote a blistering letter to Colonel Jack Weissinger, province senior advisor of Hau Nghia, in which I bitterly complained about the lack of logistical support from U.S. channels and the thievery by Vietnamese and asked for a transfer to the rear. I had had enough. Prior to hand-delivering the letter, I went over it with both district senior advisors—Captain Wing, who was transitioning out, and his replacement, Major Cooper. Captain Wing suggested I burn it while Major Cooper suggested I follow through; otherwise, how would the province senior advisor know what was going on?

I should have listened to Captain Wing. Colonel Weissinger read the letter, looked at me, handed it back, and said, "It'll be a pleasure to transfer you."

There was no "What do you need? I'll give you more support." There was no dealing with the issues. Nevertheless the transfer never took place, so I geared myself up for the remaining tour of duty. Admittedly my handwritten letter to Colonel Weissinger equated an emotional dump. Oh, the adverse conditions were genuine—ask any soldier how he feels about lack of supplies—but the problem was in how the colonel handled the complaints. Besides, a greater concern was at stake. I was getting bored. I was also getting scared, wondering if perhaps I had depleted my share of luck. The excitement and resultant adrenaline that fueled my motivation was dying, and I needed an external spark to keep going.

The Vietcong and NVA were being pounded, pushed west and underground—time for their "one step back and two steps forward" methodology. The U.S. Corps of Engineers bulldozed the Square Lake area, where they uncovered tunnel complexes and caches of weapons and ammunition. But it seemed to me that the mystery was being trashed and buried rather than unraveled. As our situation quieted, two simple questions no one has ever answered reared their treacherous heads, trying to break through my cloudy subconscious. The questions were tauntingly simple, the answers—out of reach.

"What are we doing here?"

"Why?"

Those questions, and the onerous quest for resolution, I buried deep in my soul, but the vaporous toxins solidified.

On a tape dictated to my parents on 8 January 1970, I stated the South Vietnamese government would need us full strength for at least another two or three years. By 31 December 1972, the number of U.S. military in country was less than twenty-five thousand. I was speculating, extrapolating to the whole based on limited action, which lacked statistical substance, but I felt there were not enough Trung-Uy Hots along the South Vietnamese chain.

In the meantime, throughout January Sergeant Thanh and I allocated time between outposts and district headquarters. All told, I covered five thousand kilometers by jeep during my year. On occasion while visiting outposts on my own, I would lay a couple of grenades in the passenger seat and wedge my M-16 beside me. During my tour, however, no one on MAT III-56 was ever fired on while in a jeep.

Also I participated in filling out the HES (Hamlet Evaluation System) report, a mechanism for quantifying results of the village pacification program. HES was an elaborately contrived rating system whereby hamlets and villages were classified according to the degree of security each was assigned relative to the number, type, frequency, and severity of alleged terrorist incidents or flagrant enemy attacks against each locale. Five grades were possible with an A rating deemed the most secure and an E rating an obvious, complete failure. The rating was determined after answering eighteen pacification indicators, nine security indicators, and nine development indicators. In theory, the system made sense. In practice, however, trying to quantify the enemy's degree of penetration was subjective at best for the system failed to measure what was in the soul of the people and the questions were susceptible to misinterpretation. Another inherent risk of compiling purported or alleged facts was the temptation to report things as being better than they were. This war was not winnable by the numbers. In late November for some mysterious reason, the An Dinh area had been downgraded from a C to a D.

The South Vietnamese, meanwhile, prepared to celebrate Tet, the Vietnamese Lunar New Year occurring at the end of January. For the Vietnamese, Tet, which is equivalent to our Christmas and New

Year celebrations, gave cause to celebrate and drink, even to hope, short-lived though that may be. As the senior field lieutenant in an advisory capacity in Duc Hue District, I was invited to participate with my South Vietnamese counterparts, including Dai-Uy Nghiem, the local village chief, in a celebration to be held in Hiep Hoa Village. As the children gathered round, I noticed anxiety etched in their innocent, vulnerable faces. That look of pleading would be the same anywhere in the world. These were children who had no control over their circumstances and were totally dependent upon adults to provide an environment in which they could be safely nurtured. We apportioned to them tiny bound parcels of candy, something they rarely received.

As the celebration progressed, our moods, as if in concert with the fading light, became blacker. To anesthetize our souls, we did what so many human beings do to forget that which ails or eludes— we imbibed. Remembering Thanksgiving, I had no desire to get as crocked as I did then.

The celebration started out harmlessly. Twelve participants positioned themselves at a long, rectangular table in the Hiep Hoa meeting hall. I was the token American. We began our toasts with the ubiquitous Coca-Cola. Beer soon displaced the Cokes. I was neither a heavy drinker nor a fast one, and I fell behind the Vietnamese pace of consumption. They chugged their beer as if they had just crawled through a parched desert, resolutely tossing empty beer cans out open windows, and they were goading me.

A scene from the movie *Auntie Mame* materialized, the one in which the heroine feigned downing honey-spiked daiquiris. Pretending to sip the drink, she deceptively discharged the contents by tossing the offending nectar over her shoulder while leaning back and laughing boisterously. I decided to replicate the maneuver.

I popped a fresh can of beer, put it to my lips, took one swallow, swirled the liquid around my mouth, swallowed hard, then hurled the nearly full can across the table through an open window. In the process the can flipped over and spilled some beer. A couple of soldiers jumped up, pointed at me, and hollered unfathomable diatribes in Vietnamese. I was now a marked man and they watched me more closely.

After consuming a couple more beers, I said, "Hey, I've had a great time, but it's time for me to go."

As I got up to leave, a Vietnamese officer stood as well. "No! You stay," he said in broken English.

The words did not bother me; it was his .45-caliber pistol pointed directly at my chest. Deciding discretion was the better part of valor, I willingly accepted his invitation and reclaimed my seat, wondering at the same time if that .45-caliber had once belonged to me.

FEBRUARY 1970

The month began with two new men being assigned to MAT III-56. Sergeant Isaac Charleston, an E-7 from Houston, Texas, assigned to his second tour, was black, and his youthful appearance belied his experience and age. Even though he expressed distaste about being assigned to another tour in Vietnam, his professionalism and sense of duty overcame his displeasure.

Sergeant Charleston had received his return orders after spending only nine months in the States. He reasoned Uncle Sam purposefully assigned near-retirement age personnel to high-risk positions; if they were killed, the government would not have to dole out as much pension money. In Charleston's view, a younger man should have been sent. But it was more than that for Charleston had experienced an unpleasant incident during his first advisory tour. Assigned to Advisory Team 87, which was attached to an ARVN division based in Xuan Loc in Long Khanh Province—about eighty kilometers northeast of Saigon—Charleston was participating in a two-day sweep. They made light contact about four in the afternoon, followed up by a heavy engagement the next day. It was then Charleston experienced a defining moment: during the firefight, he maneuvered to another position, and an ARVN soldier who replaced him took the round that would have ended Charleston's life. After breaking contact, the ARVN unit and its advisors humped some more until they came to a stream and took a break.

In his words: "We finally broke contact. The enemy pulled away from our platoon and moved farther into the jungle. That's when we came upon a cool stream of water that everybody wanted to get in and cool off. I was the only black out there. Everybody got in the cool, clear water; one of the Vietnamese said something, and everyone turned around and looked at me. Then the Vietnamese captain came over and told me, 'I want you to move further downstream, away from my troops.' Here I am, thinking that in my own country, I ain't got what I'm supposed to have and then my country sends me way around the world to help somebody else and then this is what . . . it really pissed me off."

The fact that Charleston overcame his disaffection and performed professionally is a credit to his character. He was a team player.

The second addition to the team, a young captain, became the team leader as the ranking officer. I resented him because I felt seasoned and had proven myself in tight situations, earning the right to continue leading MAT III-56. Colonel Weissinger saw it otherwise. Nevertheless I tried to put these feelings aside. In other circumstances I might have liked our new team member, but frankly his cockiness turned me off. This captain, with no previous combat experience, was zealous and impetuous. I tried to stress the importance of working within his limits, and not going off half-cocked, yet he would not, and did not, listen—to me or to anyone else. His know-it-all attitude, while frustrating to me, resulted in incapacitating him and destroying our interpreter.

While I was away from the outpost, a young Vietnamese boy came by and alleged he knew the whereabouts of a booby trap. The young captain wanted to get his feet wet, just as I did when I first got there, only Jim and the sergeants made me earn my keep. Somehow the captain connected with a small element from the 2nd Battalion (Mechanized), 22nd Infantry, 3rd Brigade, 25th Infantry Division. Since this was not a planned mission, the captain asked for volunteers to accompany him despite the fact that this intended action violated all semblance of common sense. While there is no way the new team leader could have known what to do, he should have known what not to do.

Sergeant Charleston firmly declined to participate; if the captain had commanded that Charleston accompany him, most likely Charleston would not be here with us today. The captain took Sergeant Thanh and a squad of Vietnamese, along with some U.S. grunts, to investigate. As the story unfolded, this youth led them to the alleged booby trap site. When they reached it, the youth, who was not hurt, pointed to an object, then dropped to the ground and disappeared.

The jagged truth was borne out by the enormity of the explosion that carried to the outpost. (Charleston surmised, based upon the strength of the explosion, that an artillery shell had been rigged to detonate.)

The captain and Sergeant Thanh, who certainly should have known better, had been standing where they were not supposed to be, in front of the abbreviated column, and absorbed the brunt of the explosion. Both were dusted off, and American soldiers from the mechanized infantry unit brought the captain's bloody, shredded flak jacket and his bowie knife back to An Dinh.

Thanh, who had served with Jim in Duc Hoa, had previously missed six weeks of action due to shrapnel wounds. His loyalty and diligence were without question, as he accompanied us on almost every operation.

Through a series of radio transmissions, I ascertained the captain's location. I visited him at the hospital and learned his prognosis for recovery was favorable. One of his arms had almost been severed from his body, but they were able to save it; he was lucky not to have been more seriously wounded or killed. He was smart enough to have worn his flak jacket, in contrast to most of us who seldom slipped one on. I wrote a letter to his parents, embellishing as best I could the circumstances of his condition. But I could not write what I really felt or wanted to say. His parents wrote back, thanking me for the letter. The captain's youth, strength, and flak jacket saved him, and his attitude on recovery was solid. I was sorry he was hurt but furious he had not listened, and even more furious at what happened to Sergeant Thanh.

Yet, in a twisted knot of guilt and remorse, I wondered whether we would have been spared the tragedy had I been more forceful in indoctrination efforts. It made no sense, for in spite of the captain's impetuousness, it could be said that he was in the wrong place at the wrong time. Or was he simply a victim of his own arrogance? Survivor's guilt—same old question, same no answer. They transferred the captain to the 106th General Hospital in Yokohama, Japan, and I inventoried his personal items for shipment. I choose to believe he felt bad about what happened—to Sergeant Thanh and himself. The captain lasted three weeks in country.

I also visited Thanh in the amputee ward. He was so bundled in bandages I could not tell if he had lost a limb, and I was too afraid to ask, fearful any question might negate my denial that a part of him might be missing. When I greeted him, however, his indomitable spirit shone through his winsome smile. He said he was okay and would be okay. We visited for a while and then I took my leave.

When visiting Thanh, I looked around the room. All I saw were maimed bodies, almost all having lost at least one limb and, in several cases, multiple limbs. Each step I took to leave the ward became more difficult as if my own strength and virility were being drained by the patients' *man-made* physical defects. It was like walking through a bad dream in which some unseen force dragged you down, rendering you impotent. I did not see Sergeant Thanh again, and I am sorry I never went back. Yet I did see him once more. On 30 September 1987 I piloted my BMW K100RS motorcycle into Carrizozo, New Mexico. It was late Wednesday night and the town was basically shut down. Only one of the few motels had a vacancy. The room featured a jammed entry door and a broken window, and I had to crawl through the window to get inside. Feeling uneasy, I set my Beretta 9mm by my side. In my fitful sleep . . . *Thanh materializes. He flashes his engaging smile once more and through time and space silently mouths, "I'm okay."*

After the booby trap explosion, calm reigned at An Dinh and produced an unexpected consequence. It was like flipping a double-edged knife. I realized that our once-sharp team had become dull from lack of action, the situation exacerbated by Kerbow's DEROS and his short-timer's attitude. Nerves became more frayed, and grumbling more pronounced.

Without question, my most difficult interpersonal relationship was the one with Sergeant Kerbow. This bothered me because I liked him and he taught me a lot. We participated together in many operations, and I thought he was a good soldier. After returning from R & R in Hawaii, where he had met his wife, he sank into an increasingly depressed state. He missed his family and wanted to go home. Sergeant Kerbow confided, "I was not the man I should have been" (who of us was?) and beat himself up about it. I felt there was much more to the story, but that is all he revealed. He drank too much, and I called him on it after witnessing a critical episode one night in the bunker.

The team had settled down for the night, and frankly I do not remember if we pulled radio watch. Three of us—Kerbow, Charleston, and I—were present. I fell asleep, but soon the sound of running water awakened me. We did not have running water.

"Kerbow, goddamn it, go outside to urinate."

I tried talking to him about it the next morning, but he just gave me his customary blank stare. If the team had come under attack, he would have been nonfunctional. A contact never occurred when Kerbow drank excessively, but between us there developed a rift that never healed. I judged him. He denied the problem.

I was not the only one bothered by Kerbow's drinking. Jim had experienced a run-in with Kerbow as well and had been concerned about the possibility of alcohol hampering his performance. In that instance, however, Kerbow had responded to Lieutenant Smith with a not-so-thinly veiled threat, "Have you heard of fragging?" (This is the art of using a fragmentation grenade to disable or kill a disliked superior, usually at night when the intended victim is asleep or else during a firefight in which it may be difficult to affix responsibility.)

Afterward Kerbow professed he did not remember his bouts of drinking or what he had said. It was a shame. He refused to face his demons. At the time, however, we did not talk effectively about such issues or, perhaps more apropos, we did not know how to deal with that kind of conflict. Any confrontation resulted in denial. I should have taken stronger action and confronted Kerbow further, but I diluted my effort under the guise of compassion. One of the last things I overheard Kerbow say was that he did not want me to have his custom-built bunk with built-in storage.

Still I wondered whether there might have been other reasons for the fracture with Kerbow. There were two incidents whereby my performance or behavior may have caused him to lose respect for me. The first incident with Kerbow occurred as he neared the end of his tour. Knowing his head was not in the game, I was reluctant to take him out on more patrols, due to my concern we might encounter hostile activity. This bothered Charleston, who made his point succinctly: "Sir, a younger man than I might claim prejudice, but we're a team and all team members should participate to the end."

I told him, "I would do the same for you if the situation were reversed."

That rationale did not hold water with Charleston, who pointed out, "But sir, this is now, and you are not going to be here at the end of my tour. You'll be in the States."

Charleston was correct. I took Kerbow on a couple of harmless patrols. In reality, none of us wanted to go out any more, but my waffling hurt the team. Hell, I just wanted everyone to go home safe.

The second incident had occurred on an earlier patrol in which Kerbow and I were accompanying the 221 Regional Force Company. We encountered an entangled, brush-infested area the RFs said was heavily laden with booby traps.

The company commander, through our interpreter, turned to me and asked, "Can we go around?"

I thought for a moment, and then replied, "Yeah, we'll go around," deciding the "damn the torpedoes and plow straight ahead" attitude made no sense. Kerbow did not say a word, just gave me his look. But I had already dusted off numerous Vietnamese casualties the past several months and saw no need to evacuate any more. Besides, we did not possess the requisite skills to detect and disarm booby traps except by stumbling into them.

So we went around, and the operation ended without incident.

On occasion during the postwar years I have wondered whether I cheapened my mission on earth because I did not take more risks in Vietnam. Courage is overcoming fear, taking the risk to step out and reach out into worlds unknown. During the above patrol the Vietnamese were scared, and I had no more confidence in their ability to ferret out booby traps than I did in ours; in fact, only once on all the patrols I accompanied did they actually spot a booby trap. If they could not do it, and it was their country, their turf, then I damn sure could not do it either. I was scared too.

Perhaps I should have commanded that we march on in spite of the risk, yet it was more risk for the militia than for me since I would not be on point or flank. But I did not want to be responsible for taking casualties, particularly in this instance when my regional force soldiers asked for permission to avoid the area. I believe they would have gone forward had I told them to do so, but maybe they were sensing the same futility I did. Did that make me an ineffective leader, one unwilling to make the tough decisions necessary to win a war, the kind of tough decision America needs to claim glorious victory? To have been truly courageous, should I have said, "I'll take point. Show you how it's done"?

Did I make selfish choices to avoid the ultimate sacrifice? Should I have died, and then learned the broader meaning and purpose of life from God? On the other hand, I might have made it through unscathed. If so, later in life, would I have taken more risks, become more successful, and attained higher fulfillment?

The adage, "A coward dies a thousand deaths," merits reflection. My conviction at the time, that the risk of reward relative to the integrity of our involvement was not worth loss of life or limb, created a paradox. Did I act cowardly? Or have I died unnecessary deaths for even broaching the question? The decision not to take the most dangerous route may have been the smartest, but not the most courageous, because at that instant my biggest fear was getting killed or maimed. I never overcame it. In terms of an individual's courage, must you always choose the most difficult path when it involves the risk of death, and is that the only way to achieve maximum fulfillment?

What would my father have thought about my decision? Dad possessed a matching mental acuity and toughness, yet he professed inadequacy. In his early sixties he once said to me, "Aw, Jack, I've felt *inferior* all my life," and, "I'm a jack-of-all-trades, master of none." Still that did not help the intimidation I felt when he solved algebra word problems in his head or the confusion I felt when he told me he could have been a great singer if he had received coaching. And while he could not read a lick of music, he could mouth tunes on the harmonica. *Inferior*? No, he was not.

Would Dad have gone through the minefield? Would he have ordered me to go through it?

My brothers—the naval officer, the chopper pilot and ranger, the combat engineer—what would they have done?

If I had been killed, however, a different hypothetical scenario presents itself.

My three older brothers are sitting at an outdoor cafe having coffee and sharing stories when an old friend walks over and asks, "Hey, how are you all doing? Say, weren't there four of you? Didn't you have a younger brother? What happened to him?"

"We lost him in Vietnam."

"What about his two daughters?"

"Oh, they were never born."

20

Winding Down

"I am not a deserter."

"Some South Vietnamese think you are."

Silly reasons.

Just because we raised some hopes
of those who tried.
Just because we left them
a desecrated countryside.
Just because we left them.

Carrots.
Lots of carrots—yanked away.

Silly reasons.

"Carrots," a poem.

March and April, 1970

For most of these two months I was bored stiff. The most exciting incident occurred at La Cua, a hamlet about three kilometers northeast of Hiep Hoa. A PF platoon occupied a small outpost nearby. Partially delineated by pools of stale, brackish water that served as a reservoir, waste dump, and breeding ground for things that slithered and scampered, La Cua stank. Before my arrival in country, this outpost had seen considerable activity, with one contact resulting in the wounding of a MAT lieutenant.

One day I visited the outpost alone. As if in honor of the blistering heat, a grass fire burned through the perimeter brush. For the next hour I sat with my back to a bunker waiting for the next claymore to explode. We had no way to put out the fire and to go out in the minefield would have been suicidal. Every once in a while I thought the last mine had blown and rose to go to the jeep, only to be repulsed by more plastic explosives. The frustrating part was that I wanted to shoot back, but there was nothing to shoot at. Since there was no outlet to discharge my tension, I embarrassed myself by flinching with each detonation. I postulated that since enemy contact had diminished, we overcompensated by trying to blow ourselves up.

Other than that, routine assignments and planning for R & R occupied my time.

Taiwan

Transitioning from pioneer life to civilization spawned discombobulating feelings. Nevertheless I looked forward to leaving the jungle boots, jungle fatigues, M-16, and accompanying paraphernalia behind. For my week's leave I purchased civilian clothes that would never grace the cover of *GQ*, but who cared. If the enemy was going to take a vacation, then I was too. On 7 April I caught a plane at Tan Son Nhut Air Base and flew to a small island northeast of Vietnam, about one hundred sixty kilometers east of China.

Allegedly the Portuguese sailed to this island in 1590 and named it Formosa, which means "beautiful one." Now known as Taiwan or the Republic of China, its capital is Taipei, which lies twenty-five kilometers south of the northern tip of the island. Numerous landlords have occupied Formosa, the most notable being China, Holland, and Japan. On 8 December 1949 noncommunist General Chiang Kai-shek initiated the migration of his Chinese followers to the island, a land mass approximating the combined territory of Massachusetts, Connecticut, and Rhode Island. In 1970 roughly 14.8 million residents called Taiwan home.

Upon arrival I elected to stay fifteen kilometers out of town at the Hotel Peitou, a small enclave nestled in a hillside cleft enveloped by lush vegetation. Taipei swarmed with activity, and among those swarming were a large coterie of prostitutes—a legal venture in this country, as evidenced by the professionals wearing government-provided health cards. The hotel desk manager even gave me a ten-minute briefing on available services.

I heard a knock on the door. "Who is it?"

"The concierge, sir. Would you come out to the hall, please?"

There, provided for my entertainment, stood a lineup of young women—available choices being none, one, or several. Or I could have sent them all back and selected from a different cafeteria-style lineup. Pricing depended on degree of specialization versus commodity services. Like it or not, it was part of life, and they catered to a large GI trade.

There was a lot more than women to see in this land. The sculptured countryside embodies steep, rugged mountains rising to 3,997 meters and fertile, terraced glades providing nutritious loam for rice, wheat, and sugarcane. Pristine forests cover fifty-five percent of the country.

The coastal village of Hualien overlooks the Pacific approximately one hundred twenty kilometers south of Taipei. I rode the coastal railway twenty kilometers north of Hualien and then descended by bus into an enchanting, marble-lined canyon—the Taroko Gorge. Mineral-laden waterfalls cascaded from high marble cliffs, cutting swaths through emerald-hued clusters of thick flora. A narrow wooden suspension bridge swung recklessly in the wind. Local artisans shaped and carved marble vases. Once the vases had cured, painters, like pistol shooters steadying their gun hands, cradled their brushes, and deftly hand painted the transformed natural resource. Jewelry, chess sets, birds, and animals were crafted from jade, the more exotic pieces speckled with black.

In Taipei electronics simmered in the embryonic stage while craftsmen fashioned desks and tables out of hard teak, softer woods laced with intricate carving, and inlaid polished marble. For a short while I was a tourist and the war was far away. I left Taiwan with two impressions: I would have hated fighting in their jungles, and war is not only destructive; it also changes your vision forever.

I returned to Vietnam on 15 April and hustled up to Cu Chi, then boarded a chopper to Hiep Hoa. MAT III-56 now consisted of Sergeant Charleston and me as Kerbow had rotated to the States. In concert with the reduction in enemy activity and size of our team, we moved out of the An Dinh outpost. I experienced some regret upon leaving the site where the Vietcong/NVA had tested, challenged, and pushed us. In a convoluted way, our work had been gratifying because we had thwarted their efforts.

A rumor was circulating that two regional force companies and MAT III-56 were to join forces and occupy a vacant ARVN battalion compound. We would establish a group headquarters with additional firepower and personnel. Unfortunately the concept never came to pass, leaving to flounder in an increasingly uncertain sea my short-lived resurgence of initiative and desire. Excitement and anticipation became lost companions, replaced by feelings of futility and yearning. The sense of disillusionment and disaffection grew stronger, and I was disappointed in my disillusionment.

Lieutenant Shanklin

When MACV assigned to MAT III-56 a green, untested lieutenant, I wondered whether he thought they had dropped him into an enemy camp by mistake. The cliché, "All is fair in love and war," needed to be revised to, "Nothing is fair in war," for I was sure that is what Lieutenant George Shanklin felt on 23 April 1970 after he disembarked from a chopper. Assigned to be my assistant, his jaw dropped to Australia once he recognized me for I had harassed him as an officer candidate in my platoon at OCS. I know he wanted to get right back on that chopper and get the hell out of there.

MAY 1970 TO DEROS

I introduced Lieutenant Shanklin to the various RF companies and PF platoons. Together we accompanied some operations but never established a rapport. My time in country was getting short, and I still had another week's R & R coming.

I decided to release Lieutenant Shanklin to Sergeant Charleston to accompany an operation. They made contact—in the daytime. Shanklin stepped on a relatively benign booby trap and was fortunate to have sustained only a bruised foot. After they returned from the operation, Charleston, snared by the flow of adrenaline, described the action. "Sir, you should have seen it. Our patrol flushed out this guy, and our RFs opened up on this Vietcong. They kept shooting at each other, and the guy apparently got hit or something, but anyway he kept shooting—I was close enough to see that he changed from his shooting arm to the other arm. He ran off and the RFs chased after him, and they came back with a weapon, a Thompson submachine gun." As young interpreter Khanh said, "He was tough."

I wished I had been there. When elements of the 25th Infantry Division and ARVN units, accompanied by American advisors, began penetrating eastern Cambodia, a part of me longed to go. I could have extended and asked for the assignment, but my instinct for survival prevailed. As history has borne out, those actions too proved fruitless. Still there existed a feeling of incompleteness for leaving both a job and a country undone.

AUSTRALIA

Mid-May found me in Sydney, Australia, where, after tantalizing exposure to people of my own kind, my desire to return to the field completely crumbled. Wandering the streets of Sydney, lusting after Australian women, hiking in the country at dusk to observe a pack of kangaroos serenely bounding through the forest, and taking a boat cruise through placid Sydney harbor were so diametrically opposed to the avowed purposes of war that to return was folly. The benefit of R & R was the anticipation of a temporary reprieve from a Neanderthal world, but the price paid for the return trip to hell was hell. I remembered how Jim had felt after returning from R & R with his wife in Hawaii. No matter when or where you went, there was a mountain to climb upon return. It was devastating.

In Australia an enterprising frontiersman took me on a four-wheel-drive tour in the wilderness. There, nestled against a hillside, surrounded by a canopy of trees, was his homemade cabin, where he prepared a homespun meal. He piped running water directly from a stream and used an old steam radiator as the indoor conduit; by the time the water completed its circuitous route, it was hot because the radiator hung over a wood fire.

My father, who, as a boy affixed sails to wagons and flew with the West Texas winds, hunted rabbits with a prized .22-caliber rifle and searched for arrowheads and rusted guns amid rattlesnake-infested farmland, would have loved both the resourcefulness of the Australian and his wild country. As a kid, Dad claimed assorted pets gathered from the prairie; included in this menagerie was a coyote he named Jack. The coyote remained a favorite until he bit Dad's grandmother. I often wonder . . . was I named after the coyote?

I left Australia and returned to Duc Hue one last time. Appropriately, on my final operation in Vietnam, I accompanied Trung-Uy Hot and his infantry company. Naval PBRs surged south down the choppy Vam Co Dong. Hot and I, along with a few RFs, were in the lead PBR while the remainder of his soldiers occupied the other boats. Positioning himself in the bow near the craft's .50-caliber machine gun, Hot's resplendent smile characterized his resilient spirit and character. He was dressed in green fatigues, with a jungle hat and sunglasses. A lensatic compass protruded from beneath an orange bandanna tied Western-style around his neck. On his left wrist he sported a watch, and a .45-caliber pistol hung from the web belt clasped around his waist. He carried a map as did I.

After cruising a few kilometers, the PBRs nudged their way

into the eastern bank, where we disembarked. We regrouped, got in a single column with point and flank security, and headed east through thick swamp and brush. The regional forces sank up to their necks in the canals. Scattered bomb craters—instant man-made reservoirs—still held milky water. A couple of kilometers inland I heard a muffled explosion and shouts of anguish. One of the RFs had tripped a booby trap.

"This is Restful Fires Four Six. I need a dustoff. Over."

That was it for me. I was done. I never saw Hot again.

Yet, as happened with Thanh, I did see Hot once more. On 9 September 2002 while touring on a 1998 BMW K1200RS motorcycle, I pulled in for the night at the Lariat Motel in Glenwood, New Mexico, near the Arizona border. As I was drifting in slumber, Lieutenant Hot returned. The apparition was short.

> *"I've been looking for you for over twenty-five years,"*
> *I say.*
>
> *Hot doesn't respond, just stares at me. Then it seems as if my whole body uncontrollably erupts in tears. Silently, he leans forward, puts his cheek against mine, and cradles my neck.*

21

PARTING SHOT

It is over.
My war is over.

I have left my foreign rural home.
Though a temporary one—
it is a home I will forever remember.

My South Vietnamese comrades . . .

The highway.
I am on the highway to Saigon—
the number is one as I recall.

Flashing red light . . .

"You're speeding, sir!"

"Speeding Irony," a poem.

◄━ ━►

Though my time had passed, the playing field and its conditions remained unchanged. While the roster of Americans rotating through this corridor continued to revolve, the names and lives of the enemy and South Vietnamese forces did not because, unless they were killed on the battlefield, they were in for the duration. And MAT III-56, its chemistry dissipated, had lost its cohesion and, during the latter part of my tour, never regained its peak.

Leaving the villa for the last time, I said my goodbyes to Major Cooper, Sergeant Charleston, and Lieutenant Shanklin; loaded my field gear in the jeep; and departed for Tan Son Nhut. Alone, fittingly I headed northeast over Route 7A, the ruddy road that bisected the lamentable village of Hiep Hoa. I turned right on Route 10, proceeding southeast until reaching Bao Trai.

There I met Colonel Weissinger for my exit interview. Neither one of us mentioned my blistering letter. The final meeting was amiable. He asked if I was going to stay in the Army. My response was simple: "No, sir!"

I wanted civilian life, but a deeper, unspoken reason prevailed: if I stayed in, I would spend one year in the States, be promoted to captain, then return to Vietnam in a combat role. That there would be a considerable number of things—mostly the camaraderie—I would miss about the Army was true, but there was no way I wanted to return to Vietnam and fight for questionable ideals.

Departing Bao Trai, I turned left and drove northeast on Route 8A toward Cu Chi. At Cu Chi I turned right, catching Highway 1 leading to Saigon. Here the highway was paved, and I floored the accelerator, as if trying to outrun and leave behind forever those experiences from another world. Five minutes later I heard a siren. I could not believe the image that appeared in the rearview mirror. I stopped the jeep. An MP pulled alongside, stepped down from his jeep, and said, "Sir, you were speeding."

Ironic and ludicrous, trying to civilize a war!

22

POOL OF REFLECTIONS

Defensiveness, coupled with a strong sense of denial, is a lethal weapon in the war against awareness, growth, and change, the origin of which, I suppose, is that it is never right to be wrong. For the one in denial, to admit being wrong or to accept another point of view as perhaps more valid than his own, is tantamount to admitting imperfection. Admitting imperfection is a self-deprecating value judgment rendering himself less than worthy. So he defends his position at all costs, planting seeds for an intractable defense of untenable positions, laying groundwork for cultivating, harvesting, and perpetuating acts of evil.

HEALING

In New Mexico, south of Eagle Nest and north of Angel Fire, lies a chapel nestled among the gentle eastern slopes of the Sangre de Cristo Mountains. A strong, solitary wind sweeps the landscape, healing rattling emotions stirred by the war mementos inside the chapel. The dominant promontory affords an expansive view of the Moreno Valley, where pain and sorrow can be gathered up and cast upon the chapel wing pointing to heaven.

Originally known as the Vietnam Veterans Peace and Brotherhood Chapel, it was built by Dr. Victor Westphall as a tribute to his son who, as a twenty-eight-year-old First Lieutenant, U.S.M.C., lost his life on 22 May 1968 in an ambush near Quang Tri. Now known as the Vietnam Veterans National Memorial, it also boasts a visitor's center. I had read about the chapel in the early seventies, dreamed about it, and then crafted a poem about it.

On my first visit to the chapel during the summer of 1982 Alicia and our six-year-old daughter, Summer, remained in the car while I harvested memories—by choice, alone. Pictures of young men who had lost their lives hung on one wall. If you visit there, study the eyes. After a while they get to you, follow you.

When I returned to the car, I said, "All those young men . . ." but I could not finish the sentence and burst into tears.

Startled, Alicia looked at Summer and said, "Your daddy was a hero."

I have thought a lot about her comment. Certainly many soldiers performed much more heroically as evidenced by the military's medals and awards hierarchy. And I am sure other soldiers never received the recognition they should have. Nevertheless I took pride in Alicia's tribute, even though she was unaware of everything else that had transpired.

As time passed, I felt a strong urge to return to the chapel. On an October day in 1985 a new, poignant photograph of a handsome young man in football uniform, posed in the classic punting position, had taken its place on the wall of the dead. I could picture him running down the field on a cool, crisp autumn day. Cheers then, none now. Friends we had then, gone now. Why do some live and some die? I could only feel man's risk for God's gift of life. We do it to ourselves, suffering the consequences of our mistakes, the mistakes of others, and willful acts of destruction. There are also many of us quite ill. We are human.

CONTEXT

When I served in Vietnam, word spread that the Vietnamese placed less value on human life than did Americans or other Western cultures. I did not experience it that way. That more intrinsic worth was assigned to the indomitable Vietnamese water buffalo and sundry farm animals than to their own children—allegedly brought into the world as a labor force—was a cultural myth cultivated by Americans. Not all of us believed this, of course, but the *message* was troublesome.

Perhaps it was a self-imposed rationalization on our part to compensate for the destruction we wreaked. Certain Asian religions believe in reincarnation and repetitious life cycles. This does not mitigate grief over the loss of a loved one. I know what I saw and felt. When I saw Vietnamese children maimed, I saw mothers grieve. When I saw a Vietnamese soldier's dead body, I saw the grief of those who loved him. Relatives cried, wailed, and mourned. The loss of a loved one hurts, and no one can ever convince me that that hurt is unique to a certain race, culture, or religion.

While some of my feelings and insights retain their original definition, others have changed shape for the superficial, protective shells have peeled away, exposing their cores to fresher, expanded views.

That the conflict was one of mass confusion is unassailable. The absence of front lines, the twisted entanglements of loyalties, Christian-based religions versus those without claim to a savior incarnate, the Vietnamese elite versus bourgeoisie versus peasants, the lack of clear definition of objectives commensurate with a dearth of consistent, effective continuity of leadership from Washington, and South Vietnam's ineffectual leadership and ambivalence toward the conflict itself fought against one other in a convoluted amalgam with no principal ingredient strong enough to unify South Vietnam.

Ho Chi Minh achieved his espoused objective of unifying his country as one people under one nation, whether or not one agrees with his methods. Nationalism and Communism won over fragmentation. Yet, if anyone had a callous disregard for life, consider that the leaders of both North Vietnam and the Vietcong sent to their deaths more than eighteen times the number of people the U.S. did . . . all for the purpose of subjugating their people to virtual enslavement.

The only way the United States could have won the war would have been to bomb North Vietnam into submission, to have pounded them relentlessly until their will to continue disintegrated. Even if we had bombed the North into submission, however, America would have had to maintain a protracted in-country presence, an intricately deeper involvement designed to meld together the multifactious elements.

That smells of occupation and colonialism and would not have addressed the folly of our dismissing their culture, our unjustified arrogance in thinking we could successfully impose our culture over theirs, or integrate the two. The American public would not have tolerated occupation. And there was no way to gauge smoldering desires of revolution residing in the heart of the South. The fact that the overrunning of Saigon 30 April 1975 was attributable to the NVA and not the guerrillas is well documented. It is also true that no foreign country, including the United States, has ever obliterated the will in the South for self-determination, much less linking and coordinating the disparate factions of divisiveness.

Regardless of the reasons why we lost the war, we lost the war. To have fought in the only war that America had ever lost carried with it shame—shame I added to my basket of perceived failures. The search for glory, the desire to carve out a legacy of sacrifice, honor, and duty to God and country as our fathers and grandfathers did in World War II vanished. There was no romanticism attached to this conflict. We saved the American public from nothing.

Among the participants themselves, however, there occurred infinite numbers of individual acts of heroism and compassion, such as a soldier lifting up a buddy when he was down, sharing food and laughter, giving a smile of understanding to a villager or a captured soldier, and gathering oneself again and again to walk patrol, fly missions, or motor upriver. Regarding supreme acts of combat heroism, whether the soldiers, airmen, or sailors lived or died, nothing written here is intended to diminish their courage and sacrifice or the value of their mustering from within the fortitude to do what they did. As individuals, I hold them in awe.

As for the advisory effort, I believe in the "pebble in the pond" theory that the ripple, however imperceptible, ultimately reaches the other shore and makes an impact, however slight. But was this more like throwing a rock into a black hole? What impact did MAT III-56 have? What legacy did we leave? Yes, we saved the An Dinh outpost on 9 November 1969 as well as on nights before and after. With the aid of American support, we saved or, perhaps more accurately, prolonged, many South Vietnamese lives. In a broader context, this applies to the entire advisory effort. But what happened after we left? Once we disengaged from Vietnam this measuring stick had to be discarded because, with the exception of the refugees, we did not collectively save the South Vietnamese.

I often wonder how the South Vietnamese who tried to establish a representative coalition government strong enough to stand on its own must have felt as we pulled out in stages—militarily (by 31 December 1973) and then financially (on 20 August 1974 U.S. Congress cut financial aid from the original request of $1.4 billion to an ultimate appropriation of $700 million). Nixon's Watergate and a Democratic Congress elected in 1972 were also contributing factors. Regardless, I surmise the South Vietnamese felt deserted, just as I feel our country abandoned them.

Buoyed by America's powerful presence, technology, weaponry, and promises, but unaware the boost was being provided by an ever-inflating, yet increasingly delicate balloon, when it burst, South Vietnam's last remnants of hope collapsed. Hindsight has 20/20 vision, but my simple conclusion is that we should never have been there because our country did not stay the course.

Finally my naïve hope was and is that some regional and popular forces and their families survived the Communist onslaught and *reeducation*, that the survivors' innate rejection of suppression was strengthened and fostered through our presence, and that those seeds will ultimately help Vietnam evolve into a truly free country—but it is a fragile, slender thread to hold on to.

DEATH, GOVERNMENT, AND GOD

I did not want to die. I did not want to be maimed. At times in Vietnam, deep in the solitude of night, I cried for to die was a waste of life not yet lived. More than once I felt the nudge to write a last letter, signing off from life, and giving directions for disposal of my meager possessions. For me, that would have been equivalent to giving up. I never wrote one. But some soldiers did, and after posting the letter, some of them died. Why? Did they want to die? Were they afraid? Did they have a premonition of impending death? Did God send a message? There is no answer here on earth, and I will never sit in judgment of those who constructed such a letter.

Americans who served, who lost buddies in combat, or saw them maimed, suffered tremendous loss and pain, not to mention the grief families back home experienced from the loss of loved ones. I believe the experience and significance of death for surviving American combatants varies in direct proportion to the intensity of combat they experienced, the closeness of their relationships, their youth, their religious and moral beliefs, their integrity, their views on war, and their willingness to feel. As mentioned previously, I did not see an American soldier lose his life in Vietnam, yet if Jim Smith had lost his life there—his gentle chiding, his sense of humor and wry smile gone but for memory—I imagine my feelings of the senselessness of this war would have escalated.

During our 1996 return to Vietnam Jim and I stopped at the Cu Chi visitors' center, which houses an assorted display of punji-stake booby traps. Cruel, they were designed to demoralize and discourage the American soldier.

One design calls for an eight-inch spike to be embedded in a hole in the ground. If you fell into it, the natural reaction would be to yank out your foot. That would be impossible, for positioned several inches higher up were four more sharpened eight-inch metal stakes slanted at a forty-five-degree angle. You could not extract your leg from the hole because your thigh would become impaled.

Another barbaric device consists of two cylinders, each impregnated with six- to eight-inch metal spikes, which rotate in opposite directions. If a soldier became wedged between the cylinders, the design is such that if he tried to claw his way free, the opposing cylinders rolled, enmeshing him deeper until both sides of the body became inextricably impaled.

Envisioning being snared in one of these lethal devices left me with both a sickening hatred and a fearful admiration for those who fabricated them. I am still amazed by the Vietcong's dedication and determination.

Later I burrowed one hundred fifty meters through the Cu Chi tunnel complex and came out feeling claustrophobic. I cannot imagine living in them as the enemy often did. I emerged with the feeling that the combination of tunnels and booby traps emanated from the bowels of the earth, that the direction from which they came intensified the aura of evil intention to perpetrate horror.

In large measure, however, we rained our destruction from above. Does the fact that our destruction and devastation came from on high make it righteous? We blew people apart, but it was less personal. How do you keep from becoming desensitized if you never see the results of what you do?

Fixed-wing pilots—except those shot down or incarcerated—seldom got a close look at the devastation, the human carnage. They had to face their fear, perhaps stretch their competency, but if a pilot survived his sortie, he might sleep the night away in an air-conditioned Quonset hut. Chopper pilots and door gunners engaged in hot LZ insertions and extractions were closer to intimate action. Artillerymen—the exceptions being firing point-blank or being overrun—lobbed in shells. But who swept the kill zone? The infantry!

The more detached you are, the more diffused the responsibility becomes. As the line of accountability grows dim—no bodies, no tangible connection to the end result—it becomes difficult to reconcile the consequences of actions taken, like trying to derive substance from a thick fog. Specifically, who do I settle with, and for what? An uneasiness lingers.

Soldiers are taught to kill. In bayonet training we were encouraged to yell the word "kill" every time we made a practice thrust. We had to believe it and practice it for, if not sufficiently desensitized, we might not have been able to do what we needed to do in order to survive. One of my OCS classmates, Little John, fought the system his way. Whenever he made a practice bayonet thrust, he yelled oaths of "love" and "peace." How many lost their lives, I wonder, because they were too sensitive to what was going on?

We were asked by our government to fight, kill, and maim for our country, absorbing into our souls government-implanted ethics. When setting foot on free soil again, I was not prepared to deal with the consequences of my actions nor, I think, were many veterans. We were supposed to drop our uniforms at the back door, assimilate the past into the present or, if unable to do that, bury the past by ignoring and forgetting it while reintegrating ourselves into society as if nothing had happened.

If there is blame to pin, I stick it to our government, which, at least theoretically, represents all of us. Neither the civilians who administered the war nor the career officers who ran the field war were aware of a much-needed path for transition and adjustment, or worse, did not care.

Americans, young and middle-aged, were sacrificed for our government's failure to extricate us more expeditiously from this tangled engagement. Reflecting upon the pieces of Vietcong propaganda that castigated Johnson and McNamara, I now believe they contained an element of truth, even though they were written from a hypocritical perspective. The twisted corollary is also true. Americans who vigorously protested against the Vietnam War gave the enemy hope, which might well have resulted in additional American causalities.

I can only hope that in the future civilian leaders who orchestrate armed conflict have sufficient insight as to the magnitude of the mission to be undertaken and exemplary foresight as to the ramifications of its consequences. I suggest the leaders go first, but of course that will never happen.

Blaming the government, however, does not absolve individual responsibility. Displacement of blame is a veneer unable to stand the test of time. As my specious shell eroded, I encountered individual moral issues tauntingly staring me in the face. While it may be easier to say "we" killed x number than it is to say "I" killed x number, I do not believe the individual can look to the collective for absolution from what he must come to grips with on his own. It is, in my opinion, an abdication of personal and moral responsibility not to make that quest. For when I see the results of war, when I see bodies that no longer breathe or limbs that are no longer attached to the body, I believe God has been deeply wounded.

GUILT AND SURVIVAL

I would have felt better if the United States had won the war—keep the cancer from spreading by killing the carrier, if not the source, of the disease. Yet neither the theory of Communism nor the spirit of democracy was being killed; people were. When the avowed purposes of halting the spread of Communism and preparing South Viet-

nam to become a free country were exposed for what they were—
nothingness—any affirming feelings attached to the global cause, by
definition, also dissolved into nothingness. The lack of a substantive
grand cause mocked conventional military rhetoric. It created instead a dichotomy of either lonely searches for understanding or a
fruitless entombing of the war's myriad tentacles. It is as if the for-
mula for living has no symbolic expression to dial in effects from the
impact of war. In the absence of a grand plan, therefore, my battle
narrowed down to two questions:

> How could I extract from the complete chaos of this
> war a personal sense of meaningfulness and significance,
> then integrate the multitude of conflicting emotions
> into a semblance of normalcy?

> How could I reconcile sorrow and shame for deaths
> and maiming of others versus feelings of gratitude and
> superiority for survival?

Not everyone felt guilt. I did. Yet I never had to lay out an enemy
soldier with my M-16, leaving therefore a paradoxical void caused by
not fulfilling part of the infantry mission—a twisted childhood fantasy
left forever unrealized, which diminishes the significance of my survival.
That I felt the need to kill by rifle fire to justify my assignment as an
infantry officer conflicted with not wanting to kill at all.

Nevertheless I feel deprived for not having an O'Hare-like encounter. But I also cannot dispute the fact that—in supporting regional forces less than thirty yards distant from the command post—
by directing artillery and helicopter gunship support, I am responsible
for the deaths of fellow human beings. Also the girl on the bicycle, the
baby in the box, and the near miss with the grenade still on occasion
scream for attention. From a selfish perspective I am disgusted with
the taint of imperfection while from a selfless perspective I believe that
I was capable of a better performance. Of course, that was one of my
father's messages: *No matter what you do, son, it is never good enough.*
My brothers heard this as well.

My search for meaning has led to a broader definition of the combat high for it was much more than the excitement of sophisticated weaponry, nerve-tingling explosions, and fear. It was a time of life when emotion and fervor peaked, the peak created by the intensity and raw power of relationships, whether good or bad, or between friend or foe. The possibility of being betrayed by the South Vietnamese with whom I served and the simple risk of walking down a trail or pulling an ambush instilled within an exaggerated sense of self-importance. I miss the intensity and excitement for, in spite of the fear of death or perhaps because of it, I was more alive that year, cared more that year than any other year before or after. But it was a life thrust upon me, not one created on my own, and, except for occasional bursts of living, I, along with those who tried to become close, have suffered for my not reaching out more fully.

At times, when depressed, I have had difficulty justifying my existence for there were those who did more, risked more, accomplished more, and suffered more. Each individual has to wrestle with his own demons and come to his own terms of self-forgiveness. Ultimately my search led to counseling and stumbling into Christ. From counseling I found understanding. From Christ I found forgiveness. While at times both the understanding and self-forgiveness slip away, they are far better than what I initially prescribed as my cure.

I thought that if my fellow Americans had embraced the returning veterans, welcomed us back with love, acceptance, and appreciation for sacrifice, then these *sanctions*—along with civilian accomplishments meriting the right to acclamation and approbation—from my fellow man would have healed the inner wounds and justified my right to live as well as imbued self-respect. I considered the Bronze Star with "V" device to be the foundation. I have kept the medal and occasionally read the words accompanying the award. On one level I am proud of it for it represents the fact that I kept my head under fire, and I am thankful to Captain Ray Wing for the recognition. However, since it was not a Silver Star, much less a Distinguished Service Cross or Congressional Medal of Honor, I have tended to discount it since only loftier medals merited the rights to higher self-esteem.

And this prompted a third question:

How could I reconcile with my father?

My reasons for wanting to be judged heroic had more to do with pretense—setting myself apart from my brothers, establishing an identity separate and apart from their being, and of even higher consequence, earning distinct recognition and approval from my father—than with altruistic motives. How shallow, and certainly no substitute for love! For just as it hurts to lose someone you love, it also hurts to come home feeling unloved. Did my father ever see me?

Shortly after my return from Vietnam, I visited a Sunday school class my parents sponsored. Dad came up behind me and clasped my shoulder. I was startled, my hair stood on end, and when I turned and faced him, I saw in his face an affirming expression, that he was giving me credit for having traveled a tough road. Yet we never talked about the war. I never heard from him the question I yearned to hear. "What was it really like, son?"

Several years later, though in a different vein, Dad came and watched Steve and me playing flag football in one of Houston's primary leagues. After observing my quarterbacking for a couple of games, he came up to me and said, "Boy, if you'd only had some coaching." And in a letter written on 19 December 1979 that came to light after my mother's death described below, Dad wrote:

> It would take hours for me to say what I would
> like to say but I simply don't have the energy to do it.
> You four boys and Mom have been my life and I
> should have told all of you this every day of my life. I
> was not thoughtful enough nor unselfish enough
> during the early stage of my marriage and raising four
> fine men. I agree with you, I am the father of four of
> the finest men ever. I was not the father I should have
> been to you, too selfish and too thoughtless. I have
> thought about these things a million times in these
> later years and now it is too late to make up for my
> failure to do so.
> . . . I sit around here regretting the things I didn't

do that I should have done . . . in other words I'm paying for all those mistakes believe me. . . . and praying that I will be forgiven by God and by all of you.

In my late thirties, as Dad lay dying, I told him I loved him, the first and only time I ever did so. He broke down in tears and said, "Oh, Jack, I don't want to go." And while he had signed his letters to me with love, he still could not verbalize, "Jack, I love you too."

In reality, however, he was ready to die, his heart eaten up by age, hard work, and the internalization of his pain and shame, and he did not want to live with a physical incapacitation that had robbed him of his blustery love for the physical, the ability to see and feel the world around him. His heart, once incredibly strong, ceased to function. On an early Saturday evening, 15 November 1980, after eating some homemade tollhouse cookies and drinking a glass of milk, he passed away, not quite eighty-three years old.

My mother, who was to live another twenty-three years, died on 13 January 2004 at the age of ninety-nine. During the intervening years after her husband's death, she and I talked a lot, becoming great friends. Once I asked Mom why she had not stood up more to Dad. She replied, "My parents yelled and screamed at each other all the time. I was determined going into my marriage that I was not going to do that. I was going to make peace."

A simple statement, understandable, yet profound. My mother was one of the brightest women I have ever known and, from pictures of her youth and adulthood, one of the most beautiful. After Dad died, she became the focal point for the family. Her grandchildren and great grand-children adored her as did the daughters-in-law, ex-daughters-in-law, and my former girlfriends. As she grew in age and wisdom, she continued to read, work daily crossword puzzles, play scrabble . . . and open up. She told me that her physical life with Dad had been good, but that had Dad not found the church, she might well have left him.

Rarely now do I dream of my father, where I allow my fear of him to equate to a fear of God, interfering with the concept of a benevolent, all-loving, all-forgiving, yet highly disciplined and disciplining master Father. Still, when the occasional dream comes, it expresses an unresolved, disturbing conflict in which I fight intimidation and my perception of his harshness, where the hinged, heavy door of suppression slams shut quickly, allowing to escape only fleeting flurries of joy.

I believe there were times Dad chose his meanness. However, over the passing years, as writing and photographing have brought me closer to my being, I wonder: might my father have mitigated his anger had he understood the remarkable therapeutic effect of creative expression and managed to do more of it?

Dad's legacy? He raised his family's socioeconomic level from that of a poverty-stricken cotton farmer to upper middle class. No son of his had to pay for a college education, and Dad provided us opportunities he never fathomed. His four sons created nine offspring, who have created another twelve, with more likely to follow.

As I move through the world, it is up to me to toss to the winds fragments of rage and shame. And, just as I believe my children have forgiven me, I forgive my father who, I feel, loved me.

A fine line separates living true to God and to oneself, between a stern adherence to discipline and abstinence versus a right to experience and savor joy, for without a conscience you can run rampant, plunder with impunity. But it is all right to live, just as there is a right to live; the good feelings must be allowed to effervesce, just as bad feelings and sorrow must be allowed their turbulence and pain. That is the message I take from my father. That is the message I take from Vietnam.

I choose never to forget Vietnam. My battles no longer rage within, having lessened in intensity, leaving smaller skirmishes wrestling for space. I no longer feel like a wave that has its strength sucked away by the undertow, no longer feel undermined by forces I do not understand. I let my conflicting feelings jostle, knowing each is valid, each has a message, and that life cannot be viewed from one perspective. I cherish more than ever the little things—lunch with a friend, a motorcycle ride with my brothers, visits with my daughters, a crisp fall day, the pleasures of a vibrant relationship, the realization as folly that you must be perfect in order to love or be loved—the little pieces of serendipity I know will come around.

I remain hopeful that Vietnam, its land and its people, will heal. Yes, the Amerasian children have been purged. Yes, those who fought for the South have been reeducated into silence. Yes, remembrances of America's presence in Vietnam have undergone classic revisionist cleansing, resulting in a distorted view that paints the Communists as saviors. I harbor no ill will toward the people. I do harbor ill will toward the practice of Communism or any other institution that stifles the natural development and expression of mankind. Communism survives on fear and control; it does not represent the needs and feelings of its people. Communism in Vietnam will fail. It will ultimately fail as does anything that is built on a pack of deceit, lies, and manipulation, whether it is a country, a company, a marriage, or an individual.

Vietnamese who fled are free to return and visit their country. From Australia, Canada, and America, they spread to their brothers and sisters and mothers and fathers messages of hope, opportunity, and success—like poplar seeds driven by the wind to root and blossom in points unknown. Infusion from the electronic media escalates the desire. And not everyone who wants to leave the country will be able to, creating within the country itself a burgeoning, bubbling reservoir clamoring for better lives, more choices. The Vietnamese people will do it themselves. The impetus for change comes from within.

The young Vietnamese girl sits erect and elegantly on the bicycle seat, her left hand delicately cradling to the handlebar the edge of her creamy white ao dai, keeping it from becoming soiled. Gracefully and steadily, like a gentle cloud flowing with the wind, she pedals along the sandy crown of the rice paddy dike, casting nary a furtive glance backward as she floats through a turn, then disappears behind an enveloping, protective hedgerow.

APPENDICES

APPENDIX A: DD FORM 214

THIS IS AN IMPORTANT RECORD
SAFEGUARD IT.

PERSONAL DATA				
1. LAST NAME-FIRST NAME-MIDDLE NAME THOMAS, JACK LYNDON		2. SERVICE NUMBER		3. SOCIAL SECURITY NUMBER
4. DEPARTMENT, COMPONENT AND BRANCH OR CLASS ARMY USAR INF	5a. GRADE, RATE OR RANK 1LT	5. PAY GRADE 02	6. DATE OF RANK	DAY 22 MONTH JUL YEAR 69
7. U.S. CITIZEN ☑YES ☐NO	8. PLACE OF BIRTH (City and State or Country) HOUSTON, TEXAS		9. DATE OF BIRTH	DAY 5 MONTH AUG YEAR 44

SELECTIVE SERVICE DATA

10a. SELECTIVE SERVICE NUMBER 41 60 44 492	10. SELECTIVE SERVICE LOCAL BOARD NUMBER, CITY, COUNTY, STATE AND ZIP CODE LB #60 HOUSTON, TEXAS	DATE INDUCTED DAY NA MONTH YEAR

TRANSFER OR DISCHARGE DATA

11a. TYPE OF TRANSFER OR DISCHARGE RELIEVED FROM ACTIVE DUTY	8. STATION OR INSTALLATION AT WHICH EFFECTED US ARMY PERSONNEL CENTER OAKLAND CALIFORNIA	
a. REASON AND AUTHORITY SEC XI & XIV CH 3 AR 635-100 SPN 611	EFFECTIVE DATE	DAY 14 MONTH JUN YEAR 70
12. LAST DUTY ASSIGNMENT AND MAJOR COMMAND USMACV APO SF 96222 USARV	13a. CHARACTER OF SERVICE HONORABLE	b. TYPE OF CERTIFICATE ISSUED NONE
14. DISTRICT, AREA COMMAND OR CORPS TO WHICH RESERVIST TRANSFERRED REVERT TO USAR CONTROL GROUP (ANNUAL) USAAC ST LOUIS MO		15. REENLISTMENT CODE NA

SERVICE DATA

16. TERMINAL DATE OF RESERVE/UMT&S OBLIGATION DAY 10 MONTH SEP YEAR 73	17. CURRENT ACTIVE SERVICE OTHER THAN BY INDUCTION a. SOURCE OF ENTRY: ☐ENLISTED (First Enlistment) ☐ENLISTED (Prior Service) ☐REENLISTED ☑OTHER ORDERED TO AD FROM USAR	A. TERM OF SERVICE (Years) NA	b. DATE OF ENTRY DAY 22 MONTH JUL YEAR 68
18. PRIOR REGULAR ENLISTMENTS NA	19. GRADE OR RANK AT TIME OF ENTRY INTO CURRENT ACTIVE SVC 2LT	20. PLACE OF ENTRY INTO CURRENT ACTIVE SERVICE (City and State) FORT BENNING, GEORGIA	

21. HOME OF RECORD AT TIME OF ENTRY INTO ACTIVE SERVICE (Street, RFD, City, County, State and ZIP Code) 6438 VANDERBILT HOUSTON, TEXAS 77005	22. STATEMENT OF SERVICE	YEARS	MONTHS	DAYS
	a. CREDITABLE FOR BASIC PAY PURPOSES (1) NET SERVICE THIS PERIOD	1	10	23
23a. SPECIALTY NUMBER & TITLE 1542 INF	(2) OTHER SERVICE	0	10	11
b. RELATED CIVILIAN OCCUPATION AND D.O.T. NUMBER UNIT COMD NA	(3) TOTAL (Line (1) plus Line (2))	2	9	4
	b. TOTAL ACTIVE SERVICE	2	9	4
	c. FOREIGN AND/OR SEA SERVICE USARPC	0	11	25

24. DECORATIONS, MEDALS, BADGES, COMMENDATIONS, CITATIONS AND CAMPAIGN RIBBONS AWARDED OR AUTHORIZED
NATIONAL DEFENSE SERVICE MEDAL   VIETNAM SERVICE MEDAL   COMBAT INFANTRY BADGE BRONZE STAR MEDAL W/"V" DEVICE & 1ST OLC   VIETNAM CAMPAIGN MEDAL 2 O/S BARS

25. EDUCATION AND TRAINING COMPLETED			
USA INF SCH	INF OFF CAND	23 WKS 68	WODLO3-L
USASWS	MATA SECTOR UNIT	6 WKS 69	
USARV ADV SCH	ADV CRS	2 WKS 69	

VA AND EMP. SERVICE DATA

26a. NON-PAY PERIODS TIME LOST (Preceding Two Years) NA	b. DAYS ACCRUED LEAVE PAID 15	27a. INSURANCE IN FORCE (NSLI or USGLI) ☐YES ☐NO XX	b. AMOUNT OF ALLOTMENT NA	c. MONTH ALLOTMENT DISCONTINUED NA
	28. VA CLAIM NUMBER c. NA	29. SERVICEMEN'S GROUP LIFE INSURANCE COVERAGE ☑\$10,000 ☐\$5,000 ☐NONE		

REMARKS

30. REMARKS
CIVILIAN EDUCATION: 16 YEARS (BBA ACCOUNTING) BLOOD GROUP: "O+" ITEM #5A: PERM 2LT USAR APTD: 22 JUL 68 RVN: 15 JUN 69 - 10 JUN 70

AUTHENTICATION

31. PERMANENT ADDRESS FOR MAILING PURPOSES AFTER TRANSFER OR DISCHARGE (Street, RFD, City, County, State and ZIP Code) SEE ITEM #21	32. SIGNATURE OF PERSON BEING TRANSFERRED OR DISCHARGED *Jack L. Thomas*
33. TYPED NAME, GRADE AND TITLE OF AUTHORIZING OFFICER G. E. LEGNER, 2LT AGC, ASST ADJ	34. SIGNATURE OF OFFICER AUTHORIZED TO SIGN *Legner*

DD FORM 214 1 JUL 66	PREVIOUS EDITIONS OF THIS FORM ARE OBSOLETE EFFECTIVE 1 JAN 67.	☆ GPO: 1969-351-112	ARMED FORCES OF THE UNITED STATES REPORT OF TRANSFER OR DISCHARGE

Appendix B: End-of-Tour Report

Headquarters: Hau Nghia Province—III CTZ
Duc Hue S/S Advisory Team 43
APO 96225
5 June 1970

To: Province Senior Advisor
Advisory Team 43
APO 96225

Through: District Senior Advisor
Duc Hue Subsector
Advisory Team 43
APO 96225

From: 1st Lt. Jack L. Thomas
Team Leader—MAT 56
Duc Hue District
Hau Nghia Province

Subject: End-of-Tour Report
(Based on eleven months
on MAT 56, both as assistant team
leader and team leader.)

1. I arrived at Hau Nhgia province on 11 July 69 at which time
Major James W. F. Pruitt, Senior RF/PF advisor, gave an adequate briefing. The province senior advisor (PSA) at that time
gave me no audience at all. I feel that the PSA should, if he is
not doing so now, give each new officer assigned to a MAT a
briefing welcoming him to the province and especially emphasiz-
ing what will be expected of that officer while he is on a MAT.

Having the highest-ranking officer in the province laying it on the line will impress a new officer.

2. I have had no financial problems that were not easily handled.

3. The administration section in Bao Trai, with the addition of Capt. Patton, has improved greatly during my tour of duty.

4. S-4 [supplies and logistics] in Bao Trai has improved its allocation of expendable items to an adequate level. If a MAT properly requisitions expendable items by the sixteenth of each month, the MAT is more likely to receive closer attention to its requests.

    • Concerning non-expendable items, a full MAT needs two vehicles. I have had only one jeep assigned from Bao Trai. I recommend that the second vehicle be either a three-quarter-ton or one-ton truck for ferrying heavy supplies and otherwise assisting the MAT in carrying out its mission.

    • The availability of good refrigerators (butane) has increased to an adequate level. However, I have never had a generator or a stove as authorized on the Table of Allowances for MATs. For a team living in the field at an outpost, I did find that the lack of the items mentioned above did add to the difficulty of my living conditions. Requisitions were put in for these two items.

    • The problems mentioned above were prevalent under the former S-4 at Bao Trai. With the new personnel now at S-4 I expect conditions to improve in the future. I believe it should be stressed to MATs that they put in requisitions for needed items from the S-4 in Bao Trai. I have received faster results (when I got results) putting in requisitions. For items that have proven difficult to obtain over an extended period of time, I have to recommend scrounging, out of necessity of survival.

5. A & L Company has performed adequate maintenance service on my vehicle. However, when a major part had to be replaced,

or an essential part had to be repaired in order to keep the vehicle running, I found it necessary to use other methods than A & L Company to fix the vehicle. The need for expediency arose out of our team having only one vehicle; thus, another reason for having two vehicles. The A & L Company has been too slow in repairing or replacing major components of a vehicle.

- I have been able to obtain necessary resupply of ammunition from A & L Company through the help of Lieutenant Reynolds.

- I strongly urge all DSAs to give sufficient notice to a MAT in regard to moving to a new location. Sufficient notice means enough time for a MAT leader to make out a requisition for the necessary building and barrier materials to build a bunker, and enough time for the requisitioned material to arrive. Back in November, our team took approximately a month and a half to complete a bunker because we had to scrounge all material. This necessary scrounging actually detracted from and hampered our mission. Additionally, we were in a "hot area" at that time and received incoming on several occasions, thus jeopardizing the safety of the team. I urge all MATs to stand firm and get their supplies first.

- In relation to Vietnamese support from the A & L Company, I have seen improvement in my companies and platoons getting supplies, barrier material and ammunition, through the use of requisitions. Frankly, I recommend that MATs do not scrounge supplies for Vietnamese unless security of the team is at stake. Vietnamese commanders ask advisors to get them material because the RFs and PFs know that advisors can get the material more easily. However, every time an advisor scrounges for Vietnamese, he is defeating his purpose as an advisor. The Vietnamese must learn to rely on their own channels. Every time a Vietnamese commander asks an advisor for supplies, the advisor should listen to everything he says and then tell the commander to make out a requisition, give the advisor a copy, send a copy to the appropriate Vietnamese S-4 shop and then follow it up. This way, perhaps the weak links in the Vietnamese supply system could be eliminated by isolating the reasons supplies fail to reach RF companies and PF platoons.

- When the Vietnamese do get supplies, the advisor should make certain that the commander does not sell the material; this includes rice rations.

6. I have become convinced that the MAT concept of operations needs to be reevaluated. The concept as it now stands certainly cannot be applied on a blanket basis. With the exception of the few new units that are being organized, a MAT has lived with most RF and PF units. From my experience, I find it advantageous for a MAT to build a semi-permanent structure with at least one company of RFs and group headquarters, all in one compound. The MAT, at the center of operations, would be fully apprised of the situation of the advised units not only through the accompaniment of other units but also through daily contact with the group commander. (A MAT also loses much time if it has to build a new bunker every thirty or sixty days, even if the team has supplies.)

- In other words, where circumstances are appropriate, I recommend that the MAT operate as a sub-subsector within its own area of operations. A MAT can more easily accompany other units on operations and improve its reporting procedures. For example, a MAT component accompanies an RF company on a night patrol. After the patrol, the MAT leader has his conference with the RF commander. Then the MAT component returns to its base of operations and critiques the group commander on the RF company's ambush patrol. This negates the necessity of the MAT having to make a special trip to the group location for a critique, which they probably would not do anyway if the MAT was not living with group headquarters.

- With good reporting on unit leaders and constant contact with the group commander, I believe a MAT will be better able to find a weak commander and get him relieved if he does not shape up.

- I make these recommendations because I have found in my area that all units are capable of defending themselves against present enemy levels and that a MAT does not have to live with a PF platoon for the survival of the platoon.

7. Many RF and PF units follow the dangerous practice of taking the same route to the same ambush sites night after night. This has been proven by the in-depth study of night operations of RF and PF units recently completed by our province. I consider MAT accompaniment of this type of unit an unnecessary hazard to U.S. advisory personnel. If the MAT leader is unable to get a unit to take different routes, sites and times, I recommend that the MAT does not accompany this unit again until the local force unit agrees to pull sound APs [ambush patrols]. I realize that this is a negative incentive, but some bad units must be shaken out of their apathetic attitude. If this approach is to be used, the DSA and the MAT leader should notify the district chief, group commander, and local force leader of the decision and the reasons therefor.

8. The DSAs should attempt to be realistic in their requirements of MAT night accompaniments per week based on the number of team personnel per MAT. A team of three members should not be required to do the work of a full team.

   - Since I took over the team in mid-December, the team has not had more than three members with the exception of three weeks from late January to mid-February. During this three-week period, the team had a captain as team leader, but he was seriously wounded in mid-February. At all other times we have operated with either two or three as a team.

   - The DSA, Duc Hue, has been fair in assigning duties and requirements to MAT III-56 in proportion to the number of team members.

9. Concerning civic action, I do believe that the MATs should try to influence each unit commander to take, say, one civic project per month, depending on the time required to complete that project.

10. I have found calling and adjustment of artillery fires and map reading to be weak areas among unit commanders. I do recommend training in these two areas for local forces.

11. There is no optimum tour for a MAT leader. For example, it takes a new officer a few months to learn what is going on. The DSA and PSA have to consider any request for transfer individually. If a new officer is assigned a new job after six months, he has probably not accomplished a great deal because small-unit-force leaders will not listen to an advisor until that advisor earns respect from his counterparts.

12. The best way to influence a counterpart is to report to him all deficiencies and then report to the DSA all deficiencies of that counterpart. The DSA then notifies the district chief. Follow-up procedure is then employed to ensure corrective action is taken.

13. MAT leaders should work with the HES. For the last five months, I have worked with the HES monthly preparation, and have found that this added to my awareness of the situation in the district.

14. Finally, new team leaders and assistants should be advised that some Vietnamese soldiers will steal. All property should be secured, and where practical, radio watch should be maintained all night.

Jack L. Thomas
First Lieutenant, Infantry
Team Leader, MAT III-56

APPENDIX C: AFTERMATH

As to what happened to Trung-Uy Hot and other regional force officers and soldiers I respected, I do not know. Stuart A. Herrington, who served as an intelligence officer in Hau Nghia Province from February 1971 through August 1972, had some follow-up experiences with ruff-puffs. In a letter dated 10 October 1983 he stated, "Incidentally, Trung-Uy Hot (we called him 'the Buffalo') was still in command and I accompanied him on many an operation."

Herrington related two other incidents. One of them he had monitored on radio watch while another advisor accompanied Trung-Uy Hot on an operation. "We had a great contact one night, south of the Square Lake. Hot didn't have a functioning strobe light, so he told the dustoff he would light a bonfire to mark the LZ. Within a few minutes, the bird said he saw the fire and was beginning his descent. As he came down, green tracers erupted from all around the fire—which was north of the Square Lake. There were two bonfires, one lit by the VC, one by Trung-Uy Hot!

"On another occasion in spring '72, a PF platoon in an ambush position outside An Dinh saw a fifty-man VC unit enter the hamlet at midnight, but not on a route that was through the kill zone. The commander quietly dispatched his unit to a new ambush position between the hamlet and the Vam Co Dong, set up his claymores and waited. Two hours later, the VC unit exited the hamlet (by the same route they entered) and walked into the kill zone. The PF (no U.S. advisors were along) sprang a perfect liner ambush and killed thirty, captured four or five wounded. It was a sapper company being guided by two village guerrillas. . . . You would have been proud to see the RFs and PFs lock horns with the NVA's 271st and 24th Regiments and win decisively. It was definitely a case of good training paying off in the crunch, and the

MAT teams who struggled to get things done with the territorial forces should get a lot of the credit. Oftentimes when you were teaching them, the officer 'leader' wasn't having any of it, but some of the NCOs or aspirants were impressed. It was these men who emerged as the leaders under LTC Thanh, and they were real heroes. Hau Nghia Province didn't lose a square foot of soil during the 'cease-fire' war of '73-'75, and the NVA picked softer, easier routes to Saigon for good reasons. They knew they could not walk through Hau Nghia's territorial forces as they could through most of the ARVN."[14]

Colonel Herrington also described what happened to Major Cooper after I left. "He was wounded in an ambush by two guerrillas on the road from Bao Cong Hamlet in Tan My (the French fort). The VC had noticed that the MAT drove their maid every day at 1630 hours down the road to So Do hamlet (on the paved road north of Bao Trai). The VC set up to ambush the MAT, but Major Cooper, who had decided to visit the outpost as an afterthought, drove into the ambush. Wounded by shrapnel from an antitank grenade, he escaped by crawling into the high rice, armed only with his .45. The two VC were standing on the road ready to hose down the moving rice with their AKs when the MAT's NCOs came along and ran them off. Cooper was medevaced to Japan. . . ." That action occurred on 13 November 1970, exactly one year after the Adams incident.

Subsequent research at the National Archives uncovered a Senior Advisor Province report on Cambodia dated 5 June 1970 which stated in part, "Most significant event this period and probably the past several years was total destruction of enemy base area at Ba Thu and Dia Gai."

There were several consequences of these actions: many VCI were neutralized, there was a significant increase in the number of Hoi Chanhs, and ethnic Vietnamese moved back into the eastern portion of Hau Nghia Province, but perhaps most notably, enemy infiltration and terrorism actually increased.

The province report for 15 June 1970 stated: "Since mid-March the VC main force, 269th Battalion, has had an element working in the An Ninh area. They have heavily booby-trapped the entire area, and for that reason the RF/PF forces are extremely hesitant to operate in the area. In addition, the area is inadequately out-posted and poorly covered by a night ambush. . . . Prior to the Cambodian Campaign, the CIDG (Civilian Irregular Defense Group) from Duc Hue and Tra Cu worked the area west of the river to block infiltration. However, now the CIDG are operating in the Ba Thu area, and enemy forces moving between the Cambodian border and the Vam Co Dong River are virtually unopposed."

Were the increased booby traps effective? A report dated 7 September 1970 summarized the number of incidents in the province for the month of August:

- Civilians Wounded/Killed   10/0
- RF Wounded/Killed   30/9
- PF Wounded/Killed   4/1
- U.S. Wounded/Killed   6/0
- Other Wounded/Killed   2/0
- Totals   52/10

Trying to eliminate this enemy was like trying to eradicate red ants: burn and kill a main mound one day, only to find a few days later that a bunch of little mounds have sprouted in adjacent areas.

As for Sergeant Charleston and Lieutenant Shanklin, they too survived the rest of their respective tours, but not without some heart-stopping moments. On a heliborne operation at an LZ in the Square Lake area, Sergeant Charleston and young Sergeant Khanh bolted from the choppers, only to discover after the choppers had lifted away that they were a two-man assault team. The rest of the Vietnamese soldiers had refused to disembark. Charleston and Khanh had to be extracted. Fortunately I never experienced this kind of distress.

Over the next few months the team operated west of the river, crossing over on small wooden sampans, which bothered Charleston for he was not a strong swimmer. Years later he expressed to me his amazement at the skill and ease with which the ruff-puffs adroitly felled trees for natural bridges. An Dinh continued to be a hot spot, with the Vietcong dropping in mortar rounds. Charleston and Lieutenant Shanklin soon parted company, however, the end coming after a night contact in the Square Lake area in which gunships had to be called in for support.

Thus far, I have been unable to establish contact with any regional and popular force soldiers with whom I served.

Epilogue

O n four occasions within the last eight years former soldiers of Advisory Team 43 have met for reunions, where pretenses were dropped and realities and vulnerabilities exposed. Seven attended the first two, four the third, and seven the fourth, which was held in September 2004 in the Richmond, Virginia, area. Below is a brief description of the key people who significantly affected the author's life in Vietnam, as well as comments on family.

Ronald D. Adams (fictitious name) has not been located.

George Brevaldo has not been located.

Isaac Charleston, who served two tours in Vietnam and retired from the Army as a master sergeant, undertook a second career at the post office. He lives in Houston, Texas. Isaac is widowed and has six grown children. On 8 January 2000 I had the honor of attending his seventieth birthday party, where friends and family celebrated his life.

Louis R. Kerbow (fictitious name) is deceased.

Richard O'Hare and his wife, Martha, live in Powhatan, Virginia. He served two tours in Vietnam: the first began with the 3rd Brigade, 82nd Airborne Division, near Hue in 1968, and the second ended with his participation on Vietnamese Airborne Advisory Team 162. After the war he completed college, earning his BA degree in both business economics and American history. Rich has two sons, and his profession, insurance and benefits consultation services, allows him time to participate in various 82nd Airborne activities as well as to pursue his hobby of gun collecting.

James C. Smith left the Army after his military service. He lives in Sebastopol, California, and has retired from electrical contracting and service work. During his first marriage he fathered one daughter, Meghan, who plays the trumpet when she is not teaching. Jim and his current wife, Judy, an Englishwoman, are mulling how to spend their retirement. His interests include motorcycling, scuba diving, and carpentry.

Jack Lyndon Thomas, after serving as chief financial officer for three medium-sized companies, abandoned his CPA profession and began writing full-time. He has published a book of poetry, written two book-length collections of his motorcycling journeys, and has completed his first novel. He lives in Houston, Texas.

David Ward left the military after his Vietnam service and lives in Missouri City, Texas. A political science graduate of the University of Arkansas, David worked twenty-six years for Southwestern Bell and recently retired. He now works part-time and spends quality time with his wife, Georgia. Once a month David and Jack drink beer at a local pub.

Ray Wing spent thirty-one months in Vietnam, including twelve months on a Special Forces "A" team. After leaving the Army, Ray owned and operated two trophy businesses in Maine. He is married to Michelle, his childhood sweetheart, and now lives in Spring Hill, Florida, where he works as an accountant/tax practitioner. Ray has two adopted daughters from his first marriage and a stepdaughter and stepson from his current one. He and his wife hosted our first reunion.

Alicia Thomas (fictitious name) remarried.

Summer Thomas earned a Bachelor of Arts in business at Southwestern University in Georgetown, Texas, and now resides with her boyfriend and two cats in St. Louis, Missouri. She works as a senior compensation generalist for a digital entertainment and communications company.

Allison Thomas lives with her cat, Elvis, in New York, where she graduated from Columbia University with a degree in sociology. She is continuing her education and also pursuing her dream of theater and dance.

May 2004 again found me at Fort Benning, Georgia, this time to attend a reunion of 52nd OCS Company, 5th Student Battalion, in which I served as a tactical officer of the fifth platoon. Thirty-nine former officers—thirty-four classmates and five cadre—attended. For everyone there is a story. This OCS company lost six young lieutenants during the Vietnam War: five from hostile fire and one from non-hostile fire in Laos.

ACKNOWLEDGMENTS

I want to thank Shirin Wright, whose interest, attention to detail, and meticulous editing has much improved the presentation of this book. My critique group—Chris Rogers, Marty Braniff, Marcia Gerhardt, Rick Nelson, and John Oehler—have been instrumental in the development of my writing skills, as has Christopher Woods, a wonderful teacher and writer. Also I appreciate early suggestions for the manuscript from Jerry and Janet Weiner, David Dillingham, and Richard Jaenicke. Additionally Karen Krakower, Nancy Geyer, Elizabeth McLane Stocker, and Chalon Fontaine contributed valuable ideas.

Judy King supplied the galley edits, which helped polish the manuscript even more. Rita Mills packaged the book layout, a difficult task, and Cindy Guire designed the jacket cover and website. To all of them I owe a great deal of thanks.

And finally my advisory team members, who are mentioned throughout this book, have become an indispensable part of my life.

Any errors or omissions, and the writing style and book structure, are my responsibility.

END NOTES

1. Before I left the country, Mr. Loc gave me a sealed letter to mail to a Vietnamese girlfriend who lives in the Midwest. Also after my return to the States I sent two books, *A Bright Shining Lie: John Paul Vann and America in Vietnam,* by Neil Sheehan, and *Vietnam: A History, The First Complete Account of Vietnam at War,* by Stanley Karnow, by courier to Loc. He acknowledged receipt of both volumes and was appreciative. (Page 61)

2. Jim and I were not the first Americans to revisit the Sugar Mill. After returning stateside, I established contact with former Sergeant Richard O'Hare through the "Counterparts" organization. O'Hare disclosed that four years earlier he and a couple of friends from the 25th Infantry Division had attempted to gain access to the Sugar Mill, only to be arrested and hauled off to the former provincial capital of Bao Trai for questioning. They bartered their freedom for one hundred dollars each. (Page 66)

3. Some months after our return to the States, Ray Wing, our former district senior advisor, watched the video I took and offered a tantalizing thesis. "It looked the same to me. I just couldn't understand why the gravestones weren't there. The only thing I could think of is that they weren't really grave markers, just a goddamned ploy by the Vietcong. They had dug tunnels or a cave underneath." Speculative? Yes! Seductive? Yes! Possible? Most definitely, for undiscovered tunnels would explain much of what had transpired at An Dinh. (Page 77)

4. In 1996 I learned the myth of the water buffalo: "In the old days, people had not planted rice yet. They had to eat domestic animals. The Emperor of Jade was afraid that when the people did not have enough domestic animals, they might eat wild animals. If people ate wild animals, they would anger the wild animal gods. So the Emperor of Jade bargained with the agricultural god and asked for rice and grass to be planted in the earth. The Emperor of Jade told him: "When you descend to the earth, I will give you three packs of grass and one pack of rice. You must remember to plant grass on the mountain and rice

on the ground." But when the agricultural god arrived on earth, he met a lot of beautiful girls. He forgot what the Emperor of Jade told him. So he planted rice and grass in the same place. That is why grass grows better than rice. It made the Emperor of Jade angry. The Emperor of Jade did not let him [agricultural god] come back into the sky and turned him into the water buffalo to eat grass and help farmers. Before transforming the agricultural god, however, the Emperor of Jade told him: "I will let you back into the sky when you eat all the grasses on the earth." But he never finished his duties. That is why Vietnamese rarely eat water buffalo meat." The myth reminded me of American Indian legends. I also think of Adam and Eve, the apple, and the serpent. (Page 115)

5. I maintained Jim's policy throughout my tour. MAT III-56 advisors carried our own radios. (Page 125)

6. Jim could have been awarded the Purple Heart. Years later he disclosed that something else happened that night—he had taken a piece of shrapnel. Though not a serious wound, it bled profusely. Embarrassed by the nature of his injury, a pinpoint hit to his penis, he tended to it himself. (Page 129)

7. Is it possible a sabotaged mortar round damaged the mortar tube? In *SOG: The Secret Wars of America's Commandos in Vietnam,* Major John L. Plaster describes the incredible actions of elite Army Special Forces and Navy Seals behind enemy lines. He writes not only of sabotaged AK47 ammunition but also of booby-trapped mortar rounds and mentions that some of their teams obtained on-the-spot verification of the effectiveness of this ruse. (Page 131)

8 . In writing about the transition from village intimacy to the loneliness and isolation in the field, I experienced now, as then, the same reluctance to leave the perceived safety of the compound. Nevertheless, the field was our realm and represented the challenges to be met. (Page 153)

9. In a 6 April 1970 confidential memo the province senior advisor wrote: "In the great majority of instances, the ambush positions and the routes to and from these positions are known by the enemy. As an example of the latter, the recently captured chief of security of the village of Duc Lap stated that each evening prior to dark his lookouts positioned themselves in trees which overlooked the local RF company outpost and observed the ambush patrol go to one of the three positions it habitually occupied, and that once the ambush was settled in for the night the VC went about their business, knowing that the RF unit would not move until it returned to its outpost." (Page 200)

10. From 12 July 1969 through 23 November 1969, MAT III-56 accompanied

eleven day patrols, twenty ambush or night patrols, two airmobile operations, and one riverine operation. (Page 202)

11. During Jim's and my 1996 return trip to Vietnam, we rehashed this particular An Dinh attack. He conveyed more detail on what he had been doing that night, raising even more speculation as to the degree of intrigue, as Captain Wing subsequently did with his gravestone theory. Jim and another sergeant had accompanied an ambush patrol with a PF platoon, not too far from the An Dinh outpost, possibly at La Cua, or even An Hiep. According to Jim, the selected site had been a good one, with adequate concealment and clear fields of fire. Lieutenant Smith had undergone considerable frustration in trying to get this unit to pull an ambush in the first place. He was even more frustrated when abruptly the PF platoon leader vigorously protested their presence in that position, saying that they had to return immediately to the PF platoon's outpost because it was too dangerous not to. This was around 2200 hours, not too long before we were hit that night. I think the PFs knew. (Page 232)

12. Review of intelligence summaries stored in the National Archives for the period October 1969 through mid-December 1969 disclosed numerous sightings of elements of the Vietcong's 269th Main Force Battalion both west and south of the An Dinh outpost, a few within two thousand meters but the majority being four to seven thousand meters away. Reports came from Vietcong sympathizers as well as from S2 (Intelligence) at district or province level. When plotting the grid coordinates, making the tenuous assumption that all reports were accurate and reliable, the only clearly discernible fact was that the enemy moved fast and frequently. I believe that within Duc Hue District they could have hit anytime, anywhere, and anyone they chose, so the effect of reacting to intelligence was necessarily mitigated because you were chasing roving bands of guerrillas. Still, perhaps the most intriguing piece of intelligence was from a summary dated 11 November 1969, two days after the heavy hit, in which a Hau Nghia sympathizer reported one Vietcong battalion with an estimated strength of two hundred men, possibly from the 269th, at grid coordinates XT 422119, approximately forty-five hundred meters southwest of the outpost. Its mission—to attack An Dinh and An Hiep outposts at all costs. A separate report estimated the 9 November attack force at two VC companies. (Page 246)

13. This medal does not appear on my DD Form 214. Instead I have a letter dated 6 January 1970 addressed to my parents from Olin E. Smith, Colonel, Infantry, Headquarters, 3rd Brigade, 25th Infantry Division: "The enclosed picture of your son was taken the other day when General Camp, the Assistant Division Commander, visited his unit to present him with the Army Commendation Medal for Valor. 1LT Thomas was well and in fine spirits, and his superiors informed me that he is doing an excellent job in MAT III [-56]. As

an Infantry Brigade Commander in Vietnam, I consider it a gratifying experience and a personal pleasure to work with young soldiers like your son. He is a most valuable asset to this command in the performance of its mission, and his efforts are greatly appreciated by the United States Army and the 3rd Brigade, 25th Infantry Division." (Page 253)

14. Stuart A. Herrington served again in Vietnam from 1973 to 1975, participating in negotiations in Hanoi and the fall of and evacuation from Saigon, which he vividly relates in his informative book, *Peace With Honor? An American Reports on Vietnam 1973-1975.* Also commenting on the period 1971-1972 in *The Dynamics of Defeat: The Vietnam War in Hau Nghia Province,* Eric M. Bergerud writes that "General Nguyen Van Minh, later the commanding general of III CTZ, stated publicly that Hau Nghia had 'the best RF in the world, better than ARVN.'" (Page 300)

GLOSSARY

AK47. A 7.62mm Soviet- or Chinese-made semiautomatic and automatic assault rifle

ARVN. Army of the Republic of Vietnam

azimuth. A horizontal angle measured clockwise from a base direction. All directions originate from the center of an imaginary circle, based upon three hundred sixty equal units of measurement called degrees. Used in directing artillery fire, directing aircraft support, and plotting patrol routes.

chung-uy. An aspirant or junior officer, no equivalent rank in the U.S. Army.

co. A term most commonly used as a prefix in addressing a Vietnamese woman

COSVN. Central Office South Vietnam, created in North Vietnam to control the Vietcong in the South

dai-uy. The Vietnamese equivalent of captain

DEROS. Date eligible for return from overseas

dust off. See medevac

Eagle Flight. Helicopter assault or reaction force consisting of a command ship and several troop carriers; usually accompanied by Cobra gunships

fields of fire. Terrain conducive to effective interlocking weapons fire

KIA. Killed in action

laterite. A reddish clay

LZ. Landing zone

M-2 machine gun. A .50-caliber, metallic link belt fed, with a forty-rounds-per-minute sustained rate of fire

M-16. A 5.56mm semiautomatic and automatic rifle with a twenty- or thirty-round magazine

M-60 machine gun. A 7.62mm, disintegrating link belt fed, with one hundred-rounds-per-minute sustained rate of fire

M-79 grenade launcher. A hand-carried, single-shot, breech-loaded weapon (like a shotgun) capable of launching a grenade-type round a distance of three hundred forty meters, with a casualty radius similar to a hand grenade. White phosphorus, gas, smoke, and flechette (steel darts) rounds could also be fired from this weapon.

MACV. Military Assistance Command, Vietnam

Madame Ngo Dinh Nhu. The highly visible wife of Ngo Dinh Nhu, President Diem's brother

MAT. Mobile Advisory Team, mobile U.S. units assigned to live and work with regional and popular forces. Officially a team comprised a captain, first lieutenant, and three NCOs—a heavy weapons advisor, light weapons advisor, and medic. The teams were rarely at full strength.

medevac or dustoff. A helicopter operation designed to extract WIAs and KIAs

NCO. Noncommissioned officers; career NCOs are indispensable to the running of the U.S. Army.

NLF. National Liberation Front, formed in Hanoi in December 1960. It was designed to disguise Communist control of the organization and to draw support from non-Communist South Vietnamese.

NVA. North Vietnamese Army

OCS. Officer Candidate School, referred to here as Infantry OCS; it was a six-month program designed to churn out second lieutenants.

on-line. Soldiers positioned abreast during a combat assault

PBR Mark II. A fast, highly maneuverable, well-armed river patrol boat. Constructed with a fiberglass hull, it was used in shallow-water operations.

PRC-25. A twenty-three-pound field radio featuring a short antenna, handset, and 920 FM channels. Carried on a soldier's back, the communication device had a range of eight to twenty-five kilometers, but it was vulnerable to terrain interference and moisture.

PRG. Provisional Revolutionary Government, established in 1969 as the political arm of the Vietcong

punji stakes. Sharpened bamboo stakes embedded at the bottom of various-sized pits and designed to impale anyone unfortunate enough to fall through the camouflaged covers concealing the pits. Often covered with dung, stakes were also placed along the sides of trails.

regional forces and popular forces. RFs and PFs. Commonly called ruff-puffs or militia, these indigenous company- and platoon-sized units generally operated in areas contiguous to soldiers' homes. Regional forces performed at district level while popular forces usually worked closer to villages and hamlets.

REMF. An acronym unflatteringly defined as rear echelon mother fucker

RPG. A rocket-propelled grenade, such as the B40, used against vehicles, fortifications, and helicopters; this single-shot weapon was fired from the shoulder.

RTO. A field radio and telephone operator

sappers. Vietcong or NVA assault demolition specialists, often a suicide mission

spooky. Converted cargo planes equipped with one or more multibarreled machine guns (7.62 mm) capable of firing six thousand rounds per minute; also carried aerial flares

thieu-uy. The Vietnamese equivalent of second lieutenant

trung-uy. The Vietnamese equivalent of first lieutenant

Vietcong. Called VC for short, the guerrilla forces operating in South Vietnam

Vietcong Infrastructure. Called VCI for short, cadre who administered the covert political arm of the Vietcong guerrilla forces

WIA. Wounded in action

BIBLIOGRAPHY

Bergerud, Eric M. *The Dynamics of Defeat: The Vietnam War in Hau Nghia Province.* Boulder, CO: Westview Press, 1991.

Clark, Gregory R. *Words of the Vietnam War.* Jefferson, NC: McFarland & Company, 1990.

Combat Leader's Field Guide. Harrisburg, PA: The Stackpole Co., 1967.

Fall, Bernard B. *Street without Joy.* Mechanicsburg, PA: Stackpole Books, 1994.

———. *Last Reflections on a War.* Mechanicsburg, PA: Stackpole Books, 2000.

Herrington, Stuart A. *Silence Was a Weapon: The Vietnam War in the Villages.* Novato, CA: Presidio Press, 1982.

———. *Peace with Honor? An American Reports on Vietnam 1973-1975.* Novato, CA: Presidio Press, 1983.

Hoover, J. Edgar. *A Study of Communism.* New York: Holt, Rinehart and Winston, 1963.

Karnow, Stanley. *Vietnam: A History, The First Complete Account of Vietnam at War.* New York: The Viking Press, 1983.

Kelley, Michael P. *Where We Were in Vietnam: A Comprehensive Guide to the Firebases, Military Installations, and Naval Vessels of the Vietnam War.* Central Point, OR: Hellgate Press, 2002.

Lee, J. Edward, and Toby Haynsworth, eds. *White Christmas in April: The Collapse of South Vietnam, 1975.* New York: Peter Lang Publishing, 1999.

Plaster, John L. *SOG: The Secret Wars of America's Commandos in Vietnam.* New York: Simon & Schuster, 1997.

RF/PF Handbook for Advisors. United States Military Assistance Command, Vietnam, rev. November 1969.

Sheehan, Neil. *A Bright Shining Lie: John Paul Vann and America in Vietnam.* New York: Random House, 1988.

Stanton, Shelby L. *Vietnam: Order of Battle.* Washington, D.C.: U.S. News Books, 1981.

Summers, Harry G., Jr. *Vietnam War Almanac.* New York: Facts on File Publications, 1985.

———. *Historical Atlas of the Vietnam War.* New York: Houghton Mifflin, 1995.

Tang, Truong Nhu, et al. *A Vietcong Memoir: An Inside Account of the Vietnam War and Its Aftermath.* New York: Vintage Books, a Division of Random House, 1986.

Thomas, Jack Lyndon. *Whirling Fire*. Houston, TX: lyndonjacks publications, 1997.

Westphall, Victor. *David's Story: A Casualty of Vietnam*. Springer, NM: Center for the Advancement of Human Dignity, 1981.

www.lyndonjacks.com